*Microprocessor Architectures
and Systems*

Microprocessor Architectures and Systems

RISC, CISC and DSP

STEVE HEATH

Newnes
An imprint of Butterworth–Heinemann Ltd
Linacre House, Jordan Hill, Oxford OX2 8DP

A member of the Reed Elsevier group

OXFORD   LONDON   BOSTON
MUNICH   NEW DELHI   SINGAPORE   SYDNEY
TOKYO   TORONTO   WELLINGTON

First published 1991
Paperback edition 1993
Reprinted 1993

British Library Cataloguing in Publication Data
Heath, Steve
   Microprocessor architectures and systems: RISC, CISC and DSP.
   1. Microprocessor systems. Design.
   I. Title
   004.256

ISBN 0 7506 1628 8

Typeset by Vision Typesetting, Manchester
Printed and bound in Great Britain

*For my Mother and Father
who bought me my
first soldering iron.*

Contents

Preface

'Why are there all these different processor architectures and what do they all mean?'

'Which processor shall I use and how should I choose it?'

There has been an unparalleled introduction of new processor architectures in recent years, which has widened the choice available for designs, but has also caused much confusion with the claims and counterclaims. This has resulted in questions concerning the need for several different processor types. The struggle for supremacy between Complex Instruction Set Computer architectures and those of Reduced Instruction Set Computer purveyors and the advent of powerful Digital Signal Processors has pulled the humble microprocessor into the realm of computer architectures, where the total system is the key to understanding and successful implementations. The days of separate hardware and software engineering are now numbered because of this close interaction between hardware and software. The effect of one decision now has definite repercussions with so many aspects throughout the design.

Given the task of selecting an architecture or design approach, both engineers and managers now require a knowledge of the whole system and an explanation of the design trade-offs and their effects. Such information rarely appears within data sheets or user manuals. This book fills that knowledge gap by closely examining the developments of Motorola's CISC, RISC and DSP processors and describing the typical system configurations and engineering trade-offs that are made. The first part of the book provides a primer and history of the three basic microprocessor architectures. The second part describes the ways in which the architectures react with the system. Chapter 5 covers memory designs, memory management and cache memories. Chapter 6 examines interrupt and exception handling and the effect on real-time applications. Chapter 7 examines basic multiprocessing ideas. Chapter 8 gives some application ideas which show how certain characteristics can be exploited. The third part of the book looks at some more commercial aspects: Chapter 9 covers semiconductor technology and what it will bring, while Chapter 10 examines the changing design cycle and its implications for the design process and commercial success. Chapter 11 looks at future processor generations and Chapter 12 describes the criteria that should be examined when selecting a processor. The appendices include further information on benchmarking and binary compatibility standards.

The examples have been based around Motorola's microprocessor families, but many of the system considerations are applicable to other processors with similar architectural characteristics. The material is based on several years of involvement with users who have gone through the decision-making process and who have frequently asked the questions at the beginning of this preface. To those of you that asked and inspired this book, I thank you.

The application note on high integrity MC68020 and MC68030 designs, the descriptions of the MC68040 processor and silicon technology in Chapters 8, 9 and 11 are based on articles that I have written for *Electronic Product Design*. Their permission to reprint the material is gratefully acknowledged.

In addition, I would like to say thank you to several of my colleagues at Motorola: to Pat McAndrew who has guided and educated me through DSP, to Ronnie Sutherland and Peter Crooks who have always been willing to discuss an architectural aspect over a beer, and to John Ralston, who has always tried to achieve the impossible whenever I have asked him! Special thanks must again go to Sue Carter for yet more editing, intelligent criticism and excellent coffee and for allowing me the use of our dining room to house my computer systems.

Steve Heath

Acknowledgements

The following trademarks mentioned within the text are acknowledged:

MC6800, MC6809, MC6801, MC68000, MC68020, MC68030, MC68040, MC68332, MC68302, MC68851, MC68881, MC68882, MC68008, MC68HC000, MC68HC001, DSP56000, DSP56001, DSP96000, MC88100, and MC88200 are all trademarks of Motorola, Inc.

UNIX is a trademark of AT&T
VRTX is a trademark of Ready Systems, Inc.
OS-9 is a trademark of Microware.
pDOS is a trademark of Eyring Research.
PDP-11, VAX 11/780 and DEC are trademarks of Digital Equipment Corporation.
iAPX8086, iAPX80286, iAPX80386 are trademarks of Intel Corporation.

While the information contained in this book has been carefully checked for accuracy, the author assumes no responsibility or liability for its use, or for any infringement of patents or other rights of third parties which would result.

As technical characteristics are subject to rapid change, the data contained are presented for guidance and education only. For exact details, consult the manufacturers' data and specifications.

1 Complex instruction set computers

8-bit microprocessors: the precursors of CISC

Ask what the definition of a CISC (Complex Instruction Set Computer) processor is and often the reply will be based around subjective comments like 'a processor that has an over-complex and inefficient instruction set', or even simply 'an MC68000 or 8086'. The problem with these definitions is that they fail to account for the facts that more CISC microprocessors are used than any other architecture, they provide more direct hardware support for the software developer than any other architecture and are often more suitable for applications than either RISC (Reduced Instruction Set Computer) or DSP (Digital Signal Processor) alternatives. A CISC processor is better described as a mature design where software compatibility and help for software are the overriding goals. Many of today's CISC processors owe their architectural philosophy to the early 8-bit microprocessors either as a foundation or as an example of how not to design a high-performance microprocessor. It is worthwhile reviewing these early designs to act as an introduction and a backdrop to further discussions.

A microprocessor can be described simply as a data processor: information is obtained, modified according to a predetermined set of instructions and either stored or passed to other elements within the system. Each instruction follows a simple set path of fetching an instruction, decoding and acting on it, fetching data from external memory as necessary and so on. In detail, such events consist of several stages based around a single or a succession of memory accesses. Figure 1.1 shows the basic functional blocks within a typical 8-bit microprocessor. The stages needed to execute an instruction to load an accumulator with a data byte are shown in italic type. Each stage is explained below.

Start of memory cycle 1

Stage 1   Here the current program counter address is used to fetch the

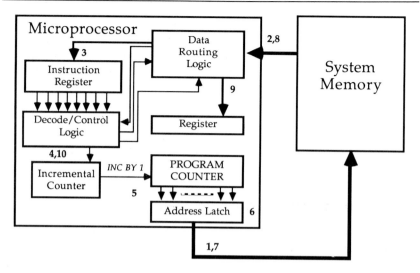

Figure 1.1   *Stages involved with instruction execution*

next instruction from system memory. This address is 16 bits in size.

Stage 2:   The 8-bit instruction is placed on to data bus and is loaded into the data routing logic from where it is passed to the instruction decode logic.

Stage 3:   The instruction decoder examines the instruction, determines what operation is required and how large the op code is. In this example, the op code requires the data value stored in the next byte location to be loaded into an internal register. This uses several control signals to start the next data fetch and route the data successfully.

Stage 4:   An incremental counter increases the program counter value by one so it points to the next location.

Stage 5:   The new program counter value is loaded into the address latch, ready for the start of a new memory cycle.

End of memory cycle 1

Stage 6:   The latched 16-bit address is placed on the external address bus.

Stage 7:   The next external memory cycle is started.

Stage 8:   The 8-bit data is placed on to the data bus by the system memory and is latched into the data routing logic. This logic has been told by the instruction decoder to route this data through to the register.

Stage 9:   The data is written into the register.
Stage 10:   The instruction decode logic is told of the successful data
            transfer, the counter incremented by one, and the next address
            stored in the program counter all ready for the next memory
            cycle.

End of memory cycle 2

This succession of events is simply repeated to create the processor flow.

8-bit microprocessor register models

The programmer has a very simple register model for this type of
processor. The model for the Motorola MC6800 8-bit processor is shown
in Figure 1.2 as an example. It has two 8-bit accumulators used for storing
data and performing arithmetic operations. The program counter is 16 bits
in size and two further 16-bit registers are provided for stack manipulations
and address indexing. On first inspection, the model seems quite primitive
and not capable of providing the basis of a computer system. There do not
seem to be enough registers to hold data, let alone manipulate it! What is
often forgotten is that many of the instructions, such as logical operations,
can operate on direct memory using the index register to act as pointer.

Figure 1.2   *The MC6800 programmer's model*

This removes the need to bring data into the processor at the expense of extra memory cycles.

The stack pointer provides additional storage for the programmer: it is used to store data like return addresses for subroutine calls and provides additional variable storage using a PUSH/POP mechanism. Data is PUSHed on to the stack to store it, and POPped off to retrieve it. Providing the programmer can track where the data resides in these stack frames, it offers a good replacement for the missing registers.

Restrictions

An 8-bit value can provide an unsigned resolution of only 256 bits, which makes it unsuitable for applications such as financial, arithmetic, high-precision servo control systems, etc. The obvious solution is to increase the data size to 16 bits, which would give a resolution of 65536 – an obvious improvement. This may be acceptable for a control system but is still not good enough for an accounting program, where a 32-bit data value may have to be defined to provide sufficient integer range. There is no difficulty with storing 8, 16, 32 or even 64 bits in external memory, even though this requires multiple bus accesses. However, due to the register model, data larger than 8 bits cannot use the standard arithmetic instructions applicable to 8-bit data stored in the accumulator. This means that even a simple 16-bit addition or multiplication has to be carried out as a series of instructions using the 8-bit model. This reduces the overall efficiency of the architecture.

The code example shown in Figure 1.3 is a routine for performing a simple 16-bit multiplication. It takes two unsigned 16-bit numbers and produces a 16-bit product. If the product is larger than 16 bits, only the least significant 16 bits are retained. The first eight or so instructions simply create a temporary storage area on the stack for the multiplicand, multiplier, return address and loop counter. Compared with internal register storage, storing data in stack frames is not as efficient, due the increased external memory access. Accessing external data consumes machine cycles which could be used to process data. Without suitable registers and the 16-bit wide accumulator, all this information must be stored externally on the stack. The algorithm used simply performs a succession of arithmetic shifts on each half of the multiplicand stored in the A and B accumulators. Once this is complete, the 16-bit result is split between the two accumulators and the temporary storage cleared off the stack. The operation takes at least 29 instructions to perform with the actual execution time totally dependent on the values being multiplied together. For comparison, an MC68000 can perform the same feat with a single instruction!

```
MULT16 LDX      #5        CLEAR WORKING REGISTERS
       CLR      A
LP1    STA      A    U-1,X
       DEX
       BNE      LP1
       LDX      #16       INITIAL SHIFT COUNTER
LP2    LDA. A   Y+1       GET Y(LSBIT)
       AND  A   #1
       TAB                SAVE Y(LSBIT) IN ACCB
       EOR  A   FF        CHECK TO SEE IF YOU ADD
       BEQ      SHIFT         OR SUBTRACT
       TST  B
       BEQ      ADD
       LDA  A   U+1
       LDA      B    U
       SUB  A   XX+1
       SBC  B   XX
       STA  A   U+1
       STA      B    U
       BRA      SHIFT     NOW GOTO SHIFT ROUTINE
ADD    LDA  A   U+1
       LDA      B    U
       ADD  A   XX+1
       ADC  B   XX
       STA  A   U+1
       STA      B    U
SHIFT  CLR      FF        SHIFT ROUTINE
       ROR      Y
       ROR      Y+1
       ROL      FF
       ASR      U
       ROR      U+1
       ROR      U+2
       ROR      U+3
       DEX
       BNE      LP2
       RTS                FINISH SUBROUTINE
                          END
```

Figure 1.3 *M6800 code for a 16-bit by 16-bit multiplication*

A simple 16-bit digit multiply is a common requirement and yet it requires a complete subroutine to perform it even crudely. Why not provide a 16-bit MUL instruction? This obvious solution is hindered by the effect of 8-bit data size on processor instructions. First, a 16-bit multiply requires extra registers to cope with the increased data size. These registers require instructions to load them, manipulate data, etc. Each new instruction requires a unique op code to define the operation, which register(s) are involved, any implicit data and addressing modes. Unfortunately, an 8-bit instruction width allows only a maximum of 255 different op codes, from which all these combinations must be encoded.

To overcome this limitation, many instruction sets use additional bytes (called operands) to contain additional data which cannot be encoded within the op code. A load accumulator LDA instruction for the MC6800 consists of an instruction plus 1 or 2 bytes containing either implicit data or some form of memory addressing. The penalty of additional machine cycles and slower execution is the resulting performance as depicted in Figure 1.1 and its description earlier. Examination of an op code list for the MC6800 shows another drawback: some instructions operate only on one special register. The advantage is that the register does not require encoding which, considering the 8-bit 255 op code limit, was beneficial. This highly non-orthogonal nature either forces a lot of data movement to and from the registers prior to execution or forces direct memory manipulation with its slower access. Code examination indicates that up to 40% of all instructions executed with such architectures simply move data from one location to another without any processing.

Addressing memory

When the first 8-bit microprocessors appeared during the middle to late 1970s, memory was expensive and available only in very small sizes: 256 bytes up to 1 kilobyte. Applications were small, due partly to their implementation in assembler rather than a high-level language, therefore the addressing range of 64 kilobytes offered by the 16-bit address seemed extraordinarily large. It was unlikely to be exceeded. As the use of these early microprocessors became more widespread, applications started to grow in size and the use of operating systems like CP/M and high-level languages increased memory requirements until the address range started to limit applications. Various techniques like bank switching and program overlays were developed to help.

Bank switching simply involves having several banks of memory with the same address locations. At any one time, only one bank on memory was enabled and accessible by the microprocessor. Bank selection, as shown in Figure 1.4, is made by driving the required bank select line. These lines come from either an external parallel port or latch whose register(s) appear as a bank switching control register within the processors's normal address

Figure 1.4   *Bank switching*

Figure 1.5 *Program overlays*

map. In the example, the binary value 1000 has been loaded into the bank selection register. This asserts the select line for bank *a* which is subsequently accessed by the processor. Even special VLSI (Very Large Scale Integration) parts were developed which provided a large number of banks and additional control facilities: the Motorola MC6883 SAM is a well known example used in the Dragon MC6809 home computer.

Program overlays are similar to bank switching except that some form of mass storage is used to contain the different overlays. If a particular subroutine is not available, the software stores part of its memory as a file on disc and loads a new program section from disc into its place (Figure 1.5). Several hundred kilobytes of program, divided into smaller sections, can be made to overlay a single block of memory, making a large program fit into the 64 kilobyte memory.

System integrity

Another disadvantage with this type of architecture is its unpredictability in handling error conditions. A bug in a software application could corrupt the whole system, causing a system to either crash, hang up or, even worse, perform some unforeseen operations. The reasons are quite simple: there is no partitioning between data and programs within the architecture. An application can update a data structure using a corrupt index pointer which overwrites a part of its program (Figure 1.6). Data are simply bytes of information which can be interpreted as instruction codes. The processor calls a subroutine within this area, starts to execute the data as code and

Figure 1.6 *System corruption via an invalid pointer*

suddenly the whole system starts performing erratically! On some machines, certain undocumented code sequences could put the processor in a test mode and start cycling through the address ranges, etc. These attributes restricted their use to non-critical applications.

It is important to put these characteristics into perspective: at the time (late 1970s), processing power offered at low cost was revolutionary and was more than sufficient for many applications. Devices were at their integration limits using the then current state of the art technology. While the deficiencies were quite apparent, better designs could be realized only using discrete implementations and minicomputers at a lot higher cost. It was the combination of reasonable performance and at a very low cost that ignited the revolution. Many applications were waiting for that balance to be achieved. But in terms of numbers, 8-bit processors like the Zilog Z80, the Intel 8080 and the Motorola MC6800 and their controller derivatives, have sold more units than any of the more powerful microprocessors. Millions are used to control car ignition systems, television remote control units, domestic appliances, etc. The list is endless. In terms of the performance race, these architectures have been left far behind – but these machines were the acorns from which today's super micros have grown.

Requirements for a new processor architecture

The deficiencies of the 8-bit processors set the goals for the new generation of processors that would use the higher integration capabilities rapidly being developed. The central aim was to provide more and more powerful facilities. The new architecture would need:

1   *A larger data size of at least 16 bits.* An obvious statement, yet is 16 bits really enough? For many computational applications, 32 bits would be a better choice. Does the external bus size need to be the same as the internal size? If a 32-bit external bus is used, is there a package with enough pins?

2   *More registers with more general purpose use.* Another obvious requirement. The questions are: how many, how big and how general purpose? Should the registers form a superset of an existing 8-bit architecture, and thus provide some form of compatibility?

3   *A larger memory addressing range.* Great, but how big? 2, 4, 8 or 16 times larger? Should it be a group of 64 Kilobyte blocks? How long will it be before that is insufficient?

4   *More complex and powerful instructions and addressing modes.* Another winner! With more powerful instructions, the less work compiler writers need to do the more efficient compilers will be. The more work an instruction can do, the less needed and, therefore, the required system memory and bus bandwidth will be smaller. However, the instruction size needs to increase to provide sufficient unique codes.

At that time, there were even suggestions that the native processor instruction set should be high-level language primitives with no assembler level support. The counter argument stated that many of the simple operations performed by such primitives could be split into several simpler lower-level instructions which would execute faster on machines with such lower-level support. This argument reappeared as part of the RISC processor philosophy.

5   *System partitioning and protection.* The processor would require resource protection mechanisms to prevent system crashes and allow the orderly recovery or shutting down of the system. Many control applications could not tolerate previous processor eccentricities.

It was against this background of larger data sizes, more powerful and complex instructions, ever increasing hardware support for compiler writers and the need for more efficient memory utilization and sophistication, that Motorola designed its MC68000 CISC processor architecture.

Software compatibility

When faced with the challenge of designing a new microprocessor architecture, one of the most critical dilemmas is how compatible must it be with preceding designs or families. Does compatibility constrain other developments and ideas which will prevent further developments? Would the best solution be a clean sheet coupled with a crystal ball to identify features that will be needed in ten years time? This was the problem faced by Motorola and the team behind the MACSS (Motorola's Advanced Computer System on Silicon) project.

The company continued development of its microprocessors and introduced the MC6809 8-bit processor in the late 1970s. The design took the basic MC6800 architecture and extended it. These extensions provided answers to many of the criticisms. The programmer's register model in Figure 1.7 shows the changes:

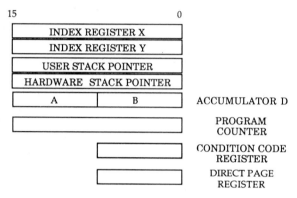

Figure 1.7 *The MC6809 programmer's model*

- the old A and B accumulators have been joined to create a new D register, while still preserving compatibility with the MC6800 model. This register provided the much needed 16-bit support
- there are two new 16-bit registers: an additional index register and a user stack pointer
- an 8-bit direct page register appeared to allow addressing into any 256 byte direct page within the 64 Kbyte memory map. This address register selects the page location within it

The instruction set and addressing modes were based on the MC6800 with new additions:

- 16-bit compare and addition instructions were added
- addressing modes were expanded to include larger offsets and indirection. Indirection allowed the contents of a memory address to be used for an address rather than the address itself

The dilemma was quite simple: should the MC6809/6800 model be extended further or start afresh? There were already hints that software compatibility would not be an unquestioned right: software was beginning to be developed in high–level languages such as PASCAL, which removed the need to code in assembler and provided a simple migration path from one architecture to another via recompilation. The question still remained unanswered: extend or start from scratch?

Enter the MC68000

The route that Motorola took with the MC68000 can be summed up with the advertising slogan used at its launch in August 1979: '*Break away from the Past.*'

The MC68000 was a complete design from scratch, with the emphasis on providing an architecture that looked forward without the restrictions of remaining compatible with past designs. The only support for the old MC6800 family was a hardware interface to allow the new processor to use the existing M6800 peripherals while new M68000 parts were being designed. Its design took many of the then current mini and mainframe computer architectural concepts and developed them using VLSI silicon technology. The programmer's register model in Figure 1.8 shows how dramatic the change was. Gone are the dedicated 8- and 16-bit registers, to be replaced by two groups of 8 data registers and 8 address registers. All these registers and the program counter are 32 bits wide. The processor

Figure 1.8 *The MC68000 USER programmer's model*

contained about 68 000 transistors – about ten times the number used by its predecessors. Folklore, if there be such a thing within a 30-year-old industry, states that the number of transistors gave the new processor its part number, and not that 68 000 was a natural successor to the MC6800 numbering. It is suspected that the transistor count was coincidental, but marketing is never slow to realize an opportunity!

Complex instructions, microcode and nanocode

The MC68000 microprocessor has a complex instruction set, where each instruction is very powerful in its processing capability and supports large numbers of registers and addressing modes. The instruction format consists of an op code followed by a source-effective address and a destination-effective address. To provide sufficient coding bits, the op code is 16 bits in size with further 16-bit operand extensions for offsets and absolute addresses. Internally, the instruction does not operate directly on the internal resources, but is decoded to a sequence of microcode instructions, which in turn calls a sequence of nanocode commands which controls the sequencers and arithmetic logic units (ALU). This is analogous to the many macro subroutines used by assembler programmers to provide higher-level 'pseudo' instructions. On the MC68000, microcoding and nanocoding allow instructions to share common lower-level routines, thus reducing the hardware needed and allowing full testing and emulation prior to fabrication. Neither the microcode nor the nanocode sequences are available to the programmer.

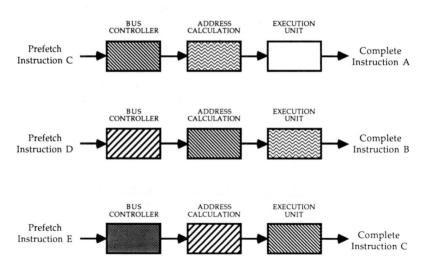

Figure 1.9   *Pipelining instructions*

These sequences, together with the sophisticated address calculations necessary for some modes, often take more clock cycles than are consumed in fetching instructions and their associated operands from external memory. This multilevel decoding automatically lends itself to a pipelined approach which also allows a prefetch mechanism to be employed. Pipelining works by splitting the instruction fetch, decode and execution into independent stages; as an instruction goes through each stage, the next instruction follows it without waiting for it to completely finish. If the instruction fetch is included within the pipeline, the next instruction can be read from memory, while the preceding instruction is still being executed, as shown in Figure 1.9.

The only disadvantage with pipelining concerns pipeline stalls. These are caused when any stage within the pipeline cannot complete its allotted task at the same time as its peers, as shown in Figure 1.10. This can occur when wait states are inserted into external memory accesses, instructions use iterative techniques or there is a change in program flow. With iterative delays, commonly used in multiply and divide instructions and complex address calculations, the only possible solutions are to provide additional hardware support, add more stages to the pipeline, or simply suffer the delays on the grounds that the performance is still better than anything else! Additional hardware support may or may not be within a designer's real estate budget (real estate refers to the silicon die area, and directly the

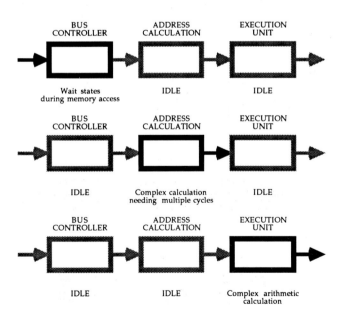

Figure 1.10 *Pipeline stalls*

number of transistors available). Adding stages also consumes real estate and increases pipeline stall delays when branching.

The main culprits are program branching and similar operations. The problem is caused by the decision whether to take the branch or not being reached late in the pipeline, i.e. after the next instruction has been prefetched. If the branch is not taken, this instruction is valid and execution can carry on. If the branch is taken, the instruction is not valid and the whole pipeline must be flushed and reloaded. This causes additional memory cycles before the processor can continue. The delay is dependent on the number of stages, hence the potential difficulty in increasing the number of stages to reduce iterative delays. This interrelation of engineering trade-offs is a common theme within microprocessor architectures. Similar problems can occur for any change of flow; they are not limited to just branch instructions and can occur with interrupts, jumps, software interrupts, etc. With the large usage of these types of instruction, it is essential to minimize delays; the longer the pipeline, the greater the potential delay.

The MC68000 hardware

The MC68000 pinout is shown in Figure 1.11. The device first appeared running at 4 MHz in a 64-pin, dual-in-line package. Fabricated in NMOS (N channel Metal Oxide Semiconductor), its 68 000 transistors were etched on to a die measuring 0.246 inches by 0.261 inches. The processor's signals can be divided into several groups.

Figure 1.11 *The MC68000 pinout*

Address bus

The address bus, signals A1 to A23, is non multiplexed and 24 bits wide, giving a single linear addressing space of 16 Mbytes. A0 is not brought out directly but is internally decoded to generate upper and lower data strobes. This allows the processor to access either or both the upper and lower bytes that comprise the 16-bit data bus.

Data bus

The data bus, D0 to D15, is also non multiplexed and provides a 16-bit wide data path to external memory and peripherals. The processor can use data in either byte, word (16-bit) or long word (32-bit) values. Both word and long word data is stored on the appropriate boundary, while bytes can be stored anywhere. Figure 1.12 shows how these data quantities are stored. All addresses specify the byte at the start of the quantity. If an instruction

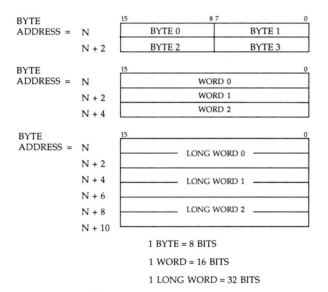

Figure 1.12 *MC68000 data organization*

needs 32 bits of data to be accessed in external memory, this is performed as two successive 16-bit accesses automatically. Instructions and operands are always 16 bits in size and accessed on word boundaries. Attempts to access instructions, operands, words or long words on odd byte boundaries cause an internal 'address' error and exception.

Function codes

The Function Codes, FC0–FC2, provide extra information describing what type of bus cycle is occurring. These codes and their meanings are shown in Figure 1.13. They appear at the same time as the address bus data and indicate program/data and supervisor/user accesses. In addition, when all three signals are asserted, the present cycle is an interrupt acknowledgement, where an interrupt vector is passed to the processor. Many designers use these codes to provide hardware partitioning. This technique is described later in Chapter 8.

Function Code			Reference Class
FC0	FC1	FC2	
0	0	0	Reserved
0	0	1	User Data
0	1	0	User Program
0	1	1	Reserved (I/O Space)
1	0	0	Reserved
1	0	1	Supervisor Data
1	1	0	Supervisor Program
1	1	1	Cpu Space/ Interrupt Ack

Figure 1.13   *The MC68000 function codes and their meanings*

M68000 asynchronous bus

The MC68000 bus is fundamentally different to the buses used on the MC6800 and MC6809 processors. Their buses were synchronous in nature and assumed that both memory and peripherals could respond within a cycle of the bus. The biggest drawback with this arrangement concerned system upgrading and compatibility. If one component was uprated, the rest of the system needed uprating as well. It was for this reason that all M6800 parts had a system rating built into their part number. If a design specified a MC6809B, then it needed 2 MHz parts and subsequently, could not use an 'A' version which ran at 1 MHz. If a design based around the 1 MHz processor and peripherals was upgraded to 2 MHz, all the parts would need replacing. If a peripheral was not available at the higher speed, the system could not be upgraded. With the increasing processor and memory speeds, this restriction was unacceptable.

The MC68000 bus is truly asynchronous: it reads and writes data in response to inputs from memory or peripherals which may appear at any stage within the bus cycle. Providing certain signals meet certain setup

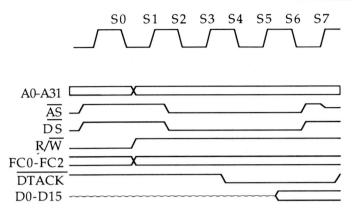

Figure 1.14   *An MC68000 asynchronous bus cycle*

times and minimum pulse widths, the processor can talk to anything. As the bus is truly asynchronous it will wait indefinitely if no reply is received. This can cause similar symptoms to a hung processor however, but most system designs use a watchdog timer and the processor bus error signal to resolve this problem.

A typical bus cycle, as shown in Figure 1.14, starts with the address, function codes and the read/write line appearing on the bus. Officially, this data is not valid until the address strobe signal AS★ appears but many designs start decoding prior to its appearance and use the AS★ to validate the output. The upper and lower data strobes, together with the address strobe signal (both shown as DS★ in Figure 1.14) are asserted to indicate which bytes are being accessed on the bus. If the upper strobe is asserted, the upper byte is selected. If the lower strobe is asserted, the lower byte is chosen. If both are asserted together, a word is being accessed.

Once complete, the processor waits until a response appears from the memory or peripheral being accessed. If the rest of the system can respond without wait states (i.e. the decoding and access times will be ready on time) a DTACK★ (Data Transfer ACKnowledge) signal is returned. In Figure 1.14, this occurs slightly before clock edge S4. The data is driven on to the bus, latched and the address and data strobes removed to acknowledge the receipt of the DTACK★ signal by the processor. The system responds by removing DTACK★ and the cycle is complete. If the DTACK★ signal is delayed for any reason, the processor will simply insert wait states into the cycle. This allows extra time for slow memory or peripherals to prepare data.

The advantages that this offers are manyfold. First, the processor can use a mixture of peripherals with different access speeds without any particular concern. A simple logic circuit can generate DTACK★ signals with the

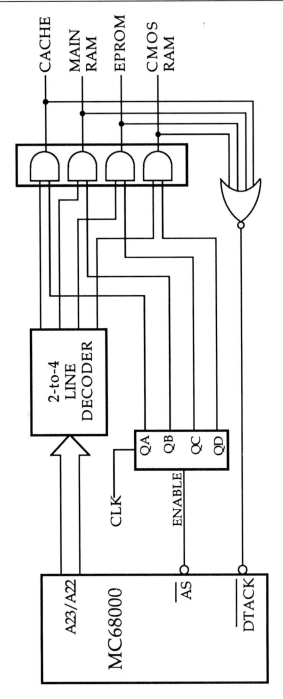

Figure 1.15   *Example DTACK* generation*

appropriate delays, as shown in Figure 1.15. If any part of the system is upgraded, it is a simple matter to adjust the DTACK★ generation accordingly. Many M68000 boards provide jumper fields for this purpose and a single board and design can support processors running at 8, 10, 12 or 16 MHz. Secondly, this type of interface is very easy to interface to other buses and peripherals. Additional time can be provided to allow signal translation and conversion.

M6800 synchronous bus

Support for the M6800 synchronous bus initially offered early M68000 system designers access to the M6800 peripherals and allowed them to build designs as soon as the processor was available. With today's range of peripherals with specific M68000 interfaces, this interface is less used. However, the M6800 parts are now extremely inexpensive and are often used in cost-sensitive applications. The additional signals involved are the E clock, Valid Memory Address VMA★ and Valid Peripheral Address VPA★. The cycle starts in a way similar to the M68000 asynchronous interface except that DTACK★ is not returned. The address decoding generates a peripheral chip select which asserts VPA★. This tells the M68000 that a synchronous cycle is being performed. It monitors the E clock signal, which is derived from the main system clock, but is divided down by 10 with 6:4 mark/space ratio. It is not referenced from any other signal and is free running. At the appropriate time (i.e. when E goes low) VMA★ is asserted. The peripheral waits for E to go high and transfers the data. When E goes low, the processor negates VMA★ and the address and data strobes to end the cycle.

For systems running at 10 MHz or lower, standard 1 MHz M6800 parts can be used. For higher speeds, 1.5 or 2 MHz versions must be employed. However, higher-speed parts running at a lower clock frequency will not perform peripheral functions at full performance.

Interrupts

Seven interrupt levels are supported and are encoded on to three interrupt pins IP0–IP2. With all three signals high, no external interrupt is requested. With all three asserted, a non-maskable level 7 interrupt is generated. Levels 1–6, generated by other combinations, can be masked internally by writing to the appropriate bits within the status register. The interrupt cycle is started by a peripheral generating an interrupt. This is usually encoded using a 148 priority encoder. The appropriate code sequence is generated and drives the interrupt pins. The processor samples the levels and requires the levels to remain constant to be recognized. It is recommended that the interrupt level remains asserted until its interrupt acknowledgement cycle commences to ensure recognition. Once the processor has recognized the interrupt, it waits until the current instruction has been completed and starts an interrupt acknowledgement cycle. This starts an external bus cycle with all three function codes driven high to indicate an interrupt acknowledgement cycle.

The interrupt level being acknowledged is placed on address bus bits A1–A3 to allow external circuitry to identify which level is being acknowledged. This is essential when one or more interrupt requests are pending. The system now has a choice over which way it will respond:

1   If the peripheral can generate an 8-bit vector number, this is placed on the lower byte of the address bus and DTACK★ asserted. The vector number is read and the cycle completed. This vector number then selects which address and subsequent software handler from the vector table.

2   If the peripheral cannot generate a vector, it can assert VPA★ and the processor will terminate the cycle using the M6800 interface. It will select the specific interrupt vector allocated for the specific interrupt level. This method is called auto-vectoring.

To prevent an interrupt request generating multiple acknowledgements, the internal interrupt mask is raised to the interrupt level, effectively masking any further requests. Only if a higher level interrupt occurs will the processor nest its interrupt service routines. The interrupt service routine must clear the interrupt source and thus remove the request before returning to normal execution. If another interrupt is pending from a different source, it will be recognized and cause another acknowledgement to occur.

A typical circuit is shown in Figure 1.16. Here, level 5 has been allocated as a vectored interrupt and level 3 autovectored. The VPA★ signal is gated with the level 3 interrupt to allow level 3 to be used with vectored or auto-vectored sources in future designs.

Error recovery and control signals

There are three signals associated with error control and recovery. The bus error BERR★, HALT★ and RESET★ signals can provide information or be used as inputs to start recovery procedures in case of system problems. The BERR★ signal is the counterpart of DTACK★. It is used during a bus cycle to indicate an error condition that may arise through parity errors or accessing non-existent memory. If BERR★ is asserted on its own, the processor halts normal processing and goes to a special bus error software

Figure 1.16   *Example MC68000 interrupt design*

handler. If HALT★ is asserted at the same time, it is possible to re-run the bus cycle. BERR★ is removed followed by HALT★ one clock later, after which the previous cycle is re-run automatically. This is useful to screen out transient errors. Many designs use external hardware to force a re-run automatically but will cause a full bus error if an error occurs during the re-run.

Without such a signal, the only recourse is to complete the transfer, generate an immediate non-maskable interrupt and let a software handler attempt to sort out the mess! Often the only way out is to reset the system or shut it down. This makes the system extremely intolerant of signal noise and other such transient errors.

The RESET★ and HALT★ signals are driven low at power up to force the MC68000 into its power up sequence. The operation takes about 100 ms, after which the signals are negated and the processor accesses the Reset vector at location 0 in memory to fetch its stack pointer and program counter from the two long words stored there. RESET★ can be driven by the processor in response to the RESET instruction. This allows the processor to reset external hardware without resetting itself. The HALT★ signal can be driven by the processor in response to a catastrophic failure or externally to halt the processor. A typical catastrophic cause may be a bus error encountered during stack frame building.

Bus arbitration

The MC68000 has a three-wire bus arbitration scheme. These signals are used in the bus arbitration process to allow another bus master, such as a DMA controller or another processor, to request and obtain the bus. While the bus is arbited away, the MC68000 bus signals are tristated. This mechanism is a more elegant replacement for the clock stretching and cycle stealing techniques used with many 8-bit processors which relied on delaying clock edges from the processor so that it did not start another cycle.

The arbitration scheme allocates the MC68000 a lower bus priority than an external request. An external master must request the bus prior to it starting a bus cycle by asserting the bus request signal BR★. The processor completes its current bus cycle, tristates its bus and control signals and asserts the bus grant signal BG★. This informs the other master that the bus is available as far as the processor is concerned. The master must check that the current cycle is complete (AS★, DTACK★, etc. negated) before asserting bus grant acknowledge BGACK★ and negating BR★. The bus is now available for use. If BR★ is negated prior to BGACK★ being asserted, the processor assumes that the request is erroneous and takes back the bus. Apart from the obvious applications with multiprocessing systems and

DMA control, this method can be used to allow circuit emulators to be used in systems without removing the processor.

Typical system

Figure 1.17 shows a typical MC68000 system. There is no differentiation between I/O and memory accesses: all peripherals, such serial and parallel ports, appear as locations within the memory map and the same instructions are used to access both memory and I/O. The memory is constructed from two byte wide memory banks forming a 16-bit data path. The MC68901 MultiFunction Peripheral has an 8-bit data bus and is connected to either the odd or even byte. Its registers therefore appear on consecutive odd or even addresses and not simply successive addresses. Just as the external hardware interface was quite different from anything previously seen, the internal architecture was a complete departure from previous designs: the architecture had more in common with a Digital Equipment Corporation PDP–11 minicomputer than a microprocessor! The first fundamental difference was the register set.

The register set

The MC68000 register set supports 8, 16 and 32-bit wide data as standard and with the large number of registers allows data to be stored internally rather than on an external stack, with the benefit of reduced stack manipulation. This was important, considering that internal register storage was faster to access and thus offered quicker instruction execution. With a complex iterative process, the ability to store data internally, so that after initial loading any further data fetches were removed from the execution time, was an obvious benefit. If the system had to suffer wait states when accessing memory, this benefit increased.

The general-purpose nature of the data and address registers further improves performance: whatever operation can be performed on data register 1 can be performed on any of the other seven. Similarly, any addressing mode can be used with any one of the eight address registers. All the overhead of moving data to and from a specific register for address calculations or manipulation is removed. This overhead can be as high as 40% on the total number of executed instructions within a dedicated register approach, although it is application dependent.

The condition code register looks very similar to that found within an 8-bit processor, except that almost every instruction execution updates it automatically without having to perform a separate compare operation. This is beneficial in performing branch determination and allows single

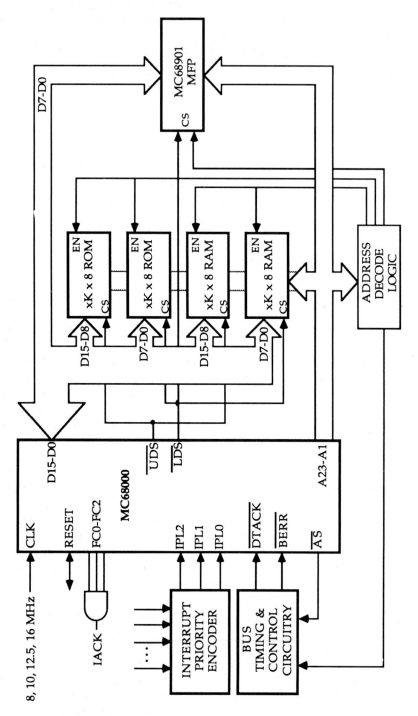

Figure 1.17 *Typical MC68000 system*

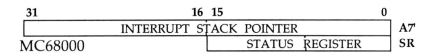

Figure 1.18 *The supervisor registers for the MC68000*

instructions to test for a condition and decide to change the program flow. The program counter is specified as a full 32 bits, but only the lower 24 bits are bonded out to provide a 24-bit external address bus.

Some additional supervisor registers are shown in Figure 1.18.

The USER/SUPERVISOR concept

Many earlier 8-bit microprocessor systems could easily be crashed by bad programming and/or software errors, associated usually with application tasks rather than the operating systems that were being used. The reason was quite simple: there was little or no separation or protection of the controlling software and application tasks running under it. To solve this deficiency, the MC68000 family uses the concept of two separate states with separate and protected resources. The processor can either be halted or execute in the USER or SUPERVISOR state. It normally executes code in the USER state but when an exception occurs, it switches into a SUPERVISOR state with its own separate stack pointer, A7', and access to the processor control registers (Figure 1.18). The SUPERVISOR stack pointer is used for the stack frames that are generated as part of the exception process. They contain essential information to restore the program flow prior to the exception and allow nesting, given that there is sufficient stack memory allocated to store all the generated frames.

The transition can be caused by a processing error, external interrupts or a software interrupt TRAP instruction (Figure 1.19). The duplicated stack pointer allows separate stacks to be maintained and also allows application software, running in USER mode, to cause errors without destroying an operating system kernel running in SUPERVISOR mode. Using these two states permits application and operating system software to be separated, preventing rogue applications from corrupting the whole system.

However, the processor's dual status needs to be repeated in the external design. If the whole of the external memory were available to both the USER and SUPERVISOR states, each other's programs would be put at risk from corruption. The memory system must be partitioned so that programs can be protected. This function is performed by the three function code signals referenced in the previous hardware interface

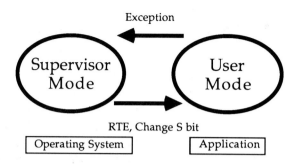

Figure 1.19 *The MC68000 USER/SUPERVISOR concept*

description. The three pins offer eight codes which indicate the type of transfer that is taking place, i.e. program or data, SUPERVISOR or USER, or interrupt acknowledge/CPU space cycle. By taking these outputs and including them in the address decode logic, blocks of memory can be reserved for specific use and can therefore be protected.

Once in SUPERVISOR mode, the exception is serviced via a specific exception handler, depending on what caused the exception to occur. Up to 255×32 bit pointers are stored in a vector table stored in the bottom 1024 bytes of memory.

Exceptions and the vector table

As described previously, the MC68000 processor responds to external interrupts and bus errors by treating them as an exception, switching into supervisor mode, selecting the appropriate vector and executing its software exception handler. Due to the internal microcoding within it, the MC68000 can identify further error and potential error conditions caused by incorrect software or hardware failures and treat them as separate entities rather than a general fault condition. This allows fault conditions to be identified early, and gives a far better indication as to the problem. Figure 1.20 shows the vector table and the conditions associated with each vector.

The first entry in the table contains the RESET vector used by the processor on power up. The bus error vector is followed by the address error. This is selected if an attempt is made to fetch an instruction or word on an odd byte boundary. The next location is used for any attempt to execute an illegal instruction. The processor detects any such attempts and will not go into an undocumented state. This vector is often used to implement breakpoints: the original instruction is overwritten by an illegal one, which on execution, passes control to the exception handler. Divide by zero is self explanatory. The next two vectors are accessed if certain conditions are met. The TRAPV instruction causes this handler to be invoked if the V flag within the condition code register is set, i.e. when an overflow condition exists. The CHECK handler is used if data is found to be out of bounds as a result of a CHECK instruction. The privilege violation handler is invoked if the processor in USER mode attempts to perform a SUPERVISOR operation, such as changing the interrupt mask. Within the handler, the SUPERVISOR can decide whether to perform the operation or not. The TRACE exception vector provides processor debug facilities: if the T bit is set in the SUPERVISOR status register, the processor takes the TRACE exception after each instruction is completed. This allows a debugger to single step through a program.

The next pair of vectors is used when certain types of instructions are executed. These are the famous F-line and A-line instructions. Their names come from the bit pattern encoded into the four highest order bits within the instruction. None of the standard instructions uses that encoding, thus allowing programmers to define their own additional A-line and F-line instructions, which will invoke their own exception handler during execution. The handler can simulate the instruction execution. Motorola used the F-line mechanism for its Floating Point Coprocessor instructions, so that software could perform the calculations if no hardware support was

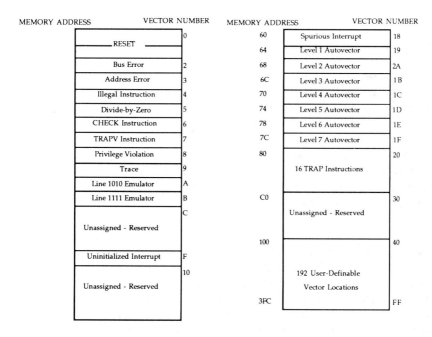

Figure 1.20 *The MC68000 exception table*

available. The A-line vector is often used for breakpoints as an alternative to the illegal instruction vector. Vector F, sandwiched between two banks of reserved vectors, handles errors during the hardware interrupt sequence when an incorrect vector is passed to the processor. The spurious interrupt vector which follows it is similar: it is selected when a bus error signal terminates the interrupt acknowledge cycle. The next seven locations are for the autovectored interrupts, with each interrupt level assigned its own handler.

The 16 TRAP vectors are next. They are the equivalent of a software interrupt and allow USER code to make requests of the SUPERVISOR. Operating system calls are made in this way and commands like TRAP # 1 and TRAP # 2 are very common. Parameters are often passed via a register to further define the request.

After another bank of reserved vectors, there are 192 allocated for the user to define. This may seem to be an overkill, but it does allow a group of different handlers to be assigned to a particular peripheral, providing a faster response. This is advantageous with peripherals that generate vector numbers. With a multiprotocol serial port, one vector could be assigned to handle interrupts when the port is in asynchronous mode, a second when in SDLC, a third for bisync support and so on. When the port is configured, the vector register is loaded to redirect the interrupt to the correct handler. This removes the overhead of determining what mode the device is in and subsequently how to handle the interrupt. Similar techniques can be used to dynamically reallocate interrupt handlers for particular ports. An operating system may decide to take a printer port offline by simply reprogramming its vector register, thus changing the vector number it generates to request servicing. Instead of being handled by a device driver, an error handler can take over and simply discard any data, thus taking it offline.

It is important to remember that any vector number from 0 to 255 can be passed during an interrupt acknowledgement cycle. It is prudent to have all vectors assigned to a handler. If unused vectors are set to non-existent or random memory locations, any external hardware faults or software errors could cause the processor to halt without providing any information as to the cause. Once the MC68000 has halted, only a system reset can start it again with the subsequent data loss.

Addressing modes

The MC68000 has a far greater range of addressing modes than its predecessors. Figure 1.21 lists their form and names. The reason for this expansion is to reduce the number of calculations needed to locate and process data. The (An)+ and −(An) modes perform automatic post-increment and pre-decrement of their respective register contents. This

Dn	Data Register Direct
An	Address Register Direct
(An)+	Address Reg. Indirect w/ Post-Increment
-(An)	Address Reg. Indirect w/ Pre-Decrement
d(An)	Displaced Address Register Indirect
d(An,Rx)	Indexed, Displaced Address Reg. Indirect
d(PC)	Program Counter Relative
d(PC,Rx)	Indexed Program Counter Relative
#xxxxxxxx	Immediate
$xxxx	Absolute Short
$xxxxxxxx	Absolute Long

Figure 1.21   *The MC68000 addressing modes*

allows pointers to be used to access data stored in a table and not have to perform register increment or decrement instructions after every access. Another advantage of these modes is their automatic size adjustment. If the pointer is used to access a long word, it is incremented by 4 to position it at the next valid byte location. Similarly, word and byte accesses are adjusted by 2 and 1 respectively. These modes reduce the number of instructions that an 8-bit architecture without these facilities would need.

The Program Counter relative addressing modes allow the easy development of relocatable and position independent code. If an instruction specifies one of these modes, an offset from the data location relative to the current program counter is encoded into an operand. If the program and the data areas are then moved into a different memory location, while retaining the same offset, the data can still be located correctly. If complete programs are written in such manner, multitasking can be achieved without hardware memory management.

Instruction set

The instruction set mnemonics are shown in Figure 1.22. Each mnemonic has a single letter suffix which defines the data size:

- B for byte
- W for a 16-bit word
- L for a 32-bit long word

Most assemblers assume word data size if no suffix is specified. Each instruction is based around a 16-bit format with optional operands depending on selected addressing modes. It takes a diadic form using two

ABCD	Bcc	DIVS	MOVE	OR	SBCD
ADD	BCHG	DIVU	MOVE to	ORI	Scc
ADDA	BCLR	EOR	CCR	ORI to	STOP
ADDI	BRA	EORI	MOVE SR	CCR	SUB
ADDQ	BSET	EORI to	MOVE	ORI to	SUBA
ADDX	BSR	CCR	USP	SR	SUBI
AND	BTST	EORI to	MOVEA	PEA	SUBQ
ANDI	CHK	SR	MOVEM	RESET	SUBX
ANDI to CCR	CLR	EXG	MOVEP	ROL	SWAP
ANDI to SR	CMP	EXT	MOVEQ	ROR	TAS
ASL	CMPA	JMP	MULU	ROXL	TRAP
ASR	CMPI	JSR	MULS	ROXR	TRAPV
	CMPM	LEA	NEG	RTE	TST
	DBcc	LINK	NEGX	RTR	UNLK
		LSL	NOP	RTS	
		LSR	NOT		

Figure 1.22   *The MC68000 instruction set*

effective addresses to form two sources AND destination, i.e. if two registers are multiplied together, the result is stored in one of them, overwriting the original value. However, it must be noted that although the encoding appears regular (i.e. bits 9 to 11 specify a source register and bits 0 to 5 specify a destination effective address) there are many instructions where this regularity is not observed such as the CMPI (compare immediate), LSL and LSR logical shift instructions. This greatly increases the decoding complexity and, as will be seen later on, became a major criticism of CISC architectures like the M68000 family.

With all these new and powerful commands, addressing modes and sophisticated hardware, CISC processors like the M68000 family catalysed the migration of software techniques and applications from mini and mainframe computers to the microprocessor arena.

Multitasking operating systems

Perhaps the most apparent reaction to this high-performance CISC architecture was the sudden appearance of sophisticated multitasking operating systems for microprocessors. Most 8-bit architectures could offer operating system support, such as CP/M for 8080 and Z80 families and MDOS for the MC6800 and MC6809 processors, but these were restricted in memory size and system response speeds and could only execute a single task at a time. Code development was often performed in assembler or BASIC with very rudimentary debugging. There was no system protection, with application errors often crashing the system and thus further hindering debugging investigations.

The MC68000 offered several solutions. Its linear 16 Mbyte memory addressing space obviously removed any memory limitations, providing sufficient memory could be afforded or installed. Its linear addressing, coupled with the addressing mode support for relocatable code, allowed multiple programs or tasks to be relocated into memory, even though they originally may have been designed to run at the same nominal location. Without this support, such relocation could be performed only with a memory management unit which, at this time, inserted delays within the bus cycles and increased software overhead. The Intel 80×86 architecture took a different approach and used a segmentation scheme based on 64 Kbyte segments. This allowed them to preserve compatibility with their previous 8-bit architectures, although adding software overhead to recognize 64 Kbyte boundaries and reprogram segment registers. This was a trade-off that Motorola did not agree with.

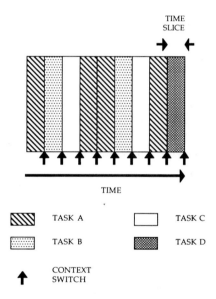

Figure 1.23 *Time slicing*

With the ability to load and hold multiple tasks, all that was required to make a multitasking operating system was a timer to control a scheduler or kernel. A multitasking operating system works by dividing the processors' time into discrete time slots (Figure 1.23). Each application or task requires a certain number of time slots to complete its execution. The operating system kernel decides which task can have the next slot, so instead of a task executing continuously until completion, its execution is interleaved with other tasks. This sharing of processor time between tasks gives the illusion to each user that he is the only one using the system.

Context switching, task tables and kernels

Multitasking operating systems are based around a multitasking kernel which controls the time slicing mechanisms. A time slice is the time period each task has for execution before it is stopped and replaced during a Context Switch. This is periodically triggered by a hardware interrupt from the system Timer. This interrupt may provide the system clock and several interrupts may be executed and counted before a Context Switch is performed. When a Context Switch is performed, as shown in Figure 1.24, the current task is interrupted, the processor's registers are saved in a special table for that particular task and the task is placed back on the 'ready' list to await another Time Slice.

Special tables, often called Task control blocks, store all the information the system requires about the task, for example, its memory usage, its priority level within the system and its error handling. It is this context information that is switched when one task is replaced by another. The 'ready' list contains all the tasks and their status and is used by the Scheduler to decide which task is allocated the next Time Slice. The scheduling algorithm determines the sequence and takes into account a task's priority

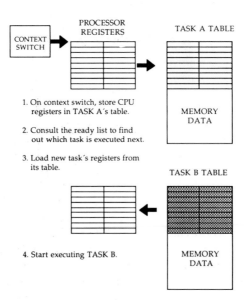

Figure 1.24　*Context switching*

and present status. If a task is waiting for an I/O call to complete, it will be held in limbo until the call is complete. Once a task is selected, the processor registers and status at the time of its last Context Switch are loaded back into the processor and the processor is started. The new task carries on as if nothing had happened until the next Context Switch takes place. This is the basic method behind all multitasking operating systems.

The M68000 architecture has extensive support for such operating systems: its SUPERVISOR/USER partitioning allows the kernel to run in SUPERVISOR mode with application tasks executing in the USER state. The timer interrupts can be given a specific interrupt vector number and handler, which will automatically switch the processor from running application tasks in its USER mode into SUPERVISOR mode to perform the context switch. The MOVEM provides a single instruction which will then load or reload the register set from a task control block in memory. This system partitioning prevents any exceptions caused by application tasks from corrupting the kernel, which could simply abort the erroneous task and carry on without it. The 16 different TRAP instructions provide an elegant method of implementing operating system calls by causing an exception and allowing a handler, within the kernel, to perform the request. The single-step facility through the TRACE exception facilitates system debuggers (many 8-bit single-step routines required special external hardware) and so on.

Multitasking and communication support

Support for intertask communication via semaphores was made possible via the TAS instruction and its associated Read-Modify-Write cycles. If a resource is to be shared between processors or tasks running under a multiprocessor operating system, any shared resource such as I/O, peripherals and memory must be controlled so that only one processor or task can access it at one time. This is essential to prevent task A from overwriting data that Task B was using and thus cause system corruption. A semaphore is frequently used to control such access. Before accessing such resources, the associated semaphore is checked. If it is clear, then no one else is using it and access is permitted. The task must then set the semaphore to lock out other tasks. If it is set, the task must repeatedly check the semaphore until it is clear and the resource is available. This can be done by the Test and Set instruction, TAS. However there is a potential problem: in between checking and setting the semaphore, another task could also check and set the semaphore with the result that both tasks now have access. This is highly undesirable! This can occur if the read cycle, i.e. testing the semaphore status, and the write cycle, i.e. the semaphore setting, can be split from two consecutive cycles into two independent ones. This can occur if another processor requests the bus in the middle or if context switch occurs in a multiprocessing operating system. To prevent this, the M68000 family has an indivisible Read Modify Write cycle. This cannot be interrupted and neatly prevents the problem. This cycle type is indicated by continued assertion of AS★ through both the cycles.

High-level language support

The M68000 provides substantial help for high-level languages by providing many specific instructions and functions to reduce the amount of work that a compiler has to perform. Condition codes are set after the completion of virtually every instruction, thus removing many comparisons that might otherwise have to be made. Procedure calls are helped by the LINK and UNLINK instructions which allow data frames to be attached and removed from the stack with a single instruction. These allow nested subroutines to use the stack areas as temporary data storage without losing track or control. The bit manipulation instructions are ideal for real-time applications, semaphore control, or any other applications which need to control data at the individual bit level. The alternative to this involves bit masking or a series of logical functions: both take multiple instructions to implement.

For compilers the biggest advantage is the large general-purpose register set. Figure 1.25 shows the main advantage of general-purpose registers: with a dedicated register set, the existing data must be moved out to other registers or to the external memory stack, the new data moved into its place and finally the specific operation performed. This sequence must be repeated each time fresh data is involved. This needs multiple instructions

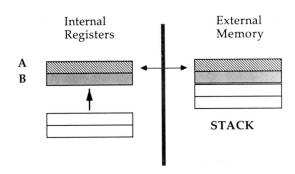

1. Store dedicated register contents on stack.
2. Move new values into dedicated registers.
3. Perform operation.

Figure 1.25 *Data movement with dedicated registers*

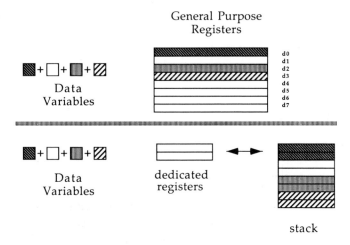

Figure 1.26 *Variable allocation*

and results in a considerable amount of time being spent simply moving data from one place to another without actually processing it. With a large number of variables as shown in Figure 1.26, this problem is even worse. The data is stored on the stack and therefore any access must go to external memory with the performance impact associated with the slower memory access. The M68000 register set allows variables to be stored in registers, allowing easy and fast access. The M6800 code example which multiplied two 16-bit numbers shows the code expansion that occurs when dealing with data larger than the processor can handle. The M68000 family with its 32-bit wide data paths does not suffer from this problem and thus allowed the easy development of 32-bit software right from day one.

The concept of a large linear addressing space is of importance to compilers and other applications. The large space does not suffer from the problem and overhead incurred through segmentation. A segmented architecture like the Intel 80×86 splits the memory into individual 64 KByte segments which are controlled by a segment register (Figure 1.27). Each time an address crosses a segment boundary, software has to reload the segment register. While this did not seem to be a problem in 1979 when most applications would fit in a segment, it contributes to the overhead involved in using larger memory spaces. For compilers this simply restricts the direct addressing to only 64 Kbytes, which is reminiscent of the problems associated with bank switching techniques used with the older 8-bit generations. The M68000 family's ability to use large linear addressing has encouraged programmers to generate large applications with many facilities: the Apple Macintosh wordprocessor used to write this text uses 1.5 Mbytes for its application and 1.2 MBytes for its system software!

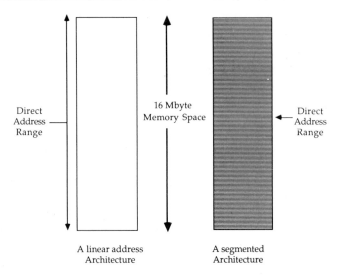

Direct Address Range

16 Mbyte Memory Space

Direct Address Range

A linear address
Architecture

A segmented
Architecture

Figure 1.27 *The linear v. segmented address ranges*

Start of a revolution

The architecture's similarity to a mini computer, rather than its 8-bit predecessors, was now providing the necessary support for software developers to move operating systems, compilers and applications to the cheaper microprocessor environment and away from the discrete and more expensive mini and mainframe computers. This pull down effect was to catalyse a rapid increase in their use and sounded ominous warnings to the computer-manufacturing industry. However, the development of the basic M68000 architecture had another iteration to perform before the appearance of the full 32-bit implementations, the MC68020 and MC68030.

The MC68010 virtual memory processor

To replace mini and mainframes, the MC68000 needed to provide a more efficient mechanism to handle external memory faults, necessary for virtual memory operating systems such as UNIX, and provide a virtual machine capability. These two concepts came directly from mini and mainframe environments and were necessary to allow M68000 systems to become cost-effective platforms for these types of application. The MC68010 was a simple superset of the MC68000, with virtual memory and machine support built in. It appeared in 1983, four years after the MC68000, and had the same USER register set and ran MC68000 USER binary code without modification, but faster by virtue of some microcode changes. From a hardware perspective, the parts were interchangeable and acted as plug-in replacements for each other.

Virtual memory support

A virtual memory operating system allows a program or task to access memory that is physically not present or is being used by another task. The technique usually involves splitting a task into smaller blocks, a memory management unit being used to translate each block's logical addresses into physical ones, some form of mass storage to act as a memory reservoir to store unused blocks and a protection system to protect all the blocks from corruption. There are usually two reasons behind using such a system: one occurs when the application requires more memory than is physically available (Figure 1.28) and the second is when two or more tasks need to access separate memory but at the same address, as may happen within a multitasking operating system.

Figure 1.28 *Using virtual memory to support large applications*

For this system to work, page faults must be detected and signalled back to the processor to halt the current bus cycle. Such faults occur when the processor tries to access non–existent or non-allocated memory, where an access goes across a page boundary or when the required block is resident on disc and needs to be swapped with an unused block. In addition, bus faults may be generated by memory parity or EDC (Error Detection and Correction) problems. These functions are easily performed by an MMU (Memory Management Unit) like the MC68451 and some bus error routing logic, as shown in Figure 1.29.

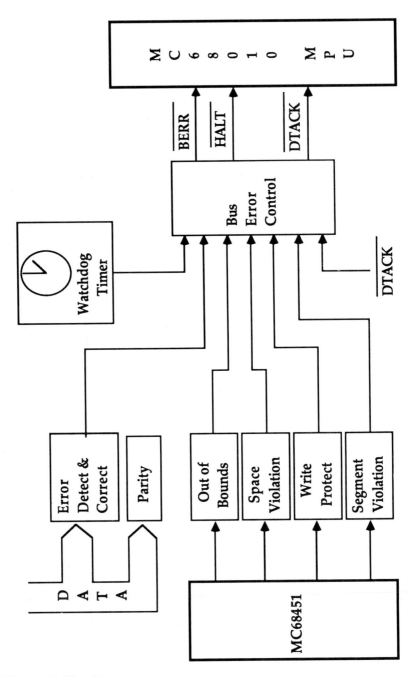

Figure 1.29   *Bus error sources*

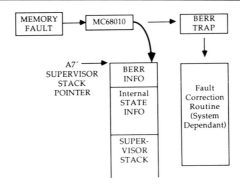

Figure 1.30 *MC68010 bus error recovery – stack building*

The real difficulty is what the processor should do once the page fault has been corrected and the cycle needs re-running. The MC68000 can be halted in mid-instruction but has to restart the interrupted instruction. This can cause a lot of challenges for the software handler to resolve: has the data within the processor been changed? If so, how? Has the external data been partially modified? If so, how can the instruction be restarted? The MC68010 provides a hardware solution to solve this dilemma. When it receives a bus error (Figure 1.30), it switches into SUPERVISOR mode and starts to build an external stack frame using the SUPERVISOR stack pointer, A7′, just like the MC68000. However, the frame is different and internal state information is added, in addition to the normal stack frame information containing the program counter, access address, etc. This state information is the contents of the processor's internal registers, latches, etc., which direct the execution of the instruction. This block is not defined or described and therefore is strictly 'off limits' to any manipulation or modification. The only publicly defined information within it is a processor mask number.

After the page fault has been corrected (Figure 1.31), an RTE (ReTurn from Exception) instruction is executed, which reloads the processor with its previous contents to restore its state at the time of the error. Once

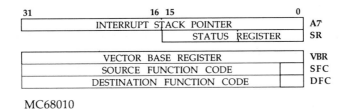

MC68010

Figure 1.31 *The MC68010 supervisor register model*

finished, the MC68010 automatically completes the instruction execution by re-running the bus cycle that had previously failed. This time, no failure should be encountered.

This mechanism offers a couple of interesting possibilities. First, *any* MC68010 can recover this state information and continue the program that encountered the error. This allows freedom for any processor within a distributed multiprocessor system to complete an instruction that another has been unable to do. Secondly, it allows systems to use the RTE instruction with a predefined stack frame to set up the processor in an exact predetermined state. Both of these are valuable techniques for robust or fault-tolerant system design.

Virtual machine support

A virtual machine environment allows several operating systems to execute concurrently on a single processor system, with each operating system thinking that it has total control of the system! In practice, one operating system is defined as the governing operating system, with the others running subservient to it. The Governing Operating System (GOS) executes in SUPERVISOR mode while all other virtual operating systems (VOS) and applications run in USER mode. Any requests for or attempts at system access by such applications or operating systems are detected by an M68000 privilege violation exception. This immediately invokes the GOS, which either rejects the request, performs it directly or performs it via the appropriate VOS.

To keep control of such a system requires a mechanism similar to that described for a multitasking operating system. Tables describing each operating system environment must be kept. When an exception occurs, the GOS always handles it initially. It first determines where the exception came from. If it was from an application or utility, the appropriate VOS will handle it. If it was from a VOS, possibly as a result of an application request, the GOS will service the request and pass the results to the VOS which will have appeared to have performed the service itself. Such interaction is simplified if different vector tables can be allocated to each operating system and selected as necessary. It would also be useful to be able to move data from SUPERVISOR to USER space to allow a VOS to receive data from the GOS, even if external hardware partitioning has been implemented. These functions are provided via additional registers and instructions available to the SUPERVISOR.

MC68010 SUPERVISOR resource

Figure 1.31 shows the MC68010 SUPERVISOR programming model. The additional registers are the Vector Base Register (VBR) and two alternate function code registers, one source and the other destination. Both of these registers can be loaded using the new MOVEC instruction. Loading the VBR with a value will offset the vector table from its original location at $000000 to anywhere in the memory map. This can provide a unique vector table for each VOS. The VBR is set to zero and is compatible with the MC68000 on power up.

The MOVES instruction will move data from one location to another but the contents of the alternate function code registers are output on the three function code pins instead of the normal code. With separate source and destination registers, data can be accessed from one space and transferred to another while maintaining the appropriate function codes necessary for correct external hardware decode. To provide a completely secure SUPERVISOR environment, the MOVE from SR (Status Register) instruction was made privileged, whereas it was non privileged with the MC68000. Although this instruction was hardly ever used, a small exception handler was necessary to ensure compatibility. It took the exception, identified the MOVE from SR command and then decided if the information could be passed to the USER.

Generic exception handlers were better supported by the inclusion of a vector number within the exception stack frame. A single handler could then be written to support multiple hardware resources within a system (e.g. one serial driver could control six serial ports). By checking the vector offset in the stack frame, the handler can immediately determine which port has interrupted it and use the appropriate addresses to access it directly.

Other improvements

The opportunity was taken with the MC68010 to re-evaluate the many of the microcode sequences used internally to execute instructions. An example is the well known anomaly concerning the CLR instruction and the MC68000. It simply sets a memory location to zero, yet it actually performs an additional read cycle before writing zero into the location. In very fast code, a move immediate instruction is often used instead. This raises the question of why two instructions are needed to perform the same operation? They do have different effects on the condition codes but is that sufficient to warrant a separate instruction? The answer is probably not; however, it was present in the original M68000 design and to maintain software compatibility, it had to be included. All 32-bit register-based operations were speeded up, along with the shift and rotate functions and the arithmetic functions. The new divide algorithm was 25% faster than the MC68000 in performing that operation.

The most impressive improvement came with the implementation of 'Loop mode'. A block move of any size from anywhere to anywhere within the 16 Mbyte memory map can be performed by a simple 2

```
START    MOVE.L   $NO_WORDS,D0  ; move number of words
                                ; into register D0
         MOVEA.L  $BLK1,A0      ; point A0 at start of BLK1
         MOVEA.L  $BLK2,A1      ; point A1 at start of BLK2
LOOP     MOVE.W   (A0)+,(A1)+   ; move word, move pointers
DBEQ.L   D0,LOOP                ; decrement D0,if not zero,
                                ; goto LOOP
```

Figure 1.32 *Example MC68000 block move*

instruction loop as shown in Figure 1.32. Examination of the MC68000 bus cycles shows that each time the two instruction LOOP is executed, both the MOVE and DBEQ instructions are fetched. This is not too efficient, as the internal pipelines already have them loaded and decoded. The MC68010 detects this software structure, automatically locks the pipeline and will not repeatedly fetch the two instructions. This frees up the bus, allowing it to be dedicated to moving the data from one block to another, which is performed much faster. 'Loop mode' works only with loops involving the DBcc (Decrement and Branch on condition) instruction and another with no absolute or offset addressing and the decrement. Inserting another instruction, even an NOP, between the two will destroy the loop mode and force the repeated instruction fetches. This is done often in benchmarks and system testing to force the MC68010 to act like an MC68000.

While most of the improvements centred on software, the MC68010 bus interface did offer help to designers using fast memory systems. The bus error signal BERR★ timing was relaxed so that it could be asserted after DTACK★ and would be recognized by the processor, which would then ignore the original DTACK★. This allowed a designer to assume that every access would complete correctly and gain an extra half clock cycle for an error detection circuit to determine an erroneous cycle. Figure 1.33 shows the new timing diagram.

The MC68008

The MC68008 also appeared at this time: it was an external 8-bit data bus version of the MC68000 in a 40-pin package. Its address bus was limited to 20 pins, giving a 1 Mbyte linear address space. It was aimed at low-cost systems and provides about 60% of the performance of the MC68000 at the same clock speed – not 50%, as even 16/32 bit machines need to fetch bytes occasionally!

Its main claim to fame was its inclusion in the Sinclair QL home computer, which was described as a 32-bit machine by its advertising material. This immediately created some controversy as it caused many arguments over exactly how a processor should be defined. Many people

Figure 1.33 *The MC68010 late bus error*

rang Motorola in the UK for adjudication. The answer was very simple but diplomatic: 'The MC68008 is an 8-bit external data bus microprocessor with a 16/32 bit internal architecture. Any 16- or 32-bit accesses are automatically performed as 2 or 4 sequential byte accesses and, therefore, software can use and specify 16- and 32-bit values.'

The story continues

Some observers have stated that the MC68010 is the processor that the MC68000 should have been first time around. For applications needing virtual memory, etc. this may be a valid comment. It should be remembered though, that not all applications need virtual memory support, etc. and, for these, the MC68000 is an eminently suitable and cost-effective solution due to its smaller die and cost. CISC processors, like the M68000 family, have continued to provide more and more powerful instructions, addressing modes and hardware functions to reduce the amount of work required of the software running on it, as can be seen in Chapter 2.

2   32-bit CISC processors

Almost as soon as the MC68000 and MC68010 had appeared, rumours started circulating about when the full 32-bit processor would be launched, what new features it would have and how much performance it would offer. The most common prediction was that it would be an MC68000 with simply full 32-bit data and address buses. It was argued that to offer any additional features would take too many transistors, cause heat dissipation problems and require too large a die to manufacture profitably.

This idea of simply expanding the buses appears on first inspection to be a very sensible stepping stone; it doubles the available data bus bandwidth and increases the linear address space. In reality, the performance increase it buys is not the factor of two, as one might expect. This is due primarily to the more frequent use of smaller data sizes – if software accesses bytes or words within a data structure, such an access is rarely sequential and is also fairly random. In such cases, fetching 32 bits and discarding 24 of them does not give any performance advantage. This is a similar situation, but in reverse, to that concerning the performance degradation suffered by a MC68008 mentioned in the previous chapter.

With the appearance of the MC68012, an MC68010 with a larger address bus, more fuel for the rumours of a simple upgrade was generated. When the MC68020 was announced in 1984, it surprised many in terms of its complexity, power and performance!

Enter HCMOS technology

With all microprocessor designs, it is the fabrication technology which will ultimately limit or facilitate new design ideas – a theme that will recur throughout this book.

The main catalyst for the Redwood design team, which was responsible for the new 32-bit M68000 processor, was Motorola's decision to move away from NMOS technology to High-Speed Complementary Metal Oxide Semiconductors (HCMOS). The new technology offered smaller transistor geometries, smaller power dissipation and higher packing density. This change gives the designers about 200 000 transistors to play with – almost a three times increase over the MC68000 – and allowed additional functions to be included.

The HCMOS process had another benefit – it was capable of supporting far higher clock speeds and allowed the processor to build to 16 MHz design rules. This was twice the speed of the then standard 8 MHz MC68000 and MC68010. It was realized that with a processor running at twice the current system speeds, major problems would be created with memory and there would be a great danger of designing a very fast processor whose performance was restricted by memory design. Undoubtedly, memory systems would catch up but would this hold back the processor's acceptance and development?

Architectural challenges

The main challenge for CIC architectures is to reduce the number of clocks required to execute instructions. The M68000 family took the idea of splitting the operation into several stages within a single pipeline. Unfortunately, the architecture has features which decrease the pipeline efficiencies. Instruction op codes with additional operands requiring multiple memory cycles or wait states inserted in the memory accesses can delay the transfer within the pipeline and cause stalls. Complex address calculations can cause similar delays further into the pipeline. Conflict between data and instruction accesses on a single bus and coprocessor communication also cause the same result – pipeline delays. Figure 2.1 shows some examples using a simple three-stage pipeline.

Delays caused through effective address calculations and complex arithmetic operations could be solved by providing each pipeline stage with its own arithmetic logic unit (ALU) and using the faster clock speed. By not having to share an ALU between stages, calculation delays could be reduced and the faster clock obviously reduced the time needed to perform such operations. Analysis showed the likely bottle-neck to be the memory sub system.

CISC processors have a memory-to-memory architecture – they allow direct manipulation of data in external memory without having explicitly to use internal registers. This has the benefit of helping compiler writers at the expense of multiple bus cycles – while the bus controller is busy completing a data access, the rest of the pipeline is stalled when it could be executing other instructions. What was needed was another entry point into the pipeline, allowing instructions to be inserted from a local cache

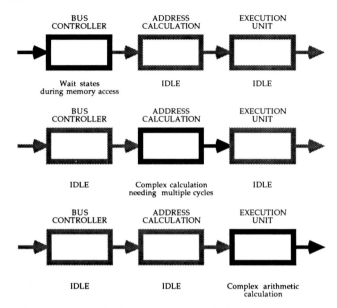

Figure 2.1 *Example of pipeline stalls and delays*

store (Figure 2.2). While an instruction is moving data to external memory as the last stage of its execution, the next instruction can be loaded into the pipeline. It can then be executed using the otherwise idle stages of the pipeline as shown in Figure 2.3. This allows the pipeline activities to be folded and the resultant instruction overlap gives the 'magical' result of zero clock cycle execution and an infinite MIPS performance! In reality, the execution time is hidden rather than reduced to nothing.

This was just one of the many revolutionary ideas implemented in the MC68020.

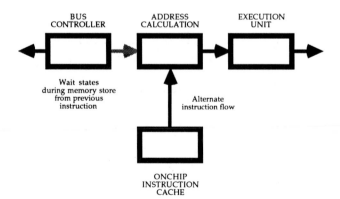

Figure 2.2 *Feeding a stalled pipeline from an onchip cache*

Figure 2.3 *Overlapping instruction execution*

The MC68020 32-bit performance standard

The MC68020 was launched in April 1984 as the '32-bit performance standard' and in those days its performance was simply staggering – 8 million instructions per second peak with 2–3 million sustained when running at 16 MHz clock speed. It was a true 32-bit processor with 32-bit wide external data and address buses, as shown in Figure 2.4. It supported all the features and functions of the MC68000 and MC68010, and it executed M68000 USER binary code without modification, but faster!

1   Virtual memory and instruction continuation were supported.
2   The bus and control signals were similar to that of its M68000 predecessors, offering an asynchronous memory interface but with a three-cycle operation (instead of four) and dynamic bus sizing.
3   Additional coprocessors could be added to provide facilities such as

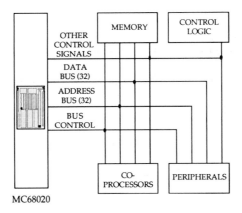

Figure 2.4 *A simple MC68020 system*

floating point arithmetic and memory management, which used this bus to provide a sophisticated communications interface.

4   The instruction set was enhanced with more data types, addressing modes and instructions.

5   Bit field data and its manipulation were supported, along with packed and unpacked BCD (Binary Coded Decimal) formats.

An instruction cache and a barrel shifter to perform high-speed shift operations were incorporated on chip to provide support for these functions.

The device was truly 'state of the art' – its die contained 200000 transistors fabricated in a 2.25 μ HCMOS technology, packaged in a 114–pin PGA (pin grid array) and typically dissipated 750 mW, the same as an MC68000. The original design was breadboarded using 14 boards, each containing 300 MSI (Medium Scale Integration) devices and tested with over 500000 lines of diagnostic software.

The internal design philosophy

The internal block diagram, Figure 2.5, shows the basic philosophy behind the design. The device has three separate ALUs (Arithmetic Logic Units):

- one for effective address calculations
- another for operand calculations
- a third for arithmetic instructions

Pipeline stalls due to oversubscribed resources are thus prevented.

The bus controller and sequencer can now operate independently of each other, allowing simultaneous data and instruction fetches. While data is being moved on the external bus, the next instruction can be fetched from the instruction cache and possibly executed. Again, this parallelism makes the best use of the design and improves performance. The actual pipeline

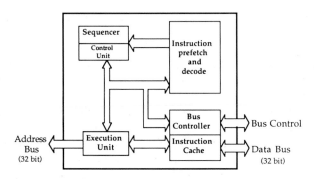

Figure 2.5   *The MC68020 internal block diagram*

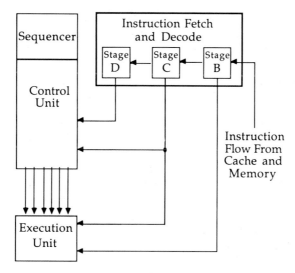

Figure 2.6 *The MC68020 internal pipelining*

used within the design, and shown in Figure 2.6, is quite sophisticated. It is a four-stage pipe with stage A consisting of an instruction router which accepts data from either the external bus controller or the internal cache. As the instruction is processed down the pipeline, either the intermediate data can cause micro and nanocode sequences to be generated to control the execution unit or, in the case of simpler instructions, the data itself can be passed directly into the execution unit with the subsequent speed improvements.

The programmer's model

The programmer's USER model is exactly the same as for the MC68000, MC68010 and MC68008. It has the same 8-data and 8-address, 32-bit register organization. The SUPERVISOR mode is a superset of its predecessors, as shown in Figure 2.7. It has all the registers found in its predecessors plus another three. Two registers are associated with controlling the instruction cache, while the third provides the Master Stack Pointer. The supervisor uses either its Master Stack Pointer or Interrupt Stack Pointer, depending on the exception cause and the status of the M bit in the status register. If this bit is clear, all stack operations default to the A7′ stack pointer. If it is set, interrupt stack frames are stored using the Interrupt Stack Pointer while other operations use the Master Pointer, which effectively allows the system to maintain two separate stacks. While

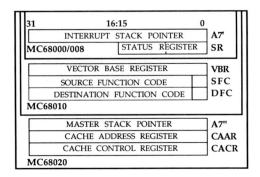

Figure 2.7 *The M68020 SUPERVISOR programming model*

primarily for operating system support, this extra register can be used for high-reliability designs.

The MC68020 instruction set is a superset of the MC68000/MC68010 sets. The main difference is the inclusion of floating point and coprocessor instructions, together with a set to manipulate bit field data. The instructions to cause a trap on condition, perform a compare-and-swap operation and a 'call–return from module' structure were also included. Other differences were the addition of 32-bit displacements for the LINK and Bcc (branch on condition) instructions, full 32-bit arithmetic with 32- or 64-bit results as appropriate and extended bounds checking for the CHK (check) and CMP (compare) instructions.

Bit field instructions were included to provide additional support for applications where data does not conveniently fall into a byte organization. Telecomms and graphics both manipulate data in odd sizes – serial data can often be 5, 6 or 7 bits in size and graphics pixels (i.e. each individual dot that makes a picture on a display) vary in size, depending on how many colours, grey scales or attributes are being depicted. The MC68020 bit field data type is 1–32 bits in size. It is defined by three terms – a starting address anywhere within the 4 Gigabyte linear addressing space, a starting bit which can be defined anywhere in a 4 Gigabit ($\pm 2^{31}$ range) and a data width which determines the size. The manipulation instructions allow data to be inserted, extended, tested, cleared, set or changed. The first set bit within a field can also be detected.

The MC68000 and MC68010 can perform these tasks by simulating instructions with software routines involving the standard logical shift and bit test instructions. However, the execution time is often dependent on both the number of bits involved and the number of shifts needed. Examination of the instruction timings shows that a logical shift instruction execution time is $(10 + 2n)$ clocks, where n is the number of bits. To reduce this overhead, the MC68020 has a hardware accelerator called a barrel shifter, which can perform a shift in a single clock, irrespective of the number of bits shifted. This hardware support is virtually essential for any bit field operations. It is also used when packing and unpacking BCD data.

The addressing modes, Figure 2.8, were extended from the basic M68000 modes, with memory indirection and scaling. Memory indirection allowed the contents of a memory location to be used within an effective address calculation rather than its absolute address. The scaling was a simple multiplier value 1, 2, 4 or 8 in magnitude, which multiplied (scaled) an index register to allow large data elements within data structures to be easily accessed without having to perform the scaling calculations prior to the access. These new modes were so complex that even the differentiation between data and address registers was greatly reduced; with the MC68020, it is possible to use data registers as additional address registers. In practice, there are over 50 variations available to the programmer to apply to the 16 registers.

New CAS and CAS2 'compare and swap' instructions provided an elegant solution to linked list updating within a multiprocessor system. A linked list is a series of data lists linked together by storing the address of the next list in the chain in the preceding chain. To add or delete a list simply involves modifying these addresses. In a multiprocessor system, this modification procedure must occur uninterrupted to prevent corruption; the CAS and CAS2 instruction meets this specification. The current

Dn	Data Register Direct
An	Address Register Direct
(An)+	Address Reg. Indirect w/ Post-Increment
-(An)	Address Reg. Indirect w/ Pre-Decrement
d(An)	Displaced Address Register Indirect
d(An,Rx)	Indexed, Displaced Address Reg.
d(PC)	Indirect
d(PC,Rx)	Program Counter Relative
#xxxxxxxx	Indexed Program Counter Relative
$xxxx	Immediate
$xxxxxxxx	Absolute Short
	Absolute Long

MC68000/008/010

(bd,An,Xn.SIZE*SCALE)	Register Indirect
	Memory Indirect
([bd,An,Xn.SIZE*SCALE],od)	Pre-Indexed
([bd,An],Xn.SIZE*SCALE,od)	Post-Indexed
	Program Counter Memory Indirect
([bd,PC,Xn.SIZE*SCALE],od)	Pre-Indexed
([bd,PC],Xn.SIZE*SCALE,od)	Post-Indexed

MC68020/MC68030

Figure 2.8 *The MC68020 addressing modes*

pointer to the next list is read and stored in Dn; the new value is calculated and stored in Dm. The CAS instruction is then executed and the current pointer value is read and compared with Dn. If they are the same, no other updating by another processor has happened and Dm is written out to update the list. If they do not match, the value is copied into Dn, ready for a repeat run. This sequence is performed using an indivisible Read-Modify-Write cycle, the condition codes being updated during each stage. The CAS2 instruction performs a similar function but with two sets of values. It is also performed as a series of indivisible cycles but with different addresses appearing during the execution.

Bus interfaces

Figure 2.9 shows the device pinout. Many of the signals are the same as those of the MC68000 – the function codes FC0–2, interrupt pins IPLO–2 and the bus request pins, RESET★, HALT★ and BERR★ perform the same functions.

With the disappearance of the M6800 style interface, separate signals are used to indicate an autovectored interrupt. The AVEC★ signal is used for this function and can be permanently asserted if only autovectored interrupts are required. The IPEND signal indicates when an interrupt has been internally recognized and is awaiting an acknowledgement cycle. RMC★ indicates an indivisible read-modify-write cycle instead of simply

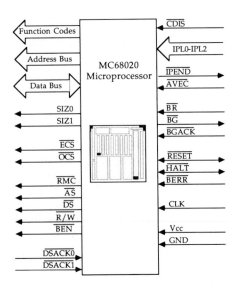

Figure 2.9 *The MC68020 device pinout*

leaving AS★ asserted between the bus cycles. The address strobe is always released at the end of a cycle. ECS★ and OCS★ provide an early warning of an impending bus cycle, and indicate when valid address information is present on the bus prior to validation by the address strobe. The M68000 upper and lower data strobes have been replaced by A0 and the two size pins, SIZE0 and SIZE1. These indicate the amount of data left to transfer on the current bus cycle and, when used with address bits A0 and A1, can provide decode information so that the correct bytes within the 4 byte wide data bus can be enabled. The old DTACK★ signal has been replaced by two new ones, DSACK0★ and DSACK1★. They provide the old DTACK★ function of indicating a successful bus cycle and are used in the dynamic bus sizing. The bus interface is asynchronous and similar to the M68000 cycle but with a shorter 3-cycle sequence, as shown in Figure 2.10.

Figure 2.10 *MC68020 bus cycle timing*

Dynamic bus sizing

Most of the systems available at the MC68020's introduction were either 8 or 16 bits in size. Even VMEbus designs were based around the 16-bit format, although today it is widely accepted and used in its full 32-bit format. The problem comes with trying to combine 8, 16, and 32-bit data paths. The processor can support these types explicitly within its instruction set so software could be forced to use certain data sizes with certain address ranges. The first 1 Mbyte could be 32 bits wide, the next 16 Mbytes be 16 bits and so on. This does, however, constrain software development – compilers cannot use the single 32-bit move instruction to fetch a 32-bit wide variable without performing some address range check. Equally, if the hardware design was changed, how would this affect software? One solution could be to adopt a standard 32-bit data path, but this would be expensive considering past design investment. While today this is totally feasible, four to five years ago there were simply not the products off the shelf!

Dynamic bus sizing allows the processor to change the data bus width on a cycle by cycle basis without prior knowledge of the memory port width. The processor always attempts the largest transfer it can (32 bits) and indicates the number of bytes needed to transfer by coding the two SIZE signals, as shown in Figure 2.11. The memory port takes as much data as possible and indicates a success and the number of bytes taken by responding with the two DSACK signals. The processor sees this, calculates how many bytes are left to transfer, shuffles the data up on its bus and automatically starts another bus cycle. Again, the port replies and the process repeats until all the data is transferred. This system means that software can specify whatever data size it needs and, providing the memory interface observed this protocol, it can fetch this data from any size or combination of external data widths. The only penalties are the extra bus cycles and increased bus activity.

DSACK1	DSACK0	MEANING
HI	HI	Insert Wait State
HI	LO	Complete cycle, Port Size = 8 bits
LO	HI	Complete cycle, Port Size = 16 bits
LO	LO	Complete cycle, Port Size = 32 bits

Figure 2.11 *MC68020 dynamic bus sizing*

This flexibility is further enhanced by the processor's ability to fetch data that lies across word and long-word boundaries. Such misaligned data is fetched as a series of aligned accesses and reconstituted internally. Again, the only penalties are extra bus cycles and increased bus activity. Instructions, however, are always fetched on a word boundary and any attempt to fetch a misaligned instruction results in an exception.

On-chip instruction cache

One of the perennial problems faced by any fast processor designer is that of slow memory accesses. Often a processor can execute instructions far faster than the system can provide them or any associated data. This von Neumann bottleneck, named after the pioneering mathematician, is caused by delays in accessing external memory, such as wait states, bus arbitration, etc. The MC68020 doubled the processor clock speed to 16 MHz overnight and reduced an MC68000 bus cycle by 25% from four clocks to three. By today's standards, these speeds are slow, but in 1984 this was state-of-the-art and presented a major obstacle. One way of solving this problem is to use cache memory. Here, instructions and/or data can be stored in local, very fast memory. The first access goes to main memory and is slow, but a copy is stored in the fast cache memory. Any subsequent access to this location is now made to the cache, giving a faster access and better performance. Providing software is written as a series of tight instruction loops, some benefit can be obtained. Cache designs and their characteristics are becoming more and more important for processor architectures and are explored more fully in Chapters 3 and 5.

The MC68020's internal 256 byte instruction cache was added to prevent the degradation expected within a system with a poor memory performance. It holds about 100 instructions and is organized as a 64 by 4 byte array. Accessing instructions from the cache can occur simultaneously with an external data fetch and this reduces the bus bandwidth needed by the processor. Cache accesses take only two cycles, giving a minimum 33% improvement over external fetches. Typically, an MC68020 uses 60% bus bandwidth compared with the 80–90% of an MC68000. By being instruction only, there are no associated stale data problems. From a programming viewpoint, it is very simple – there are two programming registers available to the SUPERVISOR which can enable/disable the cache or freeze its contents. Normally any cache updating is performed automatically using a special replacement algorithm which determines which cache entry will be used when data is fetched from external memory. When the cache is frozen, no updating is performed. In addition, either the whole cache or specific entries can be cleared. The beauty of the MC68020 cache is its simplicity – the cache is enabled and software executes

Figure 2.12 *The MC68020 internal instruction cache*

typically 15–20% faster and the maintenance and updating are performed internally and automatically. The only maintenance required is when the cache is used with memory management within a multitasking operating system. The cache appears on the logical side of the memory management unit and does not know automatically when a context switch has occurred. When a switch does take place, the cache contents is no longer valid and must be cleared. With the MC68020, this can be performed simply by an instruction within the operating system kernel.

The cache system works very simply. When an instruction fetch is started, the address is supplied to the bus controller and to the cache. If the data is present in the cache, a cache hit signal prevents the bus controller from continuing the external bus cycle. (Strictly speaking, the cycle is never really started because the address strobe, AS★, is not asserted.) If the data is not cached, a miss occurs, the external bus cycle continues and the instruction fetched from external memory. A copy of the instruction is then used to update the internal cache. By supplying the address to both the bus controller and cache, the external bus cycle is not delayed if there is a cache miss. Alternatively, if the bus controller cannot start the external cycle due to prior cycles or bus arbitration, the cache lookup is not delayed.

The lookup works by taking bits 2–8 of the access address and using them to index into the 64-element tag array (Figure 2.12). The remaining higher address bits, together with function code 2 to differentiate between SUPERVISOR and USER, are then compared with the tag memory contents. If they match, there is a cache hit and address bit 1 is used to select which of the two words stored in the cache data memory is sent via the instruction path. If there is a mismatch, or the tag is marked as not valid, a cache miss is caused. When the instruction is brought back from external memory, it and its associated tag entry replace the original cache entry. If the cache has been frozen, no updating occurs. These mechanisms are performed automatically. The cache obviously provides great benefit as can be seen from Figure 2.13. The Sperry (now Unisys) benchmarks were based around the EDN benchmark suite which tests interrupt response, bit manipulation, string sorting, etc. With fast static RAM, the improvement is about 25–30%. With slower dynamic memory, this figure increases to 50%. This performance gain is obtained by simply executing one instruction to enable the cache.

The cache causes difficulties when trying to work out how many clocks a particular instruction will take. As shown in Figure 2.14, it is possible for a register-based instruction to be executed in zero clock cycles when it can be fetched from the cache while the bus controller is completing the preceding data movement. The NOP instruction was enhanced to provide a software method of synchronizing the execution pipeline and bus controller, and thus prevent overlapping. This infinite performance is not achieved every time and is dependent on preceding instruction flow, bus activity and the

Relative Performance (Fast Static Memory)

Relative Performance (Fast Dynamic Memory)

BASED ON A RESEARCH STUDY BY SPERRY PUBLISHED IN IEEE
MICRO AUGUST 1986
(NOTE: "C" = On-chip cache enabled, "N" = On-chip cache disabled)

Figure 2.13   *MC68020 performance figures*

state of the cache. This is extremely difficult to predict without actual measurement, although the instruction timings stated in the MC68020 User's Manual are divided into three different types:

- best care with maximum overlap
- cache case
- worst case

In reality, the actual performance lies somewhere around the cache case figure, but it is totally software and system dependent.

While software engineers can exploit the cache to its full by freezing the cache contents with time critical routines, these techniques cause great difficulties for their hardware colleagues. Such small loops, including diagnostic test loops, can easily be completely cached. This removes any external instruction fetches and the processor uses the bus only for data reads and writes. If the data is register based, the processor sits there apparently doing nothing. In addition, unlike its predecessors, the MC68020 does not halt processing when the external HALT signal is asserted. It carries on executing instructions from its cache until an external fetch is needed. The halt signal is often used to provide external cycle-by-cycle single stepping but this is no longer so useful unless the cache is disabled. Further confusion is caused by the external bus cycles providing only an intermittent view of the processing going on internally. Additional support was needed to solve these problems.

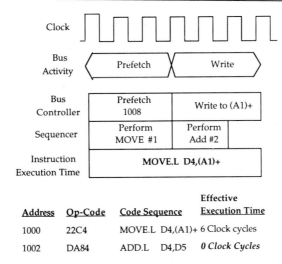

Figure 2.14 *Instruction overlapping*

Debugging support

The most important feature of debugging is the CDIS pin which disables the internal cache when asserted. With it asserted, all bus cycles take place externally, thus allowing analysers and emulators access. The cache does cause some interesting phenomena, however. The normal method of breakpointing code is to replace an instruction with an illegal one to force an exception when it is executed. Alternatively, hardware can analyse the bus cycle traffic until the breakpoint address is accessed. At this point, the hardware can take over and stop the processor. Neither of these techniques works very well with the MC68020. If the instruction is replaced after it has been cached, the cached instruction will be fetched in preference, resulting in a breakpoint that appears never to be reached. The cache must either be cleared or disabled, hence the CDIS pin. The hardware method is fine, except that it cannot determine exactly when an instruction is executed within the MC68020. In a small loop, with a breakpoint set on the first instruction after the loop, the breakpoint address is prefetched every time the loop is executed and therefore the hardware stops the processor on every loop. Again, this is not very useful.

Most emulators use a combination of the two techniques. The address traffic is analysed and when a breakpoint address appears, the hardware jams an illegal instruction on the data bus. If this is a simple prefetch, the illegal instruction is not executed and nothing happens. If the access is cached, the next access fetches the illegal instruction correctly from the cache. If the instruction is then executed, this forces an exception and stops the processor as required. Another advantage of this mechanism is its ability to set breakpoints in read-only memory. The MC68020 design provided additional support by way of the Breakpoint Instruction. This instruction forces a special Breakpoint CPU space cycle to take place and allows external hardware to supply the option of forcing the exception or providing the original instruction, thus allowing execution to continue. This process, shown in Figure 2.15, needs external hardware support and is therefore totally system dependent.

The original T trace bit of the MC68000 was also enhanced. Its function is performed by a T1 trace bit within the Status Register which, when set by the Supervisor, takes the trace exception after the completion of any instruction. If the T0 bit is set instead (is not allowed to set both bits), the trace exception is taken only after a change of flow. Such changes in flow can be caused by branching and jumping. The trace facility is best looked at as an extension of the basic instruction. If tracing is enabled, an instruction is not deemed to have completed until any trace processing has been completed. Only if an address or bus error occurs during the instruction execution will the trace processing be deferred. When the exception is taken, the trace bits are cleared, preventing any further tracing.

Coprocessor interface

Even with the large number of transitors available, there were not enough to provide memory management or floating point support on chip. The obvious solution was to use additional chips with an interface as transparent as possible. For the programmer, this means simply bringing additional registers and instructions to the software model. For the hardware designer, it should be a simple interface using standard signals and should also allow these coprocessors to be optional. The MC68020 coprocessor interface uses no special signals, supports both logical and physical caches and allows a coprocessor to act as a bus master in its own right. The basis for the mechanism are the F line exceptions and standard bus cycles.

The M68000 family treated the F and A line instructions in a special way. Their execution causes an exception and allows software to emulate their action. These instructions are used on the MC68020 to provide coprocessor instructions for floating point arithmetic and memory management facilities. When such an instruction is executed, the MC68020 starts a CPU space cycle. This is signified by the three function code outputs all going high. For the 16-bit family members, this indicated an interrupt acknowledgement cycle only. A CPU space cycle can still be an interrupt acknowledgement but can also indicate a coprocessor cycle, a breakpoint cycle or an access level control cycle. These different types are indicated by different bit patterns within the CPU space type field, bits 16–19 of the

Figure 2.15 *The MC68020 breakpoint instruction*

address bus. For a coprocessor cycle, this pattern is 0100 with bits 13–15 identifying the coprocessor identity number and bits 0–4, the register number (Figure 2.16).

The protocol allows up to eight coprocessors to be added. Usually only two sockets are used, with the MC68851 Memory Management Unit always being socket 0, together with a MC68881 or MC68882 Floating

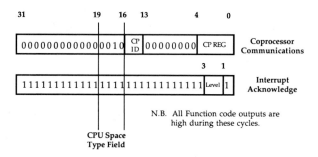

Figure 2.16 *Different CPU space cycles*

Point Unit in socket 1. The extra registers are located on the coprocessor and the processor acts as an intelligent DMA (Direct Memory Access) controller, fetching data as needed. The processor can be stalled or released to allow either sequential or concurrent operation as needed.

During the start of coprocessor instruction execution shown in Figure 2.17, the CPU sends the op code to the coprocessor using a coprocessor communications CPU space cycle. The coprocessor id is decoded and used to select physically the correct coprocessor which then takes the op code and sends a response back to the CPU. This response could indicate that the coprocessor is busy and cannot execute the op code presently, that more data or operands are needed or that no further service is needed. If the coprocessor is busy, the CPU repeatedly tries to send the op code until it is

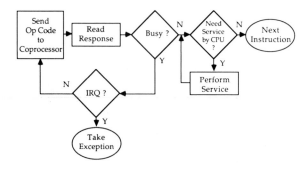

Figure 2.17 *The MC68020 coprocessor interface (simplified)*

successful or until an interrupt or other exception occurs. If the coprocessor is not capable of fetching data from memory itself, it uses the CPU as a DMA controller to perform such tasks. The coprocessor can force sequential execution by reserving the CPU for such requests and not actually requesting any. Once the CPU has finished servicing the coprocessor, it is free to execute the next instruction. If the coprocessor instruction is invalid or the coprocessor hardware is not present, the normal exception is taken and software is called to reconcile the problem. This coprocessor interface can be simulated using standard M68000 bus cycles with additional logic and software so that they can be used as peripherals with the other family members.

MC68881 and MC68882 floating point coprocessors

The MC68881 Floating Point Coprocessor provides hardware support for calculations using the full IEEE Floating Point Standard (P754 Rev 10) and transcendental functions (sin, tan, etc). All calculations are performed to 80-bit precision and many mathematical constants are stored internally in ROM for immediate use. It adds eight 80-bit floating point registers, FP0–FP7, with three control registers (Figure 2.18) to the USER programming model. The 68-pin PGA device acts as a non-DMA

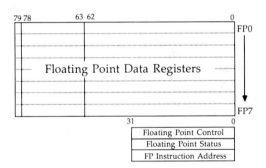

Figure 2.18 *MC68881/882 register set*

coprocessor (it relies entirely on the MC68020 for its data supply) and can be used as peripheral with MC68000/010/008 processors. The interface is very simple, requiring only simple logic to decode the processor ID and register selection from the address bus during a CPU space coprocessor cycle to generate a chip select (Figure 2.19).

Its performance was unsurpassed when it first appeared, although by today's standards, it is not a performance leader. However, considering the faster clock speeds and its wide set of functions, it still offers a cheap and easy

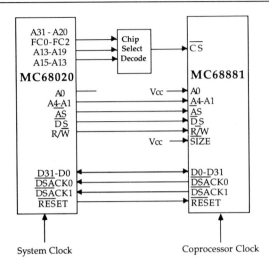

Figure 2.19   *An MC68020/MC68881 block diagram*

way of increasing performance. In extended precision, it can typically perform an addition in 2.2 µs, a multiply in 3.2 µs and a divide in 4.6 µs at a coprocessor clock of 25 MHz.

The MC68882 is a 'go-faster' version of the MC68881: it is upward and downward software compatible with MC68881, is hardware pin compatible and available in faster clock speeds (e.g. 33 and 40 MHz). It was designed to complement the MC68030 but is equally suitable for MC68020 designs. The performance is gained by increasing the onchip concurrency. The operand pre-fetch, data conversion and computation is all pipelined, with additional hardware to expedite operand loads and stores. The floating point registers are dual ported to allow simultaneous loading and computation. Figure 2.20 shows how the MC68882 achieves its optimization. If it executes standard MC68881 code, it can overlap the transfer and conversion parts of the instruction processing so that they can commence during the calculation phase, instead of waiting for its completion. This will typically improve performance by a factor of about 1.4. Further optimization can be obtained by alternating calculations with data moves where complete overlap occurs, giving a 1.7 to 2 times improvement. Both these figures are totally software dependent, however. It is possible, in certain cases, for far higher increases.

The MC68851 paged memory management unit (PMMU)

The MC68851 Paged Memory Management Unit is an intelligent coprocessor capable of external bus accesses. It provides full support for

Figure 2.20 *MC68882 optimization*

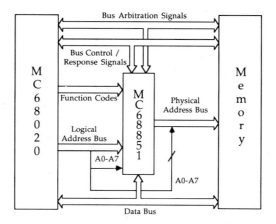

Figure 2.21 *Connecting an MC68851 to an MC68020*

systems that need memory management to allow multiple tasks to use the same or overlapping sets of logical addresses. The PMMU sits between the CPU and memory (Figure 2.21). Such sets can be declared as read only, SUPERVISOR only, etc., so that they can be protected. The device supports full 32-bit logical and physical addresses without multiplexing the buses. Address translations are performed in 45 ns due to an on chip Address Translation Cache which holds the 64 most recent translations so that they

Figure 2.22   *The MC68851 address translation mechanism*

are immediately available. This reduces the translation delay to a single cycle. When the translation entry is not held in the cache, the PMMU acts as a bus master and performs a walk through its translation tables to get the correct translation; these tables are stored in external memory. The page sizes are programmable from 256 bytes to 32 Kbytes.

The address translation mechanism uses a root pointer to select a translation table as shown in Figure 2.22. Part of the logical address, the Table Index A (TIA) is used to index into this table. The table contents are used with the lower logical address to form the physical address. The MC68851 supports multiple table levels and root pointers which allow large numbers of pages to be allocated without very large tables. Memory management techniques are described more fully later.

In retrospect, the MC68851 was too sophisticated for many applications and offered facilities that were never used. It has even been suggested that over 45% of the chip's hardware is never used. The real problem with the device (or any external memory management unit) is tracking processor speed increases. The fastest version supports only 20 MHz operation, against 33 MHz for the MC68020. With the appearance of the MC68030 together with its integrated MMU and faster clock speeds, the MC68851/MC68020 lost much of its appeal.

The MC68030 – the first commercial 50 MHz processor

The MC68030 appeared some 2–3 years after the MC68020 and used the advantage of increased silicon real estate to integrate more functions on to a MC68020-based design. The differences between the MC68020 and the

MC68030 are not radical – the newer design can be referred to as evolutionary rather than a quantum leap. The device is fully MC68020 compatible with its full instruction set, addressing modes and 32-bit wide register set. The initial clock frequency was designed to 20 MHz, some 4 MHz faster than the MC68020, and this has yielded commercially available parts running at 50 MHz. The transistor count has increased to about 300 000 but with its smaller geometries, die size and heat dissipation are similar.

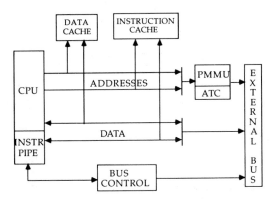

Figure 2.23 *The MC68030 internal block diagram*

Memory management has now been brought on chip with the MC68030 using a subset of the MC68851 PMMU with a smaller 22-entry on chip address translation cache. The 256 byte instruction cache of the MC68020 is still present and has been augmented with a 256 byte data cache (Figure 2.23). Both these caches are logical and are organized differently from the 64 × 4 MC68020 scheme. A 16 × 16 organization has been adopted to allow a new synchronous bus to burst fill cache lines (Figure 2.24). The cache lookup and address translations occur in parallel to improve performance. The processor supports both the coprocessor interface and the MC68020 asynchronous bus with its dynamic bus sizing and misalignment support. However, it has an alternative synchronous bus interface which supports a 2-clock access with optional single-cycle bursting. The bus interface choice can be made dynamically by external hardware.

Both cycles start with the address and other information appearing on the bus and being qualified by the address strobe. Whereas the asynchronous cycle is terminated by the DSACK signals, the hardware asserts STERM★ to indicate that a synchronous transfer is taking place. If only a single transfer is needed, the data is latched on the second clock and

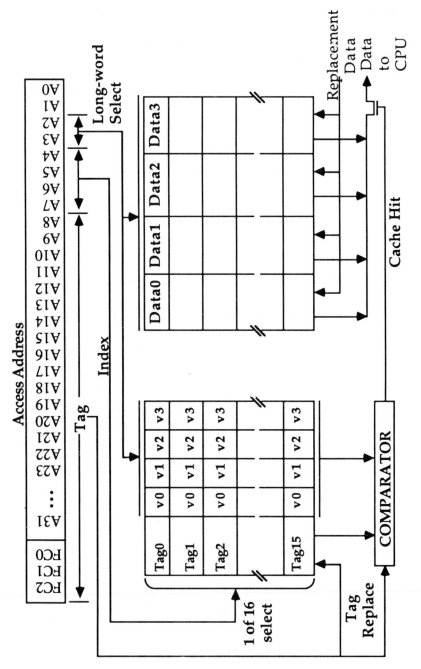

Figure 2.24   *The MC68030 internal cache organization*

STERM* is negated. If the processor read operation is filling an internal cache line (indicated by the CBREQ* Cache Burst Request Line) and the memory is capable of generating the next three addresses, a burst fill transfer can be accomplished. Here, the memory interface performs the normal synchronous access but does not negate STERM*. The processor supplies the next three locations on successive clock edges for the page or nibble mode memories to accept (Figure 2.25). The main advantage of this system is in reducing the necessity for fast static RAMs to realize the processor's performance. With 120 ns page mode DRAM, a 4-1-1-1 (four clocks for the first access, single cycle for the remaining burst) memory system can easily be built. Each 128 bits of data fetched in such a way take only seven clocks compared with five in a no-wait state system. If bursting were not supported, the same access would take 16 clocks. This translates to a very effective price performance – a 4-1-1-1 DRAM system gives about 90% of the performance of a more expensive 2-1-1-1 static RAM design.

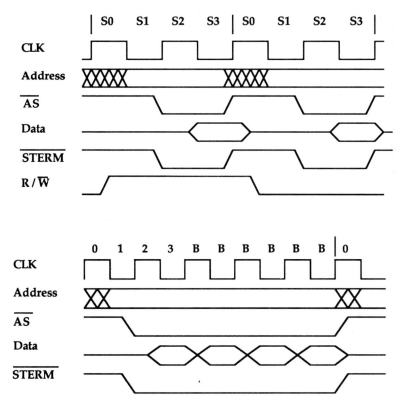

Figure 2.25 *The MC68030 synchronous and burst fill bus cycles*

Memory management

The MC68030 MMU supports 32-bit Logical and Physical Addresses with Write and Supervisor Protection. It has multiple level tables and performs its external table walks under hardware control. The onchip 22-entry ATC is used to store the most frequently used translation descriptors. The device has an extra cache inhibit bit which allows the memory management software to declare memory areas non cacheable. Accesses to these areas assert a cache inhibit signal externally, allowing the processor to tell external memory caches not to cache the data. All MMU translations are performed in parallel with the cache access and therefore, unlike the MC68851 which inserts a wait state, can perform address translations with no additional overhead. Eight page sizes are supported, ranging from 256 bytes to 32 Kbytes in size and two root pointers are allocated to Supervisor and User accesses.

To prevent system ATC entries being overwritten by applications and thus causing additional delays while performing system calls, two transparent windows have been provided (Figure 2.26). These allow two memory areas to be defined from 16 Mbytes to 2 Gbytes in size where any

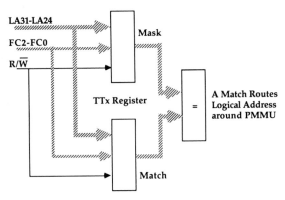

Figure 2.26 *The MC68030 transparent windows*

address translation is mapped around the normal memory management unit. Function Code and Read/Write Protection is provided. These windows are frequently used to access system memory and I/O areas without using any ATC entries or the normal memory management system.

The MMU and caches can be disabled either by external hardware using the MMUDIS★ and CDIS★ pins or by software and the control bits in the internal MMU and Cache control registers. The MMU supports only the PFLUSH, PMOVE, PTEST and PLOAD instructions. Attempted execution of any other PMMU instruction traps to an exception handler and an emulator if necessary. In addition, breakpoint registers, access levels, task aliasing, lockable CAM Entries and 'Shared Globally' Entries are not supported. This may appear to be a tremendous limitation but their disappearance was due to silicon constraints and a lack of use within software. UNIX ports from the MC68020/MC68851 environment to the MC68030 were performed extremely quickly – 24 hours in some cases!

The MC68030 did not offer the performance increase seen between the MC68000 and the MC68020; it did offer about 1.4 to 1.7 times over a straight MC68020 and over two times over MC68020/MC68851 systems. Its biggest advantage was its integration and the use of cost-effective memory to maintain the right price performance level. It is this last issue which made the appearance of a 50 MHz part feasible. Comparison of MC68020 and MC68030 designs running at 50 MHz shows that the MC68030 is more efficient due to the burst filling. Without it, there is little performance gain between a 33 MHz and a 50 MHz system, simply due to the memory delays.

While all this was going on, an alternative approach was beginning to take shape.

3 The RISC challenge

Until 1986, the expected answer to the question, 'which processor offers the most performance?' would be MC68020, MC68030 or even 386! Without exception, CISC processors such as these had established the highest perceived performances. There were more esoteric processors, such as the transputer, which offered large MIPS figures from parallel arrays but these were often considered suitable only for niche markets and applications. However, around this time, there started an interest in an alternative approach to microprocessor design, which seemed to offer more processing power from a simpler design using less transistors. Performance increases of over five times the then current CISC machines were suggested. These machines, such as the SUN SPARC architecture and the MIPS R2000 processor, were the first of a modern generation of processors based on a reduced instruction set, generically called Reduced Instruction Set Computers (RISC).

The 80/20 rule

Analysis of the instruction mix generated by CISC compilers is extremely revealing. Such studies for CISC mainframes and mini computers show that about 80% of the instructions generated and executed used only 20% of an instruction set. It was an obvious conclusion that if this 20% of instructions were speeded up, the performance benefits would be far greater. Further analysis shows that these instructions tend to perform the simpler operations and use only the simpler addressing modes. Essentially, all the effort invested in processor design to provide complex instructions and thereby reduce the compiler workload was being wasted. Instead of using them, their operation was synthesized from sequences of simpler instructions.

This has another implication: if only the simpler instructions are required, the processor hardware required to implement them could be reduced in complexity. It therefore follows that it should be possible to design a more performant processor with less transistors and less cost. With a simpler instruction set, it should be possible for a processor to execute its instructions in a single clock cycle and synthesize complex operations from sequences of instructions. If the number of instructions in a sequence, and therefore the number of clocks to execute the resultant operation, were less than the cycle count of its CISC counterpart, higher performance could be achieved. With many CISC processors taking ten or more clocks per instruction on average, there was plenty of scope for improvement.

The initial RISC research

The computer giant IBM is usually acknowledged as the first company to define a RISC architecture in the 1970s. This research was further developed by the Universities of Berkeley and Stanford to give the basic architectural models. RISC can be described as a philosophy with three basic tenets:

1 *All instructions will be executed in a single cycle*
   This is a necessary part of the performance equation. Its implement-ation calls for several features: the instruction op code must be of a fixed width which is equal to or smaller than the size of the external data bus, additional operands cannot be supported, and the instruction decode must be simple and orthogonal to prevent delays. If the op code is larger than the data width or additional operands must be fetched, multiple memory cycles are needed, increasing the execution time.

2 *Memory will be accessed only via load and store instructions*
   This naturally follows from the above. If an instruction manipulates memory directly, multiple cycles must be performed to execute it. The instruction must be fetched and memory manipulated. With a RISC processor, the memory resident data is loaded into a register, the register manipulated and, finally, its contents written out to main memory. This sequence takes a minimum of three instructions. With register-based manipulation, large numbers of general-purpose regis-ters are needed to maintain performance.

3 *All execution units will be hardwired with no microcoding*
   Microcoding requires multiple cycles to load sequencers, etc. therefore it cannot be used easily to implement single-cycle execution units.

Two generic RISC architectures form the basis of nearly all the current commercial processors. The main differences between them concern register sets and usage. They both have a Harvard external bus architecture consisting of separate buses for instructions and data, which allows data accesses to be performed in parallel with instruction fetches and removes any instruction/data conflict. If these two streams compete for a single bus, any data fetches stall the instruction flow and prevent the processor from achieving its single–cycle objective. Executing an instruction on every clock requires an instruction on every clock.

The Berkeley model

The RISC 1 computer implemented in the late 1970s used a very large register set of 138×32-bit registers. These were arranged in eight overlapping windows of 24 registers each (Figure 3.1). Each window was split so that six registers could be used for parameter passing during subroutine calls. A pointer was simply changed to select the group of six registers. To perform a simple call or return simply needed a change of pointer. The large number of registers is needed to minimize the number of fetches to the outside world. With this simple window technique, procedure calls can be performed extremely quickly. This can be very beneficial for real–time applications where fast responses are necessary.

However, it is not without its disadvantages. If the procedure calls require more than six variables, one register must be used to point to an array stored in external memory. This data must be loaded prior to any processing and the register windowing loses much of its performance. If all the overlapping windows are used, the system resolves the situation by tracking the window usage so either a window or the complete register set can be saved out to external memory. This overhead may negate any advantages that windowing gave in the first place. In realtime applications, the overhead of saving 138 registers to memory greatly increases the context switch and hence the response time.

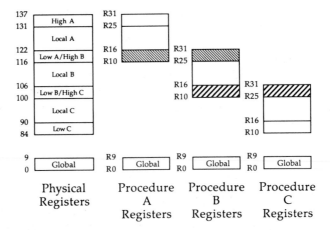

Figure 3.1 *Register windowing*

The Stanford model

This model uses a smaller number of registers (typically 32) and relies on software techniques to allocate register usage during procedural calls. Instruction execution order is optimized by its compilers to provide the most efficient way of performing the software task. This allows pipelined execution units to be used within the processor design which, in turn, allows more powerful instructions to be used.

However, RISC is not the magic panacea for all performance problems within computer designs. Its performance is extremely dependent on very good compiler technology to provide the correct optimizations and keep track of all the registers. Many of the early M68000 family compilers could not track all the 16 data and address registers and therefore would use only two or three. Some compilers even reduced register usage to one register and effectively based everything on stacks and queues. Secondly, the greater number of instructions it needed increased code size dramatically at a time when memory was both expensive and low in density. Without the compiler technology and cheap memory, a RISC system was not very practical and the ideas were effectively put back on the shelf.

The catalysts

While CISC processors, such as the MC68020, were offering state-of-the-art performance, they were also providing examples of how far CISC instructions and addressing modes could be taken and provided ideal examples of a good principle taken to an extreme. It must be stated, however that at the time the design incorporated many customer demands for these features and represented the current thinking. That wonderful debugging tool, hindsight, has shown that the CISC principles were possibly taken too far. The call-and-return module instructions, CALLM and RTM, were welcomed by many, but were never used in practice and, therefore, not supported on the MC68030 to allow space for other functions to be incorporated. Many of the memory indirection addressing modes can be performed faster by two separate address calculations, albeit at the expense of an extra register and instructions. As companies became more experienced in the MC68020, these anomalies were prompting an alternative approach. Three other ingredients appeared about the same time to complete the catalytic mixture:

1 Compiler technology had progressed sufficiently to be able to offer good optimization and register tracking.
2 Memory was now fast and cheap to cope with code expansion.
3 The up and coming ASIC technology could be used to build the processors without the expensive investment in silicon fabrication equipment.

With all these factors coming together, it was obvious that RISC technology was now a commercial proposition and offered processors with a manyfold performance increase over their CISC counterparts. It was the culmination of all these ingredients which caused RISC technology to appear apparently overnight. Coupled with the adoption of MIPS (Million Instructions per Second) as the immediate performance measurement unit, this led to claims which ranged from incredible to incorrect. RISC was so fashionable that almost any new processor would be described as RISC or RISC-like!

It was realized by Motorola that this new architecture offered potential and a project was launched in the mid-1980s to produce a RISC architecture. The remours about this work started fuelling a debate concerning the M68000 family. Was the MC68040 to be cancelled? Could CISC offer the performance that RISC promised? Was CISC a dead end? Was the M68000 family to be terminated? The answer to all accounts was an emphatic 'no', yet the hype surrounding RISC clouded the issue so much that these questions were continually being asked, even after three new M68000 processors had been announced!

In the end, Motorola used its CISC experience and developed a RISC architecture that combined the best of both worlds, and would be the start of a new family. To quote the *Unigram* newsletter: 'Only Motorola could take an apparently simple concept as RISC, and produce a processor that was more complex and advanced than a CISC!' The reason for this complexity was that the M88000 architecture was designed to go beyond a single processor and looked at achieving the right balance between processor, memory and software.

The M88000 family

The MC88100 is a concurrent RISC microprocessor which achieves its performance through the use of overlapping parallel execution units. Everything about the processor is pipelined – integer and floating-point calculations and data and instruction fetches. Indeed, early internal documents referred to it as a Concurrent Pipeline Machine; however, the CPM acronym did not bring to mind a high-technology image and the idea was quickly dropped!

Pipelining allows complex operations to be performed and yet give a single cycle performance. Fabricated using Motorola's HCMOS technology, the MC88100 has a Harvard architecture with separate external 32-bit address and data width program and data buses. It interfaces via a synchronous single-cycle transfer pipelined protocol, P-Bus, capable of 132 Mbyte/second bandwidth at 33 MHz, either directly to memory systems or to the MC88200 Cache MMU chip (Figure 3.2). The MC88200

Figure 3.2 *An M88000 processing node*

provides high-speed memory caching, address translation facilities and interfaces to external memory via a synchronous M–Bus. The processor supports either Big Endian or Little Endian byte ordering. The programming model supports user/supervisor partitioning and has a 32 by 32-bit general purpose register set, with additional access to all execution unit control registers for the supervisor. For maximum performance, IEEE P754 double and single precision floating point arithmetic is supported onchip.

The use of internal parallelism to overlap instruction pipelines and reduce execution times first appeared in the MC68020 and MC68030, where the bus controller, onchip caches and separate ALUs overlapped operations and reduced memory fetch, address translation times, etc. Such overlapping allowed some instructions and address translations to be executed effectively in zero clock cycles. However, due to the complexity of instruction decoding, a lot of hardware is required to develop this concept further and allow the majority of instructions to benefit. The M88000, with its reduced instruction set and associated simplified decoding circuitry, is able to exploit this idea fully.

M88000 concurrent functional units

The processor unit is designed as a set of execution units running in parallel to provide performance. Each execution unit is independent and fed by its own pipeline. Three separate internal buses are used to communicate between them, enabling the triadic instruction set to be supported. On every clock edge, two source buses provide the data for the next

Figure 3.3   *The MC88100 RISC processor execution units*

instruction, while a third transfers the result from the preceding instruction. By operating concurrently, one integer instruction is executed each clock cycle and, by optimizing floating-point instruction sequences, these too can be overlapped to give effective single-cycle execution. With the five independent execution units available (Figure 3.3), the M88000 can simultaneously access program and data memory spaces, execute an integer instruction and execute two integer or floating-point arithmetic instructions. In addition, as the units are pipelined, three data and three program fetches, six floating-point or four integer multiply instructions and five floating-point add or subtract instructions can be in progress at any one time.

With all these parallel operations taking place, it is becoming increasingly difficult to establish a comparative MIPS rating for such processors. The number of execution units can be multiplied by their clock rate to give a burst rating. Alternatively, a time slice can be taken on a clock edge and the execution units examined. Each full stage of each execution unit is an instruction being executed and, therefore, in excess of 220 MIPS at 20 MHz could be claimed for the M88000 family. Again, there is a danger within high-speed processing of becoming absorbed by MIPS without realizing that they often have no reference to the quality of work performed.

Multiple execution units and optimization

The MC88100 integer unit has its own arithmetic logic unit, bit field support and branch logic and is responsible for executing all integer, bit field and branch instructions. Integer multiply and divides are performed with help from the floating point units to provide faster performance. The M88000 has two onchip floating point units, an adder and a multiplier which are, in themselves, fully pipelined. Although they take multiple cycles to complete, a new instruction can be dispatched on every clock edge and by using efficient compiler optimizations, single-cycle floating point operations can be achieved. Both these units and the integer unit can execute concurrently. Unlike many other RISC architectures, there is no need to complete the preceding instruction before dispatching the next. Although a multiply takes about 4–6 clocks, depending on the precision, giving approximately 6 MFLOPS (Million FLOating Point calculations per Second) at 33 MHz, peak performances of 33 MFLOPS can be achieved.

Both the data and the instruction units are viewed as separate execution units with responsibility for moving data in and out of the processor. The data unit has its own address unit for address calculations and transfers data in and out of the processor via the PBUS. It can have up to four data accesses pending before the other internal execution units are stalled. The instruction unit provides instructions on a one per cycle basis and maintains three instruction pointers, XIP, NIP and FIP, which point to the contents of the execution pipeline for efficient exception handling. It also generates the return pointer for branch and jump instructions.

Compiler optimization for RISC processors, like the M88000, is generally based on making the most efficient use of the parallelism generated by these multiple overlapping pipelines. It identifies pipeline stalls and by re-arranging the code execution sequence, removes them while still preserving the original syntax. Such stalls can occur if execution is dependent on the availability of results from preceding instructions, or as the result of pipeline flushing during program branching. Other instructions may be inserted between dependent instructions to maintain the single cycle flow. Figure 3.4 shows the general principle involved. The effect of such optimization can be extremely dramatic – in fast Fourier

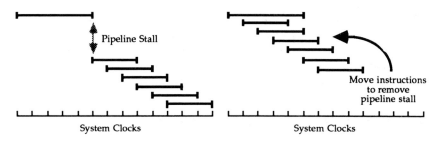

Figure 3.4 *Rescheduling instructions to improve performance*

transform calculations, execution times for a loop sequence of 22 instructions, including 10 floating-point operations, can be improved from over 50 clocks to just 23!

With all the concurrent operations being performed, there is a potential problem when instructions are executed which require data which is not yet available from previous instruction execution. Such conditions result in an erroneous operation which would not be detected. In addition, the machine hardware integrity is totally dependent on the software environment detecting such code sequences and not executing them. This is totally unacceptable for many applications. The difficulty facing compiler writers is in identifying these sequences from all the possible valid combinations that are available. Many optimizers are faced with a choice in approach. With machine integrity dependent on software, optimizers have to adopt algorithms which can guarantee total integrity. With hardware interlocking, an optimization routine can be more aggressive and not worry about the one case in a hundred where the sequence integrity is destroyed.

Scoreboarding

Figure 3.5 shows an example synchronization problem. The first instruction performs a floating-point addition where the contents of registers 1 and 2 are multiplied together and the result stored in register 3. The next instruction takes register 3, adds it to register 4 and stores the result in register 5. The problem occurs when the second instruction starts down the execution pipeline. The value of register 3 that it uses will not be the new value and the resulting calculation will be wrong. This would corrupt the system (Figure 3.6).

There are several solutions to this. The first relies on software to recognize all such situations and insert either instructions or NOPs to delay the second instruction sufficiently (Figure 3.7). This often wastes opportunities where instructions could have been executed and, as stated previously, makes the entire hardware integrity totally dependent on software. If the hardware changes with modifications to pipeline lengths, for instance, the

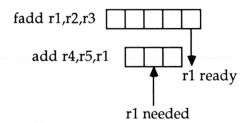

Figure 3.5 *Pipeline synchronization problem*

Figure 3.6   *Processor corruption*

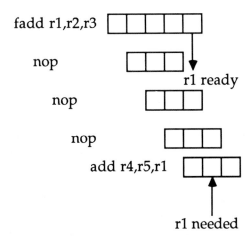

Figure 3.7   *A software solution using NOPs*

software solution may no longer be valid and binary code compatibility is lost.

The MC88100 maintains synchronization by using an internal score-board which is attached to the register file (Figure 3.8). Each register has a scoreboard bit which is set as a result of decoding an instruction which modifies the register contents. A pipeline which uses that information is delayed clock-by-clock until it is available and is fed directly from the pipeline before updating the register file. This reduces any delays to a minimum. As a result, compiler optimizers can concentrate on optimizing and not maintaining system synchronicity.

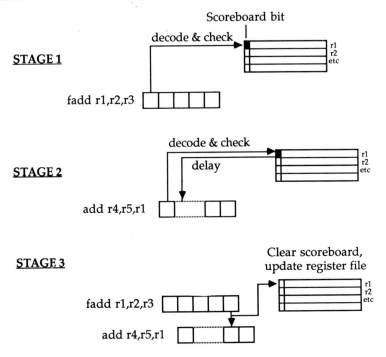

Figure 3.8   *Hardware scoreboarding*

Delayed branching

With any pipelined architecture, there is always associated stalling due to program branching or jumps, caused by an unwanted instruction being prefetched into the pipeline, which subsequently needs flushing to remove it. This obviously reduces impact and one solution is to have a branch prediction cache which stores the two instructions immediately after the branch. The cache mechanism is effective only on software loops and stores the instructions that would be taken if the flow changed. When this happens, the instructions are already available and can be fed into the execution unit. The mechanism takes large areas of silicon to implement and its performance is heavily dependent on software, cache size and hit rates.

Delayed branching is effectively a software optimizing technique which is applicable to all software, irrespective of a looping structure or not. It consumes little silicon real estate and can provide good performance increases (Figure 3.9). The technique works by reordering the instruction sequence. The preceding instruction is moved to immediately after a branch op code and executed while the next instruction is fetched. The

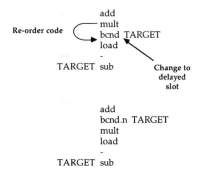

```
                               add
                             - mult
        Re-order code  (      bcnd  TARGET
                         \    load
                               -
              TARGET  sub        Change to
                                 delayed
                                 slot


              add
              bcnd.n  TARGET
              mult
              load
              -
    TARGET  sub
```

Figure 3.9 *Delayed branching*

unwanted instruction, that would normally be inserted into the pipeline, can now be executed and the pipeline not flushed to remove it. Using this technique, it is common to achieve 20 MIPS at 20 MHz.

The MC88100 programming model

The MC88100 processor supports the concept of separate supervisor and user spaces. The user programming model, shown in Figure 3.10, consists of a register file with 32×32 bit wide general purpose registers, r0 to r31. These can perform data and addressing operations without any restriction. Register r0 is read only and is hardwired to contain the value zero to provide a zero reference for the instruction set. In addition, there are two

Register	
r0	ZERO
r1	SUBROUTINE RETURN POINTER
r2	CALLED PROCEDURE PARAMETER REGISTERS
r9	
r10	CALLED PROCEDURE TEMPORARY REGISTERS
r13	
r14	CALLING PROCEDURE RESERVED REGISTERS
r25	
r26	LINKER
r27	LINKER
r28	LINKER
r29	LINKER
r30	FRAME POINTER
r31	STACK POINTER

Figure 3.10 *The M88000 user programming model*

cr0	PID	PROCESSOR IDENTIFICATION REGISTER
cr1	PSR	PROCESSOR STATUS REGISTER
cr2	TPSR	TRAP PROCESSOR STATUS REGISTER
cr3	SSBR	SHADOW SCOREBOARD REGISTER
cr4	SXIP	SHADOW EXECUTE INSTRUCTION POINTER
cr5	SNIP	SHADOW NEXT INSTRUCTION POINTER
cr6	SFIP	SHADOW FETCH INSTRUCTION POINTER
cr7	VBR	VECTOR BASE REGISTER
cr8	DMT2	TRANSACTION REGISTER #2
cr9	DMD2	DATA REGISTER #2
cr10	DMA2	ADDRESS REGISTER #2
cr11	DMT1	TRANSACTION REGISTER # 1
cr12	DMD1	DATA REGISTER # 1
cr13	DMA1	ADDRESS REGISTER #1
cr14	DMT0	TRANSACTION REGISTER # 0
cr15	DMD0	DATA REGISTER #0
cr16	DMA0	ADDRESS REGISTER #0
cr17	SR0	SUPERVISOR STORAGE REGISTER # 0
cr18	SR1	SUPERVISOR STORAGE REGISTER # 1
cr19	SR2	SUPERVISOR STORAGE REGISTER # 2
cr20	SR3	SUPERVISOR STORAGE REGISTER # 3

Figure 3.11 *The M88000 integer unit control registers*

control registers associated with the floating-point execution unit. A major difference is the lack of a condition code register containing flags. This appears to be an omission within the architecture on first sight but, in reality, the results of condition code testing through a compare operation are stored in one of the other registers. The supervisor has access to the user model and to the control registers for the integer and floating-point execution units. These registers, shown in Figure 3.11, provide the processor status and exception information.

Handling exceptions

The processor has a USER/SUPERVISOR concept similar to that of the M68000 family. Normally the processor executes code in the USER state and only moves into the SUPERVISOR state when an exception or some error condition is encountered (e.g. an interrupt or bus error). The biggest difference between the M88000 and M68000 families is the way the processor context or internal state is preserved. With the M68000 family, this is done by building an external stack frame which can take up to approximately 40 separate memory transfers. The M88000 family constantly updates a set of shadow registers so that the context is immediately preserved when an exception happens. The updating is simply stopped and this removes the delay.

The architecture of the M88000 supports two types of exception – precise and imprecise. Precise exceptions are those that require an instruction to restart and therefore the full information concerning the exception is needed. Imprecise exceptions are those such as divide by zero, where the instruction will be discontinued and the program flow started elsewhere. A range of exceptions similar to that of the M68000 family is supported via a relocatable vector table. Each vector references a 64-bit wide location which contains two instructions. These are usually a jump to the handler followed by the first handler instruction in a delayed branch mode. This allows the jump to be completed without causing a pipeline stall.

A single interrupt pin in the MC88100 is used to signal an external interrupt. If this level-sensitive pin is asserted for two successive falling clock edges, an interrupt is signalled internally and the processor context saved to an internal set of shadow registers, not to external memory. The current instruction does not have to complete and the only variable in the latency calculation is the time taken to complete any data and instruction unit memory accesses. Worst case is four operations for the data unit and two for the instruction unit. Typical values are six clock cycles which, at 25 MHz, is less than 0.25 µs, at least an order of magnitude faster than more conventional architectures.

The MC88100 instruction set

The instruction set is based on a load/store memory operation RISC architecture with triadic operations providing non-destructive data usage. By specifying two sources and a different destination, the source data is maintained and available for future use. This reduces the software overhead that a diadic instruction set needs by preserving data where the destination is one of the two sources. All instructions are 32 bits wide and aligned. The set has 51 instructions that support integer and floating-point arithmetic, logical and flow control, load/store instructions and bit field instructions. The latter are normally associated with a complex instruction set – their inclusion improves software performance without comprising the processor design goal of hardwired logic and therefore offers a clear advantage.

The M88000 instruction set has been optimized rather than reduced. This means that many conventional CISC instructions can be replaced on a one-to-one basis, which helps to keep code expansion ratios as close to this ratio as possible. With CISC processors fast approaching single-cycle execution, RISC instruction sets cannot be so reduced that they take more instructions than CISC instructions take clocks to execute. If this happens, a RISC processor may offer an outstanding MIPS figure yet actually perform less work than expected! The importance of the instruction set is discussed in a later chapter.

Addressing data

Unlike many RISC architectures, which have only one address mode and require addresses to be calculated prior to every external access, the M88000 instruction set supports seven (Figure 3.12). Probably the most useful is the register indirect with an index, which can be scaled. This allows a pointer to be assigned to the head of a table or set of tables and allows other registers to index into it, dramatically reducing the number of address calculations and instructions required. Simply changing the main pointer register to that of another table allows rapid searching of tables and linked lists. This reduces the number of instructions needed per function and increases throughput.

Addressing Mode	Syntax
Register Indirect with Unsigned Imediate	rd,rs1,imed16
Register Indirect with Index	rd,rs1,rs2
Register Indirect with Scaled Index	rd,rs1[,rs2]
Register with 9-bit Vector Number	m5,rs1,vec9
Register with 16-bit Signed Displacement	m5,rs1,d16
	b5,rs1,d16
Program Counter Relative (26-bit Signed Displacement)	d26
Register Direct	rs2

Figure 3.12   *The M88000 addressing modes*

Fetching data

Six data types are supported by the M88000 instruction set, shown in Figure 3.13. Bit field data can be from 1 to 32 bits in size. Integers can be either byte, halfword or word in length – yes, the M88000 defines 32 bits as a word, while the M68000 family defines 16 bits as word and 32 bits as a long word! (The Motorola DSP56000 family has a 24–bit word, just to add to the confusion.) Floating–point values are either 32 or 64 bits in size. The only exception to the load-store architecture used by the M88000 is the xmem instruction which exchanges a memory contents with a memory value in two successive indivisible cycles. This provides basic multiprocessor support. The load–store model effectively removes the memory access time from the instruction execution time. Such operations take only three instructions and, therefore, three cycles to complete. Direct memory modifying architectures take three instruction times plus the time for two memory accesses.

Data Type	Represented As
Bit Fields	Signed and Unsigned Bit Fields (1 to 32 bits)
Integer	Signed and Unsigned Byte (8-bits)
	Signed and Unsigned Half-word (16-bits)
	Signed and Unsigned Word (32-bits)
Floating Point	IEEE P754 Single Precision (32-bits)
	IEEE P754 Double Precision (64-bits)

Figure 3.13   *The M88000 data types*

Further consideration must be given to how much data can be fetched and how this fetching is performed. Most compiler-generated data, like 'C' variables such as char, short and int, are 8 or 16 bits in length, yet current RISC architectures are 32 bits in data size. While many RISC architectures can deal with the corresponding byte and halfword data sizes internally, they have to fetch such data using a multiple instruction sequence. The first instruction calculates the address and loads it into the address register, a 32-bit wide word of data is fetched into a register and, finally, a third instruction is needed to extract the relevant byte or halfword from that register and store it in yet another register. The MC88100 has four data byte enable signals which allow it to fetch individual bytes and halfwords directly in a single cycle. This again reduces code expansion, the number of

Figure 3.14   *Byte ordering*

Figure 3.15 *Data transfers*

cycles needed to perform the task and, ultimately, improves the system performance.

The processor can be set up on reset to use either big or little endian byte ordering. These two schemes differ in which is the most significant byte or 16-bit halfword within a 32-bit word (Figure 3.14). With big endian ordering, the most significant byte is located at bits 24–31. With little endian the same byte is located at bits 0–7. This in itself is a minor difference, although the implications for a system are immense. If an instruction tests bit 18, different data would be accessed giving differing results within a system that appeared to be compatible. Often C programs which try to be portable across many systems fail to meet this goal because of assumptions about byte ordering. The byte ordering within the M88100 processor registers is not changed. Figure 3.15 shows how data is transferred from memory to the internal registers.

MC88100 external functions

Figure 3.16 shows the functional pinout of the device. The bulk of the signals are concerned with the two PBUS memory interfaces which form the Harvard architecture. The processor clock is supplied via the CLK pin

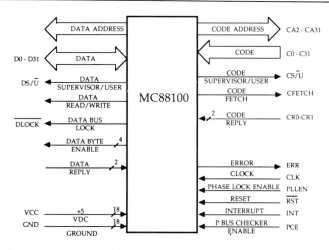

Figure 3.16 *The MC88100 signal pinout*

and the internal phase lock looping is enabled via the PLLEN signal. This reduces the problem associated with clock skewing between multiple processors or cache memory management units. There is a single reset line and a single interrupt line. The PCE signal allows the processor to be configured either as a master or a checker within a fault tolerant pair. (Fault tolerance is discussed further in Chapter 7.) The PBUS signals are shown in Figure 3.17. The data and code buses are essentially the same and use the same protocol. The instruction bus, however, cannot write to its memory space and all accesses are 32-bit wide, hence the missing CA0 and CA1 signals. The data side can perform read/write operations, indivisible cycles

DATA P BUS		INSTRUCTION P BUS	
Signal	Description	Signal	Description
DA2 - DA31	Data Address Bus	CA2 - CA31	Code Address Bus
D0 - D31	Data Bus	C0 - C31	Code Bus
DS/$\overline{\text{U}}$	Data Supervisor/User Select	CS/$\overline{\text{U}}$	Code Supervisor/User Select
DR/$\overline{\text{W}}$	Data Read/Write - asserted for read, negated for write		(no corresponding signal)
$\overline{\text{DLOCK}}$	Data Bus Lock - asserted for cache lock		(no corresponding signal)
DE0 - DE3	Data Byte Enables	CFETCH	Code Fetch - asserted for fetch
DR0 - DR1	Data Reply 0 and 1 DR0 DR1 0 0 Reserved 0 1 Success 1 0 Wait 1 1 Fault	CR0 - CR1	Code Reply 0 and 1 - CR0 CR1 0 0 Reserved 0 1 Success 1 0 Wait 1 1 Fault

Figure 3.17 *The PBUS signals*

and with the byte enable strobes access 8, 16 and 32-bit data. Both buses support the USER/SUPERVISOR partitioning. The two pairs of control registers, DR0–1 and CRO–1, tell the processor whether to insert wait states and whether the transfer has completed successfully or incorrectly.

Single-cycle memory buses

The fine-grain parallelism used in the MC88100 requires external memory systems to provide data on every clock edge in order to prevent pipeline stalls reducing performance. This effectively means that at 20 MHz memory is accessed every 50 ns and at the higher clock speeds, such as 40 MHz, this increases to every 25 ns. This places tremendous design constraints on the external memory systems. To maintain the constant flow of instructions into the processor requires a separate bus with a very high bus utilization (95–100%), hence the Harvard bus architecture with separate data and instruction buses. The insertion of a single wait state halves system performance, two wait states reduce it to a third and so on. A 20 MIPS machine can be reduced to 6 MIPS, which, considering the poorer instruction set and addressing modes available to most RISC architectures, may actually perform less work than a well-designed CISC alternative. RISC systems may have simpler processors but their memory systems are more sophisticated, often requiring cache memory subsystems.

PBUS, the processor memory interface, uses a pipelined protocol to maintain a single-cycle instruction flow using an effective 3-cycle access. An example transaction is shown in Figure 3.18. The bus cycle starts with an address with the USER/SUPERVISOR status, byte strobes and

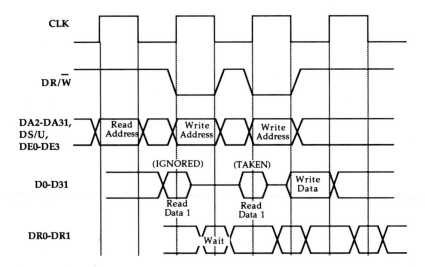

Figure 3.18 *The PBUS protocol during a READ–WAIT–WRITE cycle*

read/write status. In the example shown, a read takes place. On the next clock, the data is read in from the data bus by the processor. This always occurs due to the pipelining, however, the data is not used until the reply signals are received on the third clock. During the second clock, the address information for the next cycle is driven on to the bus. The reply to insert wait states is passed back on the third clock. The address data is maintained on the bus and the data bus is sampled again on the next clock. This time, the data is good and a success is indicated on the subsequent clock. The next operation is a write, the data appears and again success is indicated by the control signals. Each access actually consists of three stages but the pipelining allows each stage to be completed on every clock cycle, resulting in an effective single-cycle performance. Multiple cycles simply overlap each other. Any memory design must therefore latch the address. The PBUS is used normally with direct connections to M88200 CMMUs but can be connected directly to memory if required.

The biggest restriction in such direct memory designs is upgrading the system clock speed. Most of today's M68000 family designs are capable of running different speed processors on the same hardware by simply replacing the processor and keeping the memory system and peripherals the same. The insertion of wait states does not degrade the system performance too much. With a RISC architecture, both the processor and its cache memory need upgrading to prevent wait states on the processor buses from destroying performance. Faster processors need faster caches which need faster memory chips. The problem comes with the interface logic and buffering that is also needed. The buffering delays of a few nanoseconds become very significant as the cycle times become shorter. In addition, the effect of impedance mismatch and capacitive loading due to design layout and printed circuit board track lengths start exaggerating the problems. In effect, it will be virtually impossible to speed upgrade such designs without redesigning the board. The only sensible method of solving these problems is to integrate the various functions on to one piece of VLSI manufactured in the same technology. With both the processor and its cache memory system using similar fabrication techniques, they can easily track each other as the faster versions become available. A board upgrade simply becomes a processor and CMMU replacement without a redesign.

MC88200 cache MMU

The MC88200 Cache/Memory Management Unit provides 16 kbytes of one-cycle access, four ways set associative cache memory together with full support for segmented and demand paged memory management schemes. By integrating memory caches with memory management functions, translation delays can be removed by overlapping cache accesses with address translations and thus the use of memory management does not reduce system performance. This idea is present on the MC68030 but again has been further developed within the M88000 family.

Memory management functions

Integrating memory management and cache memory on a single chip allows their operations to be overlapped so there is no penalty for their use. This is done by performing the cache lookup and address translation in parallel. The logical address bus is split, allowing the lower bits to be used within the cache lookup mechanism while the address translation is done. When the correct physical address is ready, it makes the final data selection from the potential cache entries that the lookup has generated. If data and the address translation descriptor are cached on chip, the data is supplied with no wait states to the processor. If the descriptor is missing, the CMMU performs an external table walk into external memory to fetch it. If the data is not present, it is fetched from memory. The CMMU supports various memory granularity:

- 4 Gbytes User Space
- 4 Gbytes Supervisor Space
- Segment (4 Mbytes on 4 Mbyte Boundary)
- Block (512 Kbytes on 512 Kbyte Boundary)
- Page (4 Kbyte on 4 Kbyte Boundary)

Granularity is controlled by three descriptors, as shown in Figure 3.19. In addition to the more normal read/write user/supervisor protection bits,

Area

Sup'v. Segment Table Base	WT	0	G	CI	0	0	U	WP	V
User Segment Table Base	WT	0	G	CI	0	0	U	WP	V

Segment

Page Table Base	WT	SP	G	CI	0	0	U	WP	V

Page

Page Frame Base	WT	SP	G	CI	0	M	U	WP	V

V	Valid		CI	Cache Inhibit
WP	Write Protect Enable		G	Global - Snoop
U	Used		SP	Supervisor Only
M	Modified		WT	Write Through

Figure 3.19 *MC88200 MMU descriptors*

various cache coherency mechanisms, such as cache inhibit, write back, etc. can be invoked dynamically. By coupling the cache control with the memory management in this way, it is very easy to configure the system for optimum performance.

In addition to the cache memory, there are two caches for high speed address translation:

1 The Page Address Translation Cache (PATC), containing 56 descriptors.
2 A Block Address Translation Cache (BATC), with a 10 entry table of memory block descriptors.

In most systems, the operating system uses the BATC, while applications use the PATC. This prevents operating system descriptors from being overwritten by application entries as tasks are loaded and run.

Cache coherency

The 16 Kbyte memory cache is on the physical memory side, with the advantage of no flushing on every context switch and, therefore, it maintains high hit rates of about 97–99%, although such figures are highly software dependent. A typical processing node may use up to eight MC88200s, split between the data and program buses (Figure 3.20). With a maximum number, a M88000 processor node would have 128 kbytes of wait free cache along with 448 PATC and 80 BATC translation entries. This provides an elegant solution to the von Neumann bottleneck, which is often a limiting factor in both RISC and CISC architectures. By comparison, the MC68030 has 512 bytes of cache and a 22-entry translation cache.

Figure 3.20 *An MC88100/88200 processor node*

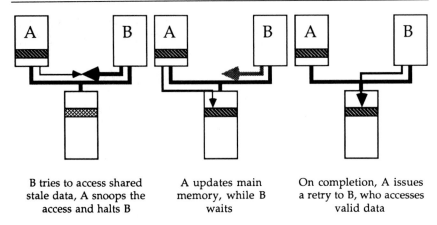

B tries to access shared
stale data, A snoops the
access and halts B

A updates main
memory, while B
waits

On completion, A issues
a retry to B, who accesses
valid data

Figure 3.21   *Cache coherency v. bus snooping*

The MC88200 provides a hardware solution for the problem of stale data cache coherency. Entries can be allocated either with a copy back policy to reduce external traffic or written through. There is a bus snoop protocol which monitors the external bus and updates the cache when a data entry is modified externally. This function is again essential to any high-performance system which uses either multiple processors or DMA to prevent corruption and the resulting system crashes (Figure 3.21). Caches, and their coherency are described in greater detail in Chapter 5.

The MBUS protocol

Each MC88200 CMMU communicates to main memory via the MBUS. This is a synchronous pipelined bus which supports both single and block transfers and concurrent arbitration. The bus has an arbitration mechanism which allows designers to use a single bus structure or maintain the Harvard architecture of the processor. At 20 MHz, it is capable of transfers up to 64 Mbytes/second. Due primarily to a pin out restriction, the bus uses a multiplexed address and data bus. The control and status signals, associated with it (Figure 3.22) have different meanings depending on which phase of the cycle is current. During the first 'request' phase, indicated by C0 = 1, the address is generated along with other information describing the bus access (Figure 3.23). This could be a non–cached global access involving a locked sequence, for example. The memory or subsystem responds either with a success, wait or error via the system status signals, SS0–3*. Wait states can be inserted to allow extra address decoding time.

Once completed, the second 'data' phase commences. Here, some control signals change meaning and become byte enable strobes to indicate

CONTROL SIGNAL	REQUEST PHASE	DATA PHASE
C0	REQUEST = 1	REQUEST = 0
C1	Intent to Modify	End of Request (EOR)
C2	Read/$\overline{\text{Write}}$	Read/$\overline{\text{Write}}$
C3	Locked	Byte Strobe 3 (I31-I24)
C4	Cache Inhibit	Byte Strobe 2 (I23-I16)
C5	Global	Byte Strobe 1 (I15-I8)
C6	reserved	Byte Strobe 0 (I7-I0)

SYSTEM STATUS SIGNAL	REQUEST PHASE	DATA PHASE
$\overline{\text{SS3}}$	ERROR	ERROR
$\overline{\text{SS2}}$	RETRY	RETRY
$\overline{\text{SS1}}$	WAIT	WAIT
$\overline{\text{SS0}}$	reserved	End of Data (EOD)

Figure 3.22 *The MBUS control and status signals*

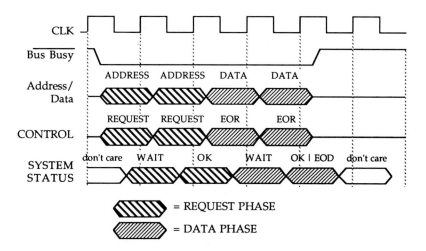

Figure 3.23 *An MBUS cycle with wait states*

whether this is the last transfer in the sequence. The data appears on the bus and the system status signals can show success or error or insert wait states. There is a special signal, however, which indicates that the memory cannot accept any more transfers and that this should be the last. The combination of these SS0* and C1 signals allow block transfers to be controlled by either the CMMU or the memory. Parity generation and checking can be selected for the bus and its control signals.

M88000 master/checker fault tolerance

One feature that has not been seen previously within the MC68000 family, is the ability to run a second processor node in a fault checking shadow mode without any additional comparator and/or synchronizing logic. Both the MC88100 and MC88200 have an external pin which, when asserted, forces the processor to execute internally without driving the external buses. Instead, the external signals from the master processor are compared by the checker processor and, if there is a discrepancy, an error signal is asserted. The checking circuits can also detect external bus faults on power up. Further protection is given by the use of four parity bits on the MC88200 M-Bus interface to external memory. This fault detection scheme has no impact on performance whatsoever and allows redundant M88000 nodes to be easily designed.

Future enhancements

With only the MC88100 and MC88200 parts available currently, it may appear to be a little difficult to see how the family is likely to progress. However, if the architecture is examined in a little more detail some ideas do come to mind.

The MC88100 diagram (Figure 3.24) shows a group of Special Function Units (SFUs). The floating-point unit is SFU 1 and up to six more can be added at a later stage. All have their own internal interface to the register file and scoreboard and 256 unique op codes are predefined for them. If such an op code is executed on a MC88100, it causes an exception and

Figure 3.24 *Special function units*

allows software to emulate the function. This situation is extremely similar to the F-line and A-line exceptions on the MC68000. They allowed extra coprocessors to be added on future generations.

If extra execution units are to be added, the next obvious step from single-cycle execution is to start executing multiple instructions per clock. For this to perform correctly, a form of hardware interlock is needed to determine when instructions can be executed without corrupting the software precedence. This can be caused by an instruction wanting the result of a preceding instruction or by multiple instructions all competing for the same resource like a condition code or status register – but the MC88100 already has a scoreboard mechanism and has no condition code registers or status registers. Is this just coincidence? All that can be certain is that the next generations are already under development.

4 Digital signal processing

When confronted with the term digital signal processing (DSP), an immediate response is an image of complex mathematical formula requiring banks of computers to perform even trivial tasks such as filtering out high-frequency signals from low-frequency ones. This tends to beg the question, why bother?

The 'mathematical complexity' is attributable to years of experience and familiarity with analogue filters and their relatively simple equations. A filter as shown in Figure 4.1 is extremely simple compared with its digital equivalent in Figure 4.2. The analogue filter works by varying the gain of the operational amplifier which is determined by the relationship between R_i and R_f. In a system with no frequency component, the capacitor C_f plays no part, as its impedance is far greater than that of R_f. As the frequency component increases, the capacitor impedance decreases until it is about equal with R_f where the effect will be to reduce gain of the system. As a result, the amplifier acts as a low-pass filter where high frequencies will be filtered out. The equation in Figure 4.1 shows the relationship where jw is the frequency component. These filters are easy to design and are cheap to build. By making the CR network more complex, different filters can be designed.

The digital equivalent is more complex, requiring several electronic stages to convert the data, process it and reconstitute the data. The equation appears to be more involved, comprising a summation of a range of calculations using sample data multiplied by a constant term. These constants take the place of the CR components in the analogue system and will define the filter's transfer function. With digital designs, like that of Figure 4.2, it is the tables of coefficients that are dynamically modified to create the different filter characteristics.

Given the complexity of digital processing, why use it? The advantages are many. Digital processing does not suffer from component ageing, drift or any adjustments which can plague an analogue design. They have high

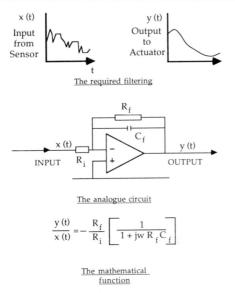

Figure 4.1   *Analogue signal processing*

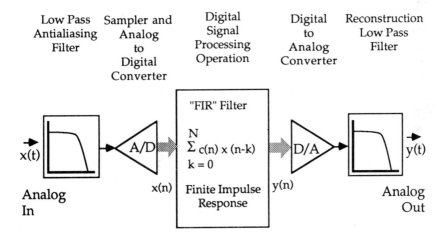

Figure 4.2   *Digital signal processing*

noise immunity and power supply rejection and due to the embedded processor can easily provide self-test features. The ability to modify the coefficients dynamically and therefore the filter characteristics, allows complex filters and other functions to be implemented easily. However, the processing power needed to complete the 'multiply–accumulate' processing of the data does pose some interesting processing requirements.

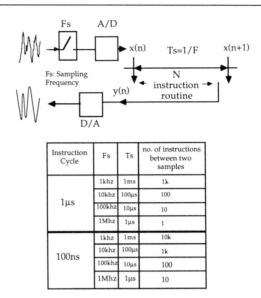

Figure 4.3   *DSP processing requirements*

Figure 4.3 shows the problem. An analogue signal is sampled at a frequency F_s and is converted by the A/D converter. This frequency will be first determined by the speed of this conversion. In every period, T_s, there will be a new sample to process using N instructions. The table shows the relationship between sampling speed, the number of instructions and the instruction execution time. It shows that the faster the sampling frequency, the more processing power is needed. To achieve the 1 MHz frequency, a 10 MIPS processor is needed whose instruction set is powerful enough to complete the processing in under 10 instructions. This analysis does not take into account A/D conversion delays. For DSP algorithms, the sampling speed is usually twice the frequency of the highest frequency signal being processed: in this case the 1 MHz sample rate would be adequate for signals up to 500 KHz. Certainly for higher frequencies up to radio frequencies, analogue filters still have a lot to offer.

The analysis also highlights one major criterion that a DSP processor must fulfil. It shows that to maintain the periodic sampling, necessary to stop distortion and maintain the algorithm's integrity, the processing must be completed within a finite number of instructions. This immediately raises the question of how to handle interrupts, program loops, etc. Most of the processor enhancements are centred around this issue.

One major difference between analogue and digital filters is the accuracy and resolution that they offer. Analogue signals may have definite limits in their range, but have infinite values between that range. Digital signal processors are forced to represent these infinite variations within a finite number of steps determined by the number of bits in the word. With an 8-bit word, the increases are in steps of 1/256 of the range. With a 16-bit word, such steps are in 1/65 536 and so on. Depicted graphically in Figure 4.4, a 16-bit word would enable a low-pass filter with a roll-off of about 90 dB. A 24-bit word would allow about 120 dB roll-off to be achieved.

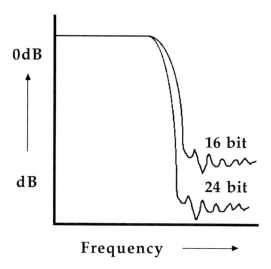

Figure 4.4 *Word size and cutoff frequencies*

DSP can be performed by ordinary microprocessors although their more general-purpose nature often limits performance and the frequency response. However, with responses of only a few hundred hertz, even simple microcontrollers can perform such tasks. As silicon technology improved, special building blocks appeared allowing digital signal processors to be developed, but their implementation was often geared to a hardware approach rather than designing a specific processor architecture for the job.

Processor requirements

A good example of a DSP function is the Finite Impulse Response (FIR) filter. This involves setting up two tables, one containing sampled data and the other filter coefficients that determine the filter response. The program then performs a series of repeated multiply and accumulates using values from the tables. As shown before, the bandwidth of such filters depends on the speed of these simple operations. With a general-purpose architecture like the MC68000 family the code structure would involve setting up two tables in external memory, with an address register allocated to each one to act as a pointer. The beginning and the end of the code would consist of the loop initialization and control, leaving the multiply–accumulate operations for the central part. The MC68000 instruction set does offer some facilities for efficient code: the incremental addressing allows pointers to progress down the tables automatically, and the decrement and branch instruction provides a good way of implementing the loop structures. However, the disadvantages are many: the multiply takes >40 clocks, the single bus is used for all the instruction fetches, and table searches, thus consuming time and bandwidth. In addition, the loop control timings vary depending on whether the branch is taken or not. This can make bandwidth predictions difficult to calculate and results in very low bandwidths and is therefore of limited use within digital signal processing. It does not mean that a MC68000 cannot perform such functions; it can, providing performance is not an issue.

RISC architectures like the M88000 family can offer some immediate improvements. The MC88100's capability to perform single-cycle arithmetic is an obvious advantage. The Harvard architecture reduces the execution time further by allowing simultaneous data and instruction fetches. The MC88100 can, by virtue of its high performance, achieve performances suitable for many DSP applications. The system cost is high involving a multiple chip solution with very fast memory, etc. In applications that need high-speed general processing as well, it too can be a suitable solution.

Another approach is to build a dedicated processor to perform certain algorithms. By using discrete building blocks, such as hardware multipliers, counters, etc. a totally hardware solution can be designed to perform such functions. Modulo counters can be used to form the loop structures and so on. The disadvantages are cost and a loss of flexibility. Such hardware solutions are difficult to alter or program. What is obviously required is a processor whose architecture is enhanced specifically for DSP applications.

The DSP56000 family

When Motorola announced its DSP56000 family of DSP processors, it was a great surprise not only to the industry but also to most of the people within Motorola! It was not the first DSP chip, as both Texas and NEC had been supplying chips in volume, but it was the first generation to take a classical microprocessor architecture and enhance it for DSP applications. It is this combination that has led it to be used in many embedded controller applications which, while not performing traditional DSP functions, can use its fast arithmetic processing, on chip peripherals and memory to great effect. There are two members of the family: the DSP56000 which has a mask programmed internal program ROM and the DSP56001 which replaces the ROM with RAM. For most applications, they are completely interchangeable.

Basic architecture

The processor is split into ten functional blocks as shown in Figure 4.5. It is a 24-bit data word processor to give increased resolution[1]. The device has an enhanced Harvard architecture with three separate external buses: one for program and X and Y memories for data. The communication between these and the outside world is controlled by two external bus switches, one for data and the other for addresses. Internally, these two switches are functionally reproduced by the internal data bus switch and the address arithmetic unit (AAU). The AAU contains 24 address registers in three banks of eight which are used to reference data so that it can be easily fetched to maintain the data flow into the data ALU. The program address generator, decode controller and interrupt controller organize the instruction flow through the processor. There are six 24-bit registers for controlling loop counts, operating mode, stack manipulation and condition codes. The program counter is 24-bit although the upper 8 bits are used only for sign extension.

The main workhorse is the data ALU, Figure 4.6, which contains two 56-bit accumulators, A and B, which each consists of three smaller registers A0, A1, A2, B0, B1 and B2. The 56-bit value is stored with the most significant 24-bit word in A1 or B1, the least significant 24-bit word in A0 or B0 and the 8-bit extension word is stored in A2 or B2. The processor uses a 24-bit word which can provide a dynamic range of some 140 dB, while intermediate 56-bit results can extend this to 330 dB. In practice, the extension byte is used for over and underflow. In addition there are four 24-bit registers X1, X0, Y1 and Y0, which can also be paired to form two 48-bit registers X and Y. The registers can read or write data from their respective data buses and are the data sources for the multiply accumulate (MAC) operation. When the MAC instruction is executed, two 24-bit values from X0, X1, Y1 or Y0 are multiplied together and then added or subtracted from either accumulator A or B. This takes place in a single machine cycle of 75 ns at 27 MHz. While this is executing, two parallel data moves can take place to update the X and Y registers with the next values. In reality, four separate operations are taking place concurrently.

The data ALU also contains two data shifters for bit manipulation and to

---

[1] Yes, Motorola does define different word lengths for its different processors! The MC68000 word is 16 bits, the M88000 word is 32 bits and the DSP56000 word is 24 bits. To avoid confusion, 16-bit words, 24-bit words, etc. are referred to.

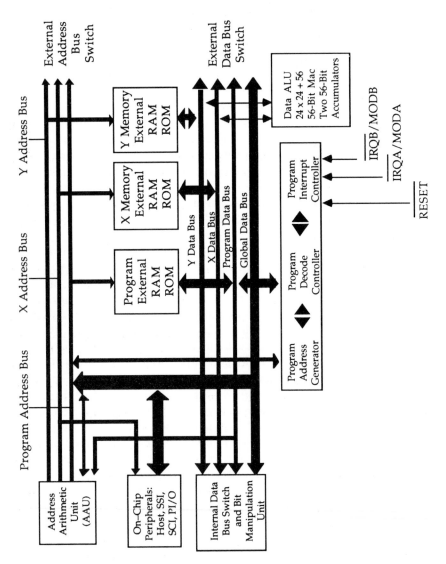

Figure 4.5   *The DSP56000 block diagram*

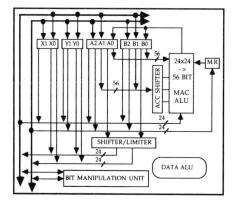

Figure 4.6 *The DSP56000 data ALU*

provide dynamic scaling of fixed point data without modifying the original program code by simply programming the scaling mode bits. The limits are used to reduce any arithmetic errors, due to overflow for example. If overflow occurs, i.e. the resultant value requires more bits to describe it than are available, then it is more accurate to write the maximum valid number than the overflowed value. This maximum or limited value is substituted by the data limiter in such cases, and sets a flag in the condition code register to indicate what has happened.

The device pinout is shown in Figure 4.7. The external signals are split into various groups. There are three ports A, B and C and seven special bus control signals, two interrupt pins, reset, power and ground and finally, clock signals. The device is very similar in design to an 8-bit Micro Controller (MCU), and it can be set into several different memory configurations. The three independent memory spaces, X data, Y data and program are configured by the MB, MA and DE bits in the Operating Mode Register. The MB and MA bits are set according to the status of the and MB and MA pins during the processor's reset sequence. These pins are used subsequently for external interupts. Within the program space, the MA and MB bits determine where the program memory is and where the reset starting address is located. The DE bit effectively either enables or disables internal data ROMs which contain a set of Mu and A Law expansion tables in the X data ROM and a four-quadrant sinewave table in the Y data ROM. The on chip peripherals are mapped into the X data space between $FFC0 and $FFFF. Each of the three spaces is 64 Kbytes in size.

These memory spaces communicate to the outside world via a shared 16-bit address bus and a 24-bit data bus. Two additional signals, PS★ and X/Y★ identify which type of access is taking place. The DSP56000 can be programmed to insert a fixed number of wait states on external accesses for

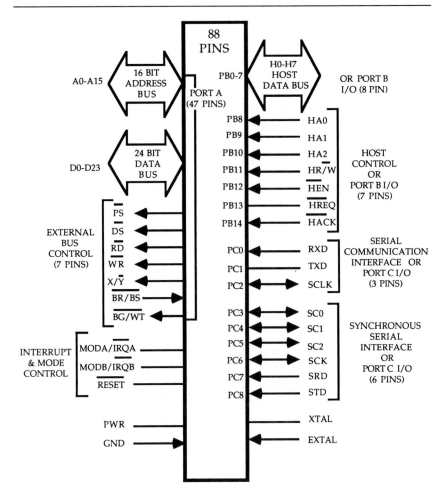

Figure 4.7 *The DSP56000/1 external pinout*

each memory space and I/O, as shown in Figure 4.8. Alternatively, an asynchronous handshake can be adopted by using the bus strobe and wait pins (BS★ and WT★). There is a special bootstrap mode which allows the DSP56001 to copy its program from a single external EPROM into its internal RAM as shown in Figure 4.9. Once loaded, the program is executed from internal memory without any speed penalty. This is a very common technique with MCUs, and again shows how the DSP56000 family has taken many MCU ideas and used them.

External communication can be performed vía three ports A, B and C. Port A is used, together with the external control signals, to provide the expansion buses to communicate with external memory. Port B has 15 pins which can be configured either as general-purpose I/O or as a byte-wide

Figure 4.8 *A mixed speed memory subsystem*

full duplex parallel port, suitable for connection to the data bus of another processor. Port C has 9 pins which can also be configured as general-purpose I/O or as two independent serial interfaces. The Serial Communication Interface (SCI) is a three-wire, full duplex serial communication port suitable for linking to other DSP processors, microprocessors, modems, etc. It can be used directly or with RS232C type transceivers. The three signals transmit data, receive data and generate a reference serial clock. It will support standard asynchronous bit rates or a 2.5 Mbit/s synchronous transfer. A programmable baud rate generator is used to generate the transmit and receive clocks or can be used as a timer if the SCI is not used. Multidrop mode is supported within the asynchronous protocols to allow Master/Slave operation.

Figure 4.9 *Bootstrapping from a single EPROM*

A synchronous serial communication interface (SSI) is also provided to communicate to a variety of serial devices like codecs (a combined A/D and D/A used in digital telephone systems), other DSP processors, microcontrollers, etc., either on a periodic basis within a network or on demand. The number of bits per word, the protocol or mode, the clock and the transmit/receive synchronization can all be defined. The Normal mode is used typically to interface on a regular or periodic basis between devices. The On-Demand mode is data driven where the communication is irregular; in this mode the clock can be gated or continuous. In the Network mode it uses time slots to effectively allow multiple devices to communicate, from 2 to 32 devices can be supported. Each time slot is allocated to a device and, either through an interrupt or by polling status bits, each device has the option of transmitting data or not. The receiver always reads the data, thus allowing the processor the choice of using or discarding the data. The SSI is often used within arrays of DSP 56000 processors to create a multiprocessing array to improve throughput or resolution.

The Host port provided on Port C can be used for general I/O but is usually configured to provide a byte-wide parallel interface between the DSP56000 and other processors. The interface simply looks like a location within its own memory map which is read or written to by any intelligent device including DMA. Using its controls signals, it is easy to connect to an MCU or M68000 processor as shown in Figure 4.10. The host interface has a simple programming model (Figure 4.11). The three address bits HA0–HA2 allow access to the three transmit and receive byte registers, the command vector register and the interrupt control, vector and status

Figure 4.10 *Using the host interface*

Figure 4.11 *The host interface registers*

registers. This can be programmed to allow either the DSP56000 or the other device to interrupt the other, thus allowing a fast, efficient data transfer. The HR/W★ signal indicates the direction of data transfer and is used in conjunction with HEN★ to enable transfers on the data bus.

The HREQ★ signal is an open drain output signal used by the DSP56000 to request service from the other DMA device, processor, etc. It is used normally to generate an interrupt. The HACK★ signal has two functions −

it can either provide a Host Acknowledge handshake for DMA transfers or be used as an M68000 host interrupt acknowledge signal which places the contents of the interrupt Vector register on the data bus to generate the interrupt vector.

An extremely innovative feature of the interface is the Host Command facility. This allows the host processor to issue vectored exception requests direct to the DSP56000. The host can select one of 32 exception routines by writing into the command vector register to perform operations such as reading and writing to the DSP56000 registers, X and Y memory, force specific exception handlers for the onchip peripherals, perform control and debugging routines, etc. In some respects, this is similar to the MC68020 coprocessor interface which uses microcoded routines and the standard processor interface to allow the seamless joining of the main processor and the floating point unit. With the host command facility, the DSP56000 can be similarly coupled with another processor to combine both architectures into an extremely powerful tightly coupled multiprocessor system. This technique will be explored further in later chapters.

The programming model

The programming model is really a cross between the dedicated register model of the older 8-bit architectures and the general-purpose, more orthogonal M68000 architecture. The register set can be divided into three main groups: the Data ALU, the Program controller and the Address Generation Unit. The Data ALU register looks similar to those of an 8-bit architecture with its accumulators and X and Y registers, rather than that of a M68000. The dedicated registers come from the specialized hardware needed to perform the multiply–accumulate function. For DSP applica-

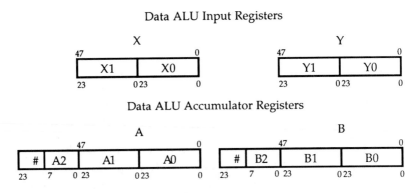

Figure 4.12 *The DSP56000 programming model – data ALU unit*

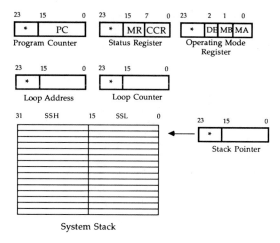

Figure 4.13   *The DSP56000 programming model – program controller*

Address Generation Unit

23	15	0
*	R7	
*	R6	
*	R5	
*	R4	
*	R3	
*	R2	
*	R1	
*	R0	

Pointer registers

23	15	0
*	N7	
*	N6	
*	N5	
*	N4	
*	N3	
*	N2	
*	N1	
*	N0	

Offset registers

23	15	0
*	M7	
*	M6	
*	M5	
*	M4	
*	M3	
*	M2	
*	M1	
*	M0	

Modifier registers

Figure 4.14   *The DSP56000 programmer's model – address generation*

tions, the dual set is sufficient for most needs – and is still an improvement over an M6800 model.

The Program generation set has two interesting components in addition to the normal program counter, status and operating mode registers. The loop address and loop counter registers allow hardware to perform do loops and instruction repetitions without any software overhead. Considering that many routines are based around small instruction loops, this is extremely beneficial. The stack pointer is different from both the M68000 and M88000 families in that it is hardware based and capable of nesting up to 15 exception routines, before requiring software intervention to extend it into RAM. The 32-bit wide stack is used only to store the program counter and status register. Other registers are saved in either X or Y memory. In reality, DSP and embedded control software do not require to context switch so much and this is therefore not a disadvantage.

The Address Generation Unit consists of three groups of eight registers, each of which provides an address pointer whose contents can be offset by the corresponding offset register and whose arithmetic function is defined by the related modifier register. The pointer and offset registers behave in a way similar to the M68000 address registers. The different arithmetic address functions defined by the modifiers are for DSP support. The linear addressing mode is the standard twos complement 16-bit arithmetic function normally associated with microprocessors. The modulo addressing mode effectively causes the address contents to remain within a predefined address range with upper and lower boundaries. This is useful for repetitive table searching and for both general-purpose processing and DSP applications.

The reverse carry arithmetic is based solely on improving the execution of Fast Fourier Transforms (FFT). The FFT is a mathematical method of analysing a waveform into its component parts. Performing an FFT on an audio signal results in a frequency spectrum giving the intensities and frequency of the various components. The basic mathematical operation is a matrix multiplication on large arrays of data. By performing these calculations in a specific order, it is possible to reduce the number of calculations, thus increasing the speed or resolution of the analysis. The disadvantage is that the data order is scrambled and needs to be reordered, with the associated software and time overhead. The scrambling is not random and is equivalent to propagating the carry bit in the reverse direction. To save the software overhead, reverse carry arithmetic allows the data to be accessed in the correct order without reordering. In large FFTs, this is extremely advantageous.

The instruction set

The instruction set looks like a hybrid between an 'M6800' 8-bit processor and a 'M68000' 16/32-bit chip and follows from the programming model, which has dedicated 'M6800'-like arithmetic accumulators with a set of 'M68000'-like, general-purpose address registers. This hybridization permeates the instruction set where these types of op codes sit side by side. The set covers six main operation types:

- Arithmetic
- Logical
- Bit manipulation
- Loop
- Move
- Program control

The instruction is coded within a 24-bit word.

Arithmetic and logical instructions

The arithmetic instructions, shown in Figure 4.15, perform all the arithmetic operations within the data ALU. They are register based and do not specify addresses on the X, Y or global data buses. The reduction in the number of bits needed to encode the operation allows the spare bits to be used to specify parallel data moves across the X and Y space. Therefore, within most of the basic commands, the programmer can specify two additional transfers which can be executed simultaneously. This is an extremely powerful technique for improving performance, allowing data and/or results to be stored while calculating the next set. All these instructions execute in a single cycle and the destination is either of the 56-bit accumulators.

ADDL	Shift Left and add Accumulators
ADDR	Shift Right and Add Accumulators
AND	Logical AND
ANDI	AND Immediate with Control Register*
ASL	Arithmetic Shift Accumulator Left
ASR	Arithmetic Shift Accumulator Right
CLR	Clear Accumulator
CMP	Compare
CMPM	Compare Magnitude
DIV	Divide Iteratlon
EOR	Logical Exclusive OR
LSL	Logical Shift Left
LSR	Logical Shift Right
MAC	Signed Multiply-Accumulate
MACR	Signed Multiply-Accumulate and Round
MPY	Signed Multiply
MPYR	Signed Multiply and Round
NEG	Negate Accumulator
NORM	Normalize Accumulator Iteration*
NOT	Logical Complement
OR	Logical Inclusive OR
ORI	OR Immediate with Control Register*
RND	Round Accumulator
ROL	Rotate Left
ROR	Rotate Right
*These instructions do not allow parallel data moves.	

Figure 4.15 *the DSP56000 arithmetic and logical instructions*

The CMPM instruction is useful in determining minima and maxima by setting the condition code bits according to the results of the subtraction of two operands. The NORM instruction performs a single-bit normaliz-ation on the contents of an accumulator and updates a specified address register accordingly. This, and the RND instruction for convergent rounding, are used extensively within floating-point and scaling oper-ations. The most powerful operation within the group is the MACR instruction. It performs a signed multiply and accumulate with convergent rounding with two parallel data moves. These four activities are executed within a single cycle.

Bit manipulation

These instructions, shown in Figure 4.16, are familiar to microcontroller programmers and can be split into two groups. They both test the state of any single bit in a memory location, but one group optionally sets, clears or inverts the bit as needed, while the other transfers program flow via a jump or jump to subroutine. Due to their use of the memory buses, parallel data moves are not allowed.

BCLR	Bit Test and Clear
BSET	Bit Test and Set
BCHG	Bit Test and Change
BTST	Bit Test on Memory
JCLR	Jump if Bit Clear
JSET	Jump if Bit Set
JSCLR	Jump to Subroutine if Bit Clear
JSSET	Jump to Subroutine if Bit Set

Figure 4.16   *The DSP56000 bit manipulation instructions*

Loop control

There are two loop instructions, DO and ENDDO. Other processor families, like the M68000 and M88000, construct program loops by setting up a loop counter, labelling the start of the loop, decrementing or incrementing the loop counter at the end of the loop and, finally, performing a comparison to decide whether to repeat the loop or drop through to the next instruction. While some support has been provided (e.g. the M68000 DBcc decrement and branch on condition instruction), it still requires a few instructions and their overhead. With the periodic and regular processing to prevent data samples being missed, such overhead cannot be tolerated. To solve this problem, many time-critical loops were unfolded and written as straight line sequential code. The disadvantage is the code expansion – a 10-instruction loop repeated 100 times would be replaced by 1000 instructions: a 100:1 expansion!

The DSP56000 has hardware loop counters which are controlled by the DO and ENDDO instructions. This allows program loops to be set up with no software overhead during the loop. The DO instruction sets up the loop. It saves the LA and LC registers on the stack, so that program loops can be nested, sets up the LA and LC registers accordingly and places the first instruction of the loop on the stack to remove any delay at the loop end. The number of counts can be specified via an indirect address, and allows single instruction loops. DO loops are interruptable. The ENDDO instruction terminates a DO loop prematurely and cleans up the stack as needed.

None of these instructions allows parallel moves, although this restriction does not apply to the instructions that form the loop itself.

MOVE commands

There are five 'MOVE' instructions (Figure 4.17) which transfer data across the X, Y and global data buses as well as the program data bus. Their execution does not affect the condition code register except for the L limiting bit when either accumulator A or B is read. The MOVE instruction can be considered as a data ALU no-op but with its two parallel data moves intact.

LUA	Load Updated Address
MOVE	Move Data Registers
MOVEC	Move Control Registers
MOVEM	Move Program Memory
MOVEP	Move Peripheral Data

Figure 4.17 *The DSP56000 move instructions*

Program control

This group of instructions, shown in Figure 4.18, includes the almost universal jump and conditional jumps to other addresses or subroutines, return from subroutine or interrupt commands, etc. However, there are some interesting newcomers. The REP instruction simply repeats the next instruction without refetching it to maximize throughput. The instruction is not interruptable because of this. A single instruction DO loop can be used instead. There are two power down modes controlled by WAIT and STOP. The WAIT instruction halts internal processing until an interrupt appears to wake it up. The STOP instruction halts all internal processing and gates off the clock.

None of this group of instructions supports the parallel data moves.

Jcc	Jump Conditionally
JMP	Jump
JScc	Jump to Subroutine Conditionally
JSR	Jump to Subroutine
NOP	No Operation
REP	Repeat Next Instruction
RESET	Reset On-Chip Peripheral Devices
RTI	Return from Interrupt
RTS	Return from Subroutine
STOP	Stop Instruction Processing*
SWI	Software Interrupt
WAIT	Wait for Interrupt*
*low power standby modes	

Figure 4.18 *The DSP56000 program control instructions*

Instruction format

The first sight of assembler source code for the DSP56000 instils a reaction of sheer terror in those more used to 'normal' assemblers. It looks as if the formatting has gone crazy and put instructions in comment fields! In reality, the assembler format is reflecting the processor's ability to perform parallel operations as shown in Figure 4.19. The opcode and operand fields are self explanatory; however, the next two fields must be considered as part of the single assembler instruction as they specify the two associated data moves.

OPCODE	OPERANDS	X Bus Data	Y Bus Data
MAC	X0,Y0,A	X:(R0)+, X0	Y:(R4)+,Y0

Figure 4.19   *The DSP56000 instruction format*

Using special addressing and loop modes

The requirement for multiple tables lends itself neatly to the adoption of multiple address spaces, allowing parallel fetches. The reasoning is similar to the adoption of Harvard architectures previously discussed. It increases bus bandwidth and reduces execution time. The DSP56000 has taken the approach a step further with a program space and two data spaces. In addition to the more common addressing modes, the DSP56000 provides modulo addressing, shown in Figure 4.20, to allow circular buffers to be created in memory without the software overhead of incrementing a pointer, testing for out of range, and jumping to the start of the table. These functions are performed by hardware with no extra overhead. This provides an elegant way to implement FIFOs, delay lines, sample buffers or shift registers where a simple pointer is moved instead of the data contents. In similar fashion, do loops can be performed by dedicated internal

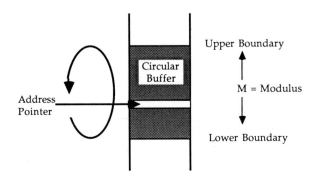

Figure 4.20   *Modulo addressing*

hardware instead of the more normal software methods and again decrease the execution overhead. A hardware loop counter register is provided internally for such applications.

Internal parallelism

The DSP56000 has specific hardware support and parallelism to perform a single-cycle, 24-bit by 24-bit multiply, a 56-bit addition, two data moves and two address pointer updates in a single cycle of 97 ns. This feat is another example of the continuing theme of making the most efficient use of the available hardware within a processor. The benefit for DSP56000 users is two instructions executed with no overhead, a reduction in the loop execution time, and an increased data throughput. The advantage of such facilities can be seen from examination of a typical FIR filter program in Figure 4.21. It uses just 11 instructions. The essential components of the

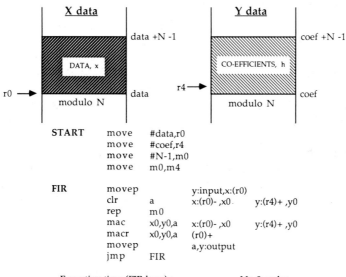

Figure 4.21 *FIR filter program for DSP56000 processor*

routine are the 'rep' and 'mac' instructions. The rep instruction is hardware supported and repeats the mac instruction m0 times. The repeated instruction performs the single-cycle multiply accumulate with two moves. Without modular addressing and the simultaneous data movements, the loop execution time could be six times greater.

Architectural differences

The DSP56000 is a microprocessor which has been enhanced for DSP applications. Through its microprocessor roots and features, it also makes an exceptionally good embedded controller, however, so does the M68000 and the M88000. The problem is now to understand the other system functions these architectures need, how they perform and their associated trade-offs. These are the next topics for discussion.

5 Memory, memory management and caches

This chapter describes the many techniques that are used to build memory subsystems for processors and describes their relevance to the RISC, CISC and DSP processor families. Each family can use similar techniques to improve its performance, although it does not follow that what is good for a M68000 is automatically good for an M88000.

Achieving processor throughput

Processor throughput depends on three separate activities: opcode and data fetching, instruction execution and finally data storage. For any processor to maintain its maximum performance, this flow of data must be maintained. If there are any wait states in the accesses, performance is lost while the processor is waiting for data. These statements are applicable to any architecture, but the effect of wait states is different depending on the processor architecture.

Figure 5.1 shows the effect of wait states on the performance of an MC68000 processor. The CPU performance data is from MacGregor and Rubenstein and has been derived from measurements of bus activity of various systems. It is relative performance, although roughly equivalent to a conservative MIPS rating. While cynics may say that there is no such thing, for this analysis, it is the relative figures that are important. Intuition would indicate that while wait states are detrimental, the processor is more computation bound than bus bound and therefore it is sensible to run the processor faster and tolerate wait states. The reasoning behind this is that CISC processors can take many cycles to execute an instruction and any additional wait states do not greatly contribute to any delays. MacGregor and Rubenstein's analysis showed that on average it took 12.576 clocks per instruction, including an average 2.698 accesses with no wait states. In this instance, the addition of a couple of clocks is not too significant.

MC68000 Performance vs Wait states

Figure 5.1   *The effect of wait states on CISC processor (based on data from MacGregor and Rubenstein, 'A performance analysis of MC68020-based systems', IEEE Micro, December 1985)*

The graph shows exactly this. The performance degradation decreases as the number of wait states increases but this is not a linear function. While any removal of wait states improves performance, closer examination confirms that it is beneficial to run the processor faster, although incurring an additional wait state. Consider the performance of an 8 MHz processor with three wait states: from the graph, it has a performance rating of 0.39. Running a 10 MHz processor with four wait states gives a rating of 0.43, some 16% improvement. If the system is performing a lot of computational work, this value will be even greater.

Unfortunately, this may not be so beneficial with RISC processors. RISC architectures simplify the instruction set so that an instruction has to be fetched on every cycle to maintain the data flow into the processor. This effectively means that, at 20 MHz, memory is accessed every 50 ns and at the higher clock speeds, such as 40 MHz, this increases to every 25 ns. This places tremendous design constraints on the external memory systems. To maintain the constant flow of instructions into the processor requires a separate bus with a very high bus utilization (95–100%), hence the Harvard bus architecture with separate data and instruction buses. The insertion of a single wait state halves system performance, two wait states reduce it by two thirds and so on, as shown in Figure 5.2. Examination shows that a RISC architecture, or any processor executing single-cycle instructions, suffers far more with wait states than a CISC processor. The graph shows that it is better to run a processor slightly slower but with less wait states. This is the opposite of the case for CISC.

Another useful maxim can be drawn from these graphs: as the average clock per instruction decreases, the more dramatic is the effect that wait

Figure 5.2 *The effect of wait states on the RISC performance*

states have on performance. RISC systems may have simpler processors but their memory systems are more sophisticated. DSP processors fall halfway between the two camps. With the DSP56000, its time-critical code and data is usually held on chip in wait state free memory. It is only when extra data or code is needed that there is a potential conflict. Depending on the CPI (clock per instruction), the effect can be similar to either CISC or RISC.

Partitioning the system

One way of making the most of the memory resources available is to partition the memory map so that the most appropriate memory is used to maximize performance. The idea is to have different types of memory with different access speeds, depending on the performance v. cost tradeoffs. These are applicable across the board. Analysis of systems shows that instructions are fetched more often than data, usually irrespective of the architecture. It follows that it is more beneficial to have faster memory allocated to instructions than data. With a CISC processor that shares a single bus between data and instruction fetches, any delay degrades performance. MacGregor and Rubenstein[1] established that for the M68000 family, there were twice as many op code fetches as data accesses and, therefore, a wait state on any data access was only equivalent to 0.33 of a total system wait state.

[1] MacGregor and Rubenstein, 'A performance analysis of MC68020-based systems', *IEEE Micro*, December 1985.

With multiple bus architectures like the M88000 and DSP56000, this effect is enhanced. The M88100 Harvard architecture decouples I/O and data fetches from the instruction traffic and allows both streams to access memory independently. Its separate data unit is pipelined and therefore three to four data fetches can be outstanding before the processor is stalled. A wait state on data fetches may not impact performance at all, provided data accesses are not performed consecutively. With the load–store architecture, this is usually the case. The DSP56000 family, with its multiple buses, offers even more scope for such manipulation.

Shadow RAM

Shadow RAM is a simple technique which is applicable to any processor architecture where essential software or data is stored in non-volatile memory, but with the penalty of slow access times. With an operating system kernel stored in an EPROM (Erasable Programmable Read Only Memory), every system call invariably results in one or more calls to the system routines stored in EPROM. Any removal of wait states from these accesses is extremely beneficial to performance. By copying EPROM contents into RAM on system initialization, the processor can access the faster RAM and retrieve its lost performance. This overlapping memory bank is called Shadow RAM. This technique is used with microcontrollers where EPROM contents are automatically transferred to internal memory on power up, as well as CISC, RISC and DSP processors. The DSP56001 is a version of the DSP56000 that has RAM instead of ROM, and it uses the same technique to load its RAM on power up.

The MC68020 and MC68030 can use shadow RAM, but also use it with dynamic bus sizing so that only a single byte wide EPROM is used to source the information for a 32-bit wide shadow RAM. Only one EPROM is needed, reducing system cost. The processor accesses the boot routines from the EPROM, albeit slower due to the multiple bus cycles needed, copies the contents into the shadow RAM, and then jumps to the software.

All these techniques map the shadow RAM into a different location, which needs software that is either relocatable or specially written for shadow RAM addressing. For some systems, like the IBM PC, this is not possible due to compatibility restrictions. Here, the shadow RAM must occupy the same address as the original EPROM. This requires special hardware to implement it, like the Motorola MCS2120, PC-AT memory controller. It implements shadow RAM with two independent 128 Kbyte segments – one for the normal BIOS and a second for BIOS extensions. Each segment is enabled before the BIOS code is transferred via a series of consecutive reads and writes at the same address. The MCS2120 routes the cycles accordingly – reads go to the EPROM and writes to the Shadow

RAM. After the transfer is completed, writing into a configuration register disables the EPROM access and switches the RAM bank into its address space.

DRAM v. SRAM

While most system designers would prefer to implement designs with static RAM, the increased cost of lower memory densities often prevents this. Dynamic memories are cheaper and have higher densities, but require refreshing regularly. The difference between the two memory types is due to the logic used to store each bit of data in a cell. With static memory, five transistors are used to create a 'flip-flop' logic circuit that can be flipped into a low or high state as needed. No refresh is needed and the data remains held as long as power is applied. Dynamic RAM reduces the transistor count to one and uses a small capacitor to store the bit. This increases the memory density, but the storage remains for only a few milliseconds before the capacitor charge disappears through internal leakage, destroying the cell data. This is why DRAM requires regular refreshing. The cell is refreshed whenever the cell is accessed.

There are generally two ways of providing this refresh: the first is to generate a regular processor interrupt and get it to access the memory systematically. This is a tremendous overhead and hinders real-time response, although it does simplify the hardware design. The second is to use a hardware refresh where sections of the memory are accessed periodically by hardware. Typically 4–5% of the memory bandwidth is consumed using these techniques.

The cell transistor count gives a good indicator of the current densities available between memory technologies. The transistor count defines the cell area and hence the densities. Static RAM is usually a factor of 4 smaller in density when compared with the single-cell memories like DRAM, EPROM, EEPROM (Electrically Erasable Programmable Read Only Memory) and Flash EPROM. Flash EPROM is a new memory technology which can perform bulk erasing quickly, allowing the device to perform as a slow RAM device. It has been hailed as the natural solid-state successor to magnetic storage devices, as it can retain data when powered down. What is uncertain is the number of read/write operations that it can sustain before the cells fail. This is extremely important if the technology is going to challenge winchester discs.

Optimizing the DRAM interface

The basic DRAM interface, shown in Figure 5.3, takes the processor-generated address, places the high-order bits on to the memory address bus to form the row address and asserts the RAS* signal. This partial address is

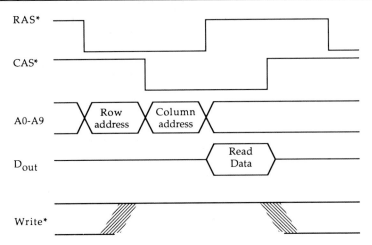

Figure 5.3 *Basic DRAM interface timings*

latched internally by the DRAM. The remaining low-order bits, forming the column address, are then driven on to the bus and the CAS★ signal asserted. After the access time has expired, the data appears on the D_{out} pin and is latched by the processor. The RAS★ and CAS★ signals are then negated. This cycle is repeated for every access.

The majority of DRAM specifications define minimum pulse widths for the RAS★ and CAS★ and these often form the major part in defining the memory access time. This direct access method limits wait state free operation to the lower processor speeds. DRAM with 100 ns access time would allow only a 12.5 MHz processor to run with zero wait states. To achieve 20 MHz operation needs 40 ns DRAM, which is unavailable today, or fast static RAM which is available, but at a price.

Page mode operation

One way of reducing the effective access time is to remove the RAS★ pulse width every time the DRAM is accessed. It needs to be pulsed on the first access, but subsequent accesses to the same page (i.e. with the same row address) do not require it and so are accessed faster. This is how the 'page mode' versions of most 256 kbit, 1 Mbit and 4 Mbit memory work. In page mode, the row address is supplied as normal, but the RAS★ signal is left asserted. This selects an internal page of memory within the DRAM where any bit of data can be accessed by simply placing the column address and asserting CAS★ (Figure 5.4). With 256 kbit memory, this gives a page of 1 Kbytes (512 column bits per DRAM row times 16 DRAMs in the array). A 2 Kbyte page is available from 1 Mbit DRAM and 4 Kbyte page with 4 Mbit DRAM. This allows fast processors to work with slower memory

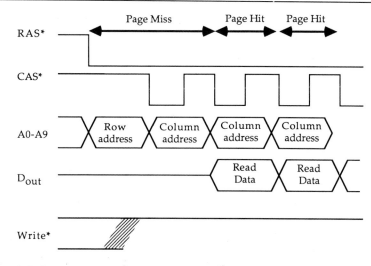

Figure 5.4 *Page mode access*

and yet achieve almost wait state free operation. The first access is slower and causes wait states, but subsequent accesses within the selected page are quicker with no wait states. There is one restriction, however. The maximum time that the RAS★ signal can be asserted during page mode operation is often specified at about 10 µs. In many designs, the refresh interval is frequently adjusted to match this time, so that a refresh cycle will always occur and prevent a specification violation.

Page interleaving

Using a page mode design provides greater performance only when the memory cycles exhibit some form of locality (i.e. stay within the page boundary). Every access outside the boundary causes a page miss and two to three wait states. The secret, as with caches, is to increase the hits and reduce the misses. Fortunately, most accesses are sequential or localized, as found in program subroutines and some data structures. However, if a program is frequently accessing data, the memory activity often follows a code–data–code–data access pattern. If the code areas and data areas are in different pages, any benefit that page mode could offer is lost. Each access changes the page selection, incurring wait states. The solution is to increase the number of pages that are available. If the memory is divided into several banks, each bank can offer a selected page, increasing the number of pages and, ultimately, the number of hits and performance. Again, extensive hardware support is needed.

Typically, a page mode system implements a 1, 2, or 4-way system, depending how much memory is in the system. With a 4-way system, there are four memory banks, each with their own RAS★ and CAS★ lines. With 4 Mbytes of DRAM per bank, this would offer 16 Mbytes of system RAM. The 4-way system allows four pages to be selected within page mode at any one time. Page 0 is in Bank 1, page 1 in bank 2 and so on, with the sequence restarting after four banks, as shown in Figure 5.5.

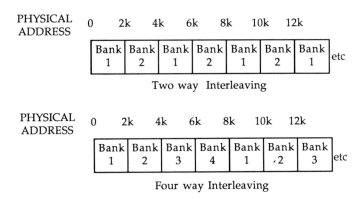

Figure 5.5 *Two and four-way interleaving*

With interleaving and Fast Page Mode devices, inexpensive 85 ns DRAM can be used with a 16 MHz processor to achieve a sub 1 wait state system. With no page mode interleaving, this system inserts two wait states on every access. With the promise of faster DRAM, future designs will be able to offer 20–25 MHz systems with very good performance, without the need for cache memory with its associated costs and complexity. These pagemode and interleaving techniques are also applicable to SRAM designs and frequently compliment burst fill caches as on the MC68030.

Alternative memory systems

Other memory systems which offer lower cost solutions can be used. Video DRAMs have an onchip shift register which can hold a complete column of data and, after the initial slow access, can provide the rest of the data in a burst mode until the shift register is empty. This provides data on a single-cycle basis once the initial access has been performed. The disadvantage is that every time there is a flow change in the code, a slow access has to be performed to reload the shift register. This slow access may insert 4/5 waitstates and therefore the average time per access may drop to two clocks per fetch. In addition, video DRAMs are more expensive and have smaller densities than standard DRAMs, which restricts their use to applications requiring small amounts of memory.

Memory management

Hardware memory management is implemented usually by a MMU (Memory Management Unit) to meet at least one of four system requirements:

1   The need to extend the current addressing range
The often–perceived need for memory management is usually the result of prior experience or background, and centres on extending the current linear addressing range. The Intel 80×86 architecture is based around a 64 Kbyte linear addressing segment which, while providing 8-bit compatibility, does require memory management to provide the higher order address bits necessary to extend the processor's address space. Software must track accesses that go beyond this segment, and change the address accordingly. The M68000 family has at least a 16 Mbyte addressing range and does not have this restriction. The M88000 family has an even larger 4 Gbyte range. The DSP56000 has a 128 Kword (1 word $= 24$ bits) address space, which is sufficient for most present-day applications; however, the intermittent delays that occur in servicing an MMU can easily destroy the accuracy of the algorithms. For this reason, the linear addressing range may increase, but it is unlikely that memory management will appear in DSP applications.

2   To remove the need to write relocatable or position-independent software
Many systems have multitasking operating systems where the software environment consists of modular blocks of code running under the control of an operating system. There are three ways of allocating memory to these blocks. The first simply distributes blocks in a pre-defined way, i.e. task A is given the memory block from \$A0000 to \$A8000, task B is given from \$C0000 to \$D8000 etc. With these addresses, the programmer can write the code to use this memory. This is fine, providing the distribution does not change and there is sufficient design discipline to adhere to the plan. However, it does make all the code hardware and position dependent. If another system has a slightly different memory configuration, the code will not run correctly.

To overcome this problem, software can be written in such a way that it is either relocatable or position independent. These two terms are often interchanged but there is a difference: both can execute anywhere in the memory map, but relocatable code must maintain the same address offsets between its data and code segments. The main technique is to avoid the use of absolute addressing modes, replacing them with relative addressing modes. The M68000, M88000 and DSP56000 families all have this basic architectural support. If this support is missing or the compiler technology cannot use it, memory management must be used to translate the logical program addresses and map them into physical memory. This effectively realigns the memory so that the processor and software think that the memory is organized specially for them, but in reality is totally different.

3   To partition the system to protect it from other tasks, users, etc.
To provide stability within a multitasking or multiuser system, it is advisable to partition the memory so that errors within one task do not corrupt others. On a more general level, operating system resources may need separating from applications. Both the M68000 and M88000 families can provide this partitioning through the use of the Function codes or by the combination of the user/supervisor signals and Harvard architecture. This partitioning is very coarse, but is often all that is necessary in many cases. For finer grain protection, memory management can be used to add extra description bits to an address to declare its status. If a task attempts to access memory that has not been allocated to it, or its status does not match (e.g. writing to a read-only declared memory location), the MMU can detect it and raise an error to the supervisor level.

4   To allow programs to access more memory than is physically present in the system
With the large linear addressing offered by today's 32-bit microprocessors, it is relatively easy to create large software applications which consume vast quantities of memory. While it may be feasible to install 64 Mbytes of RAM in a workstation, the costs are expensive compared with a 64 Mbyte winchester disc. As the memory needs go up, this differential increases. A solution is to use the disc storage as the main storage medium, divide the stored program into small blocks and keep in processor system memory only the blocks that are needed (Figure 5.6). As the program executes, the

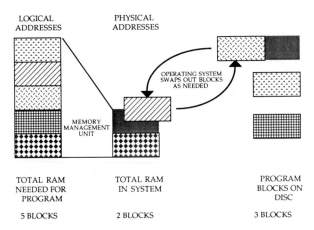

Figure 5.6   *Using virtual memory to support large applications*

MMU can track how the program uses the blocks, and swap them to and from the disc as needed. If a block is not present in memory, this causes a page fault and forces some exception processing which performs the swapping operation. In this way, the system appears to have large amounts of system RAM when, in reality, it does not. This virtual memory technique is used frequently in workstations and in the UNIX operating system.

Disadvantages of memory management

Given that memory management is necessary and beneficial, what are the trade-offs? The most obvious is the delay it inserts into the memory access cycle. Before a translation can take place, the logical address from the processor must appear. The translation usually involves some form of table look-up, where the contents of a segment register or the higher-order address bits are used to locate a descriptor within a memory block. The descriptor provides the physical address bits and any partitioning information such as read-only, etc. These signals are combined with the original lower-order address bits to form the physical memory address. This look-up takes time, which must be inserted into the memory cycle, and usually causes at least one wait state (Figure 5.7), so slowing down the processor and system performance.

Figure 5.7 *Address translation mechanism*

   In addition, there can be considerable overheads in managing all the look-up tables and checking access rights, etc. These overheads appear on loading a task, during any memory allocation and when any virtual memory system needs to swap memory blocks out to disc. The required software support is performed usually by an operating system. In the latter case, if the system memory is very small compared with the virtual memory size and application, the memory management driver will consume a lot of processing and time in simply moving data to and from the disc. In extreme cases, this overhead starts to dominate the system which is working hard but achieving very little. The addition of more memory relieves the need to swap and returns more of the system throughput to executing the application.

Segmentation and paging

There are two methods of splitting the system memory into smaller blocks for memory management. The size of these blocks is quite critical within the design. Each block requires a translation descriptor and therefore the size of the block is important. If the granularity is too small (i.e. the blocks are 1–2 Kbytes), the number of descriptors needed for a 4 Gbyte system is extremely large. If the blocks are too big, the number of descriptors reduces but granularity increases. If a program just needs a few bytes, a complete block will have to be allocated to it and this wastes the unused memory. Between these two extremes lies the ideal trade-off.

A segmented memory management scheme has a small number of descriptors but solves the granularity problem by allowing the segments to be of a variable size in a block of contiguous memory. Each segment descriptor is fairly complex and the hardware has to be able to cope with different address translation widths. The memory usage is greatly improved, although the task of assigning memory segments in the most efficient way is difficult. This problem occurs when a system has been operating for some time and the segment distribution is now right across the memory map. The free memory has been fragmented into small chunks, albeit in large numbers. In such cases, the total system memory may be more than sufficient to allocate another segment, but the memory is non-contiguous and therefore not available. There is nothing more frustrating, when using such systems, as the combination of '2 Mbytes RAM free' and 'Insufficient Memory to load' messages when trying to execute a simple utility. In such cases, the current tasks must be stopped, saved and restarted to repack them and free-up the memory. This problem can be found also with file storage systems which need contiguous disc sectors and tracks.

A paged memory system splits memory needs into multiple, same-sized blocks called pages. These are usually 1–2 Kbytes in size, which allows them to take easy advantage of fragmented memory. However, each page needs a descriptor, which greatly increases the size of the look-up tables. With a 4 Gbyte logical address space and 1 Kbyte page size, the number of descriptors needed is over 4 million. Each descriptor would be 32 bits (22 bits translation address, 10 bits for protection and status) in size and the corresponding table would occupy 16 Mbytes! This is a little impractical, to say the least. To decrease the amount of storage needed for the page tables, multi-level tree structures are used, as shown in Figure 5.8. Such mechanisms have been implemented in the MC68851 Paged Memory

Figure 5.8 *Using trees for descriptor tables*

Management Unit (PMMU), the MC68030 processor and the MC88200 CMMU.

Trees work by dividing the logical address into fields and using each of the fields to successively reference into tables until the translation address is located. This is then concatenated with the lower–order page address bits to complete a full physical address. The root pointer forms the start of the tree and there may be separate pointers for user and supervisor use. The root pointer points to separate pointer tables, which in turn point to other tables and so on, until the descriptor is finally reached. Each pointer table contains the address of the next location. Most systems differ in the number of levels and the page sizes that can be implemented. Bits can often be set to terminate the table walk when large memory areas do not need to be defined uniquely at a lower or page level. The less levels, the more efficient the table walking.

Figure 5.9 shows the three-level tree used by the MC88200 CMMU. The logical 32-bit address is extended by a user/supervisor bit which is used to select one of two possible segment table bases from the User and Supervisor area registers. The segment number if derived from bits 31 to 22 and is concatenated with a 20-bit value from the segment table base and a binary '00' to create a 32-bit address for the page number table. The page table base is derived similarly until the complete translation is obtained. The remaining 12 bits of the descriptors are used to define the page, segment or area status in terms of access and, more recently, cache

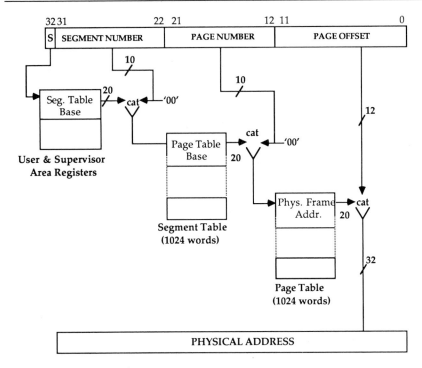

Figure 5.9 *The MC88200 table walking mechanism*

Area		
Sup'v. Segment Table	WT 0 G CI 0 0 U WP V
User Segment Table Base	WT 0 G CI 0 0 U WP V

Segment	
Page Table Base	WT SP G CI 0 0 U WP V

Page	
Page Frame Base	WT SP G CI 0 M U WP V

V	Valid	CI	Cache Inhibit
WP	Write Protect Enable	G	Global - Snoop
U	Used	SP	Supervisor Only
M	Modified	WT	Write Through

Figure 5.10 *MC88200 memory management descriptors*

coherency mechanisms. If the attempted access does not match with these bits (e.g. write to a write protected page), an error will be sent back to the processor. The descriptors used by the MC88200 are shown in Figure 5.10.

Figures 5.11 and 5.12 show a practical implementation using a two-level tree from an MC68851 PMMU. The example task occupies a 1 Mbyte logical address map consisting of a code, data and stack memory blocks.

Figure 5.11   *The required memory map*

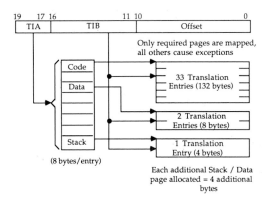

Figure 5.12   *Example multilevel tree*

With a single-level table, this would need 512 descriptors, assuming a 2 Kbyte page size. With the two-level scheme shown, only the needed pages are mapped. All other accesses cause an exception to allocate extra pages as necessary. This type of scheme is often called 'demand paged memory management'. With the two-level table mechanism, only 44 entries are needed, occupying only 208 bytes, with additional pages increasing this by 4 bytes. The example shows a relatively simple two-level table but up to five levels are often used, which leads to a fairly complex and time-consuming table walk to perform the address translation.

To improve performance, a cache or buffer is used to contain the most recently used translations, so that table walks occur only if the entry is not in the address translation cache (ATC) or translation look-aside buffer (TLB). This makes a lot of sense – due to the location of code and data, there will be frequent accesses to the same page and, by caching the descriptor, the penalty of a table walk is paid only on the first access. However, there are still some further trade-offs to consider.

Multitasking and user/supervisor conflicts

Using ATCs or TLBs (for example, with the MC68851, MC68030 and MC88200 processors) decreases memory management delays considerably. However, consider the dilemma faced when they are used within a multitasking system as shown in Figure 5.13. Two tasks with the same logical address are mapped into different physical locations. Task A executes for the first time – the TLBs are loaded with the correct translations and the system performs correctly. A context switch occurs and task B is loaded with the same logical address. The problem is – how does the MMU know whether its TLB contents are valid?

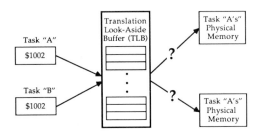

Figure 5.13 *A multi-tasking memory management dilemma*

There are three solutions to this. The first involves flushing the TLB during the context switch so that task B can start with a clean buffer. This is simple but forces several table walks to be performed to load the TLB. The second requires additional information to be appended to the each entry, so that a task identity can be used to resolve any conflict. Here, translation entries need not be flushed from the cache and, thus improve performance. The third involves preloading the TLB during the context switch with the relevant task descriptors so that the table walking overhead is removed. The first solution is simple but has the impact of external table walks. The second needs hardware and effectively splits the TLB into several smaller

TLBs and potentially suffers the problem of insufficient TLB entries, forcing further table walks. The third has the overhead of adding to the task data that must be saved and reinstated. Which solution is best?

There are no obvious indicators. The MC68851 PMMU implemented the second solution with its 'task aliasing' feature but it was little used (as were about half of the PMMU's facilities) and was not supported on the MC68030 MMU. It is difficult to define the reason accurately, but it was probably due to a combination of silicon real estate limitations on the MC68030 design (its ATC held only 22 entries, compared with 64 for the MC68851), lack of use and the effective reduction of the TLB entries per task. Between the appearance of the MC68851 and the MC68030, programs had grown considerably, processing performance had increased and systems had taken advantage of the new 256 Kbit and 1 Mbit DRAM technology to increase the available memory. In such conditions, eight entries per task is simply not big enough. The technique of preloading TLB entries and increasing the number of entries per task would be better. It is interesting to note that operating system page sizes have also increased from 1 to 4 Kbytes, with talk of even 8 or 16 Kbytes for the next generation.

A second problem with TLBs and ATCs concerns the updating and overwriting of entries. Consider an operation system memory, application memory and I/O areas. All are mapped correctly. During task A's execution time, it accesses many pages and eventually fills up the TLB with all its entries. It then makes a system call to the operating system, the processor switches into supervisor mode and starts to perform the request. With no current TLB entries, this causes an external table walk. Once completed, the request handler can now be accessed and the system call completed. It is extremely likely that multiple table walks would need to be carried out, and these would greatly increase the call execution time. Once completed, task A can restart and load in its TLB entries, overwriting the supervisor entries. The same system call is made and the table walking and subsequent overwriting repeated, which can cause an extremely poor system call response. This scenario can occur when accessing physical I/O such as memory mapped graphics, etc.

The MC68030 solves this problem by providing two transparent windows (Figure 5.14), which can be used to access directly two blocks of memory. These can be from 16 Mbytes to 2 Gbytes in size and can be user/supervisor restricted, cache inhibited and write protected, if necessary. They do not use any of the MMU functions and can be dedicated solely to operating system use. The MC88200 solution is to provide two caches – the Paged Address Translation Cache for applications and a separate Block Address Translation Cache for supervisor and operating system use. With the multiple CMMU configurations normally used with the MC88100 RISC processor to support its Harvard architecture, there are separate MMUs and ATCs for instructions and data.

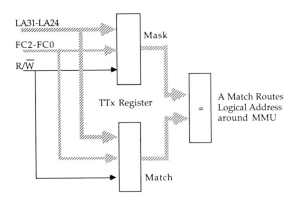

Figure 5.14   *The MC68030 transparent windows*

Instruction continuation v. restart

Another potential problem is thrashing during page swapping, caused by an instruction continuation instead of instruction restart. If, during an instruction execution, a memory access goes across a page boundary and causes a page fault, a page swap is performed; the required page is taken from disc and may replace the old page which contained the original instruction. If the processor uses instruction continuation, there is no problem; the old page is not needed and only the faulting access is attempted again to carry on as before. If the processor has to restart the instruction, the original instruction is needed; this has been swapped out to disc and the subsequent fetch causes another page fault. It is likely that the new page is chosen to swop out because it is the least recently used. The instruction is executed, the data access is attempted causing a page fault, etc. The system starts to thrash and may never resolve the situation. In reality, this can easily be detected by simply enforcing a rule of 'never swapping the previous page' and is therefore never a serious problem. However, if software is ported from a 'continuation' architecture to a 'restart' one, this must be handled.

Memory management and DSP

On first inspection, digital signal processing appears to have no need for memory management at all. The programs are relatively small and do not need virtual memory. They do not run multi-user operating systems and therefore do not need protection. They cannot tolerate the random delays caused by page faults and external table walks which would seriously reduce the signal bandwidth that they can handle, or introduce distortion errors. However, DSP processors are becoming more like general-purpose processors and, with the DSP96000, will have 32-bit addressing. It may be that future generations will start to need memory management functions so they can run both DSP and more general applications.

Cache memory

Any comments on cache memory design and its parameters are almost guaranteed to start a debate among engineers, as zealous as any discussion in a synod or other philosophical gathering! This is because there are no wrongs or rights in cache design – it results inevitably in a juggling act involving the resources available. Therefore it is important to understand the ideas behind such designs and the trade-off decisions before making instantaneous evaluations and dismissing them. It is always sobering to remember that the simple 256 byte internal cache on the MC68020 gives a performance increase of about 17–25%!

With faster (>25 MHz) processors, the wait states incurred in DRAM accesses start to reduce performance dramatically, so many designs implement a cache memory to buffer the processor from such delays. Cache memory systems work because of the cyclical structures within software. Most software structures are loops where pieces of code are repeatedly executed, albeit with different data. Cache memory systems store these loops so that after the loop has been fetched from main memory, it can be obtained from the cache for subsequent executions. Accesses from cache are faster than from main memory and thus increase system throughput. This means that caches cannot be 100% efficient – the first accesses always goes through to main memory.

Cache size and organization

There are several criteria associated with cache design which affect its performance. The most obvious is cache size and organization – the larger the cache, the more entries that are stored and the higher the hit rate. However, as the cache size increases, the return gets smaller and smaller. In practice, the cache costs and complexity place an economic limit on most designs. As the size of programs increase, larger caches are needed to maintain the same hit rate and hence the 'ideal cache size is always twice that available' comment. In reality, it is the combination of size, organization and cost that really determines the size and its efficiency.

Consider a basic cache operation. The processor generates an address which is fed into the cache memory system. The cache stores its data in an array with an address tag, each tag being compared in turn with the incoming address. If they do not match, the next tag is compared. If they do match, a cache hit occurs, the corresponding data within the array is passed on the data bus to the processor and no further comparisons are made. If no match is found (a cache miss), the data is fetched from external memory and a new entry is created in the array. This is simple to implement, needing only a memory array and a single comparator and counter. Unfortunately, the efficiency is not very good due to the serial interrogation of the tags.

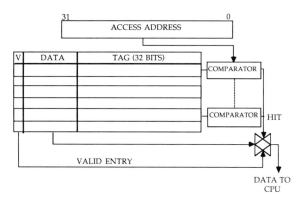

Figure 5.15   *A fully associative cache design*

A better solution is to have a comparator for each entry, so all entries can be tested simultaneously. This is the organization used in a fully associative cache shown in Figure 5.15. In the example, a valid bit is added to each entry in the cache array, so that invalid or unused entries can easily be identified. The system is very efficient from a software perspective – any entry can be used to store data from any address. A software loop using only 20 bytes (10 off 16-bit instructions) but scattered over a 1024 byte range would run as efficiently as another loop of the same size but occupying consecutive locations. The disadvantage of this approach is the amount of hardware needed to perform the comparisons, increasing in proportion to the cache size and therefore limiting these fully associative caches to about 10 entries. Address translation caches are often fully associative. The fully associative cache locates its data by effectively asking *n* questions where *n* is the number of entries within it. An alternative organization is to assume certain facts derived from the data address so that only one location can possibly have the data and only one comparator is needed, irrespective of the cache size. This is the idea behind the direct map cache shown in Figure 5.16.

The address is presented as normal but part of it is used to index into the tag array. The corresponding tag is compared and, if there is a match, the data is supplied. If there is a cache miss, the data is fetched from external memory as normal and the cache updated as necessary. The example shows

Figure 5.16 *Direct mapped cache*

how the lower address bits can be used to locate a byte, word or long word within the memory block stored within the array. This organization is simple from the hardware design but can be inefficient from a software viewpoint.

The index mechanism effectively splits external memory space into a series of consecutive memory pages, with each page the same size as the cache. Each page is mapped to resemble the cache and therefore each location in the external memory page can correspond only with its own location in the cache. Data that is offset by the cache size thus occupies the same location within the cache, albeit with different tag values. This can cause bus thrashing. Consider a case where words A and B are offset by the cache size. Here, every time word A is accessed, word B is discarded from the cache. Every time word B is accessed, word A is lost. The cache starts thrashing and the overall performance is degraded. The MC68020 is a typical direct mapped cache.

A way to solve this is to split the cache so there are two or four possible entries available for use. This increases the comparator count but provides alternative locations and prevents bus thrashing. Such designs are described as 'n way set associative', where n is the number of possible locations. Values of 2, 4, 8 are quite typical of such designs. The MC88200 CMMU is organised as a 4-way set associative cache. Figure 5.17 shows an n-way set associative cache.

The advantage of a set associative cache is its ability to prevent thrashing at the expense of extra hardware. However, all the caches so far described can be improved by further reorganizing so that each tag is associated with a line of long words which can be burst filled using a page memory interface. The logic behind this idea is based on the sequential nature of instruction execution and data access. Instruction fetches and execution

Figure 5.17 *A set associative cache design*

simply involve accesses to sequential memory locations until a program flow change happens due to the execution of a branch or jump instruction. Data accesses often follow this pattern during stack and data structure manipulation.

It follows that if a cache is organized with, say, four long words within each tag line, a hit in the first long word would usually result in hits in the rest of the line, unless a flow change took place. If a cache miss were experienced, it would be beneficial to bring in the whole line, providing this could be achieved in less time than to bring in the four long words individually. This is exactly what happens in a page mode interface. By combining these, a more efficient cache can be designed which even benefits in line code. This is exactly how the MC68030 cache works (Figure 5.19). Address bits 2 and 3 select which long word is required from the four stored in the 16 byte wide line. The remaining higher address bits and function codes are the tag which can differentiate between supervisor or user accesses, etc. If there is a cache miss, the processor uses its synchronous bus with burst fill to load up the complete line.

	W/O Burst	W/ Burst
Instruction Cache	46%	82%
Data Cache - Reads	60%	72%
Data Cache - R & W	40%	48%

Figure 5.18 *Estimated hit rates for the MC68030 caches*

Figure 5.19 *The MC68030 direct mapped burst fill cache*

With a complete line updated in the cache, the next three instructions result in a hit, providing there is no preceding flow change. These benefit from being cached, even though it is their first execution. This is a great improvement over previous designs, where the software had to loop before any benefit could be gained. Figure 5.18 shows the estimated improvements that can be obtained. The effect is similar to increasing the cache size, the largest effect being with instruction fetches which show the greatest degree of locality. Data reads are second, but with less impact due to isolated byte and word accesses. Data read and write operations are further reduced, caused by the cache's write through policy. This forces all read-modify-write and write operations to main memory. In some designs, data accesses are not sequential, in which case, system performance actually degrades when the data cache is enabled – burst filling the next three long words is simply a waste of time, bus bandwidth and performance. The solution is simple – switch off the cache!

This method is used in most high-performance cache designs.

Optimizing line length and cache size

Such performance degradation is symptomatic of external bus thrashing due to the cache line length and/or burst fill length being wrong, leading to system inefficiencies; it is therefore important to get these values correct. If the burst fill length is greater than the number of sequential instructions executed before a flow change, data is fetched which will not be used, consuming valuable external bus bandwidth. If the burst length is greater than the line length, multiple cache lines have to be updated, which may destroy a cache entry for another piece of code that will be executed later. This destroys the efficiency of the cache mechanism and increases the cache flushing, again consuming external bus bandwidth. Both of these contribute to the notorious 'bus thrashing' syndrome where the processor spends vast amounts of time fetching data that it never uses. Some cache schemes allow line lengths of 1, 4, 8, 16 or 32 to be selected; however, most systems use a line and burst fill length of 4. Where there are large blocks of data to be moved, higher values can improve performance within these moves, but this must be offset by any effect on other activities.

Cache size is another variable which can affect performance. Unfortunately, it always seems to be the case that the ideal cache is twice the size of that currently available! The biggest difficulty is that cache size and efficiency are totally software dependent – a configuration that works for one application is not necessarily the optimum for another.

Size	Associativity	Line Size	Hit Rate	Performance Ratio vs DRAM
1k	direct	4 bytes	41%	0.91
8k	direct	4 bytes	73%	1.25
16k	direct	4 bytes	81%	1.35
32k	direct	4 bytes	86%	1.38
32k	2-way	4 bytes	87%	1.39
32k	direct	8 bytes	91%	1.41
64k	direct	4 bytes	88%	1.39
64k	2-way	4 bytes	89%	1.40
64k	4-way	4 bytes'	89%	1.40
64k	direct	8 bytes	92%	1.42
64k	2-way	8 bytes	93%	1.42
128k	direct	4 bytes	89%	1.39
128k	2-way	4 bytes	89%	1.40
128k	direct	8 bytes	93%	1.42

Figure 5.20 *Cache performance*
Source: 80386 Hardware Reference Manual

Figure 5.20 shows some efficiency figures quoted by Intel in its 80386 Hardware Reference Manual and, from this data, it is apparent that there is no clear-cut advantage of one configuration over another. Common to all the cache organizations is the dependency on fast tag access and comparison. Typical access speeds for tag RAMs are 15–25 ns, with 20–25 ns Static RAMs forming the data arrays.

Logical v. physical caches

Cache memory can be located either side of a memory management unit and use either physical or logical addresses as its tag data. In terms of performance, the location of the cache can dramatically affect system performance. With a logical cache, the tag information refers to the logical addresses currently in use by the executing task. If the task is switched out during a context switch, the cache tags are no longer valid and the cache, together with its often hard-won data must be flushed and cleared. The processor must now go to main memory to fetch the first instructions and wait until the second iteration before any benefit is obtained from the cache. However, cache accesses do not need to go through the MMU and do not suffer from any associated delay.

Physical caches use physical addresses and do not need flushing on a context switch, therefore data is preserved within the cache. The disadvantage is that all accesses must go through the memory management unit, thus incurring delays. Particular care must also be exercised when pages are swapped to and from disc. If the processor does not invalidate any associated cache entries, the cache contents will be different from the main memory contents by virtue of the new page that has been swapped in.

Of the two systems, physical caches are more efficient, providing the cache coherency problem is solved and MMU delays are kept to a minimum. The MC88200 solves the MMU delay by coupling the MMU with the cache system. An MMU translation is performed in conjunction with the cache look-up, so that the translation delay overlaps the memory access and is reduced to zero. This system combines the speed advantages of a logical cache with the data efficiency of a physical cache.

Cache coherency

The biggest challenge with cache design for any system architecture is how to solve the problem of data and cache coherency. This issue arises when the data cached can be modified by more than one source. The problem normally is associated only with data but can occur with instructions in a page-swapping operating system. The stale data situation arises when a copy is held in both cache and main memory. If either copy is modified, the other becomes stale and system coherency is destroyed. The simple solution is to declare shared data as non-cacheable so that any processor access is forced to main memory. This ensures coherency but it couples the processor to slow memory and really defeats the reason for implementing a cache at all. For very simple systems, it is a suitable solution.

There are four typical methods of writing cached data, as shown in Figure 5.21. However, they all have trade-offs and many systems implement all four on a memory block-by-block basis to optimize the system performance.

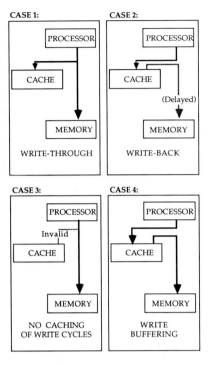

Figure 5.21 *Different Write schemes*

Case 1: Write through

In this case, all data writes go through to main memory and update the system as well as the cache; this is simple to implement but couples the processor unnecessarily to slow memory. If data is modified several times before another master needs it, the write-through policy consumes external bus bandwidth supplying data that is not needed; this is not very efficient. In its favour, the scheme is very simple to implement, providing there is only a single cache within the system. But if there are more than two caches, the stale data problem reappears in another guise. Consider such a system where two processors with caches have a copy of a global variable. Neither processor accesses main memory when reading the variable, as the data is supplied by the respective caches. Processor A now modifies the variable; its cache is updated, along with the system memory. Unfortunately, processor B's cache is left with the old stale data, creating a coherency problem. A similar problem can occur within paging systems.

DMA (Direct Memory Access) can modify memory directly without any processor intervention. Consider an UNIX paging system. Page A is in physical memory and is cached. A page fault occurs and page A is swapped

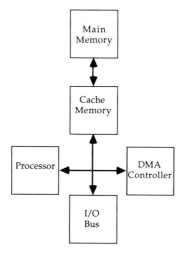

Figure 5.22 *A coherent cache architecture*

out to disc and replaced by page B at the same location; the cached data is now stale. A software solution involves flushing the cache when the page fault happens so that the previous contents are removed. But this can destroy useful cached data and needs operating system support, which can make it non-compatible. The only hardware solution is to force any access to the main memory via the cache, so that the cache can update any modifications (Figure 5.22). A transparent solution is provided, but it does force the processor to compete with the DMA channels, and restricts caching to main memory only, with the subsequent reduced performance.

Case 2: Write back

Here the cache is updated first but the main memory is not updated until later, which is probably the most efficient method of caching, giving 15–20% improvement over a straight write-through cache. This scheme needs a bus snooping mechanism for coherency, which will be described later. The usual cache implementation involves adding dirty bits to the tag to indicate which cache lines or partial lines hold modified data that has not been written out to main memory. This dirty data must be written out if there is any possibility that the information will be lost. If a cache line is to be replaced as a result of a cache miss and the line contains dirty data, the dirty data must be written out before the new cache line can be accepted, so increasing the impact of a cache miss on the system. There can be further complications if memory management page faults occur. However, these aspects must be put into perspective – yes, there will be some system impact if lines must be written out, but this will have less impact on a wider scale. It can double the time to access a cache line, but it has probably saved more performance by removing multiple accesses through to the main memory. The trick is to get the balance in your favour.

Case 3: No caching of write cycles

In this method, the data is written through but the cache is not updated. If the previous data had been cached, that entry is marked invalid and is not used, which forces the processor to access the data from main memory. In isolation, this scheme does seem to be extremely wasteful; however, it often forms the backbone of a bus snooping mechanism.

Case 4: Write buffer

This is a variation on the write-through policy. Writes are written out via a buffer to main memory, which enables the processor to update 'main memory' very quickly, allowing it to carry on processing data supplied by the cache. While this is going on, the buffer transfers the data to main memory. The main advantage is the removal of memory delays during the writes but the system still suffers from coherency problems caused through multiple caches.

Another term associated with these techniques is 'write allocation'. A write allocate cache allocates entries in the cache for any data that is written out. The idea behind it is simple – if data is being transferred to external memory, why not cache it, so that when it is accessed again, it is already waiting in the cache? This is a good idea if the cache is large but it does run the risk of overwriting other entries that may be more useful. The problem is particularly relevant if the processor performs block transfers or memory initialization. Its main use is within bus snooping mechanisms where a first write allocate policy can be used to tell other caches that their data is now invalid.

The most important need with these methods and ideas is bus snooping.

Bus snooping

With bus snooping, a memory cache monitors the external bus for any access to data within main memory that it already has. If the cache data is more recent, the cache can either supply it direct or force the other master off the bus, update main memory and start a retry, thus allowing the original master access to valid data. As an alternative to forcing a retry, the cache containing the valid data can act as memory and supply the data directly. As discussed previously, bus snooping is essential for any multimaster system to ensure cache coherency. The bus snooping mechanism used by the MC88100/MC88200 uses a combination of write

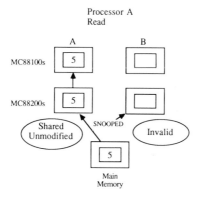

Figure 5.23   *M88000 cache coherency – i*

policies, cache tag status and bus monitoring to ensure coherency. Figures
5.23–5.31 show a typical sequence.

In Figure 5.23, processor A reads data from main memory and this data is
cached. Main memory is declared global and is shared by processors A and
B. Both caches have bus snooping enabled for this global memory, so
causing the cached data to be tagged as shared unmodified – i.e. another
master may need it and the data is identical to that of main memory. A's
access is snooped by processor B, who does nothing as its cache entry is
invalid. It should be noted that snooping does not require any direct
processor or software intervention and is entirely automatic. Processor B
accesses main memory, as shown in Figure 5.24 and updates its cache as
well. This is snooped by A but the current tag of shared unmodified is still
correct and nothing is done.

Processor A modifies its data (Figure 5.25) and, by virtue of a first write

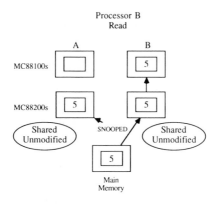

Figure 5.24   *M88000 cache coherency – ii*

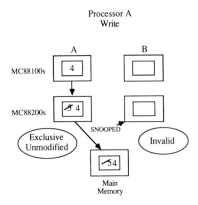

Figure 5.25   *M88000 cache coherency – iii*

allocate policy, writes through to main memory. It changes the tag to exclusive unmodified, i.e. the data is cached exclusively by A and is coherent with main memory. B snoops the access and immediately invalidates its old copy within its cache. When processor B needs the data, it is accessed from main memory and written into the cache as shared unmodified data. This is snooped by A, which changes its data to the same status. Both processors now know that the data they have is coherent with main memory and is shared (Figure 5.26). Processor A now modifies the data which is written out to main memory and snooped by B which marks its cache entry as invalid. Again, this is a first write allocate policy in effect (Figure 5.27).

Processor A modifies the data again but, by virtue of the copyback selection, the data is not written out to main memory (Figure 5.28). Its cache entry is now tagged as exclusive modified, i.e. this may be the only

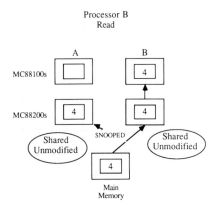

Figure 5.26   *M88000 cache coherency – iv*

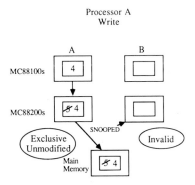

Figure 5.27 *M88000 cache coherency – v*

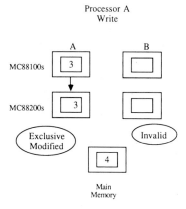

Figure 5.28 *M88000 cache coherency – vi*

valid copy within the system. Processor B tries to get the data and starts an external memory access, as shown in Figure 5.29. Processor A snoops this access, recognizes that it has the valid copy and so asserts a retry response to processor B, which comes off the bus and allows processor A to update main memory and change its cache tag status to shared unmodified (Figure 5.30). Once completed, processor B is allowed back on to the bus to complete its original access, this time with the main memory containing the correct data (Figure 5.31).

This sequence is relatively simple compared with those encountered in real life, where page faults, cache flushing, etc., etc. further complicate the state diagrams. The control logic for the CMMU is far more complex than that of the M88100 processor itself and this demonstrates the complexity involved in ensuring cache coherency within multiprocessor systems.

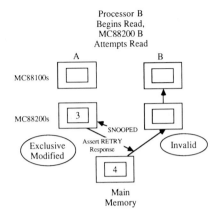

Figure 5.29 *M88000 cache coherency – vii*

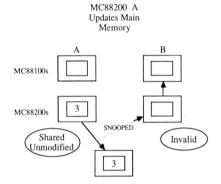

Figure 5.30 *M88000 cache coherency – viii*

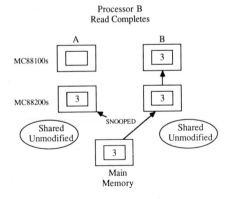

Figure 5.31 *M88000 cache cherency – ix*

Implementing memory systems

While many system designs use cache memory to buffer the fast processor from the slower system memory, it should be remembered that access to system memory is required on the first execution of an instruction or software loop and whenever a cache miss is incurred. If this access is too slow, these overheads greatly diminish the efficiency of the cache and, ultimately, the processor's performance. Great store is made of cache implementations, but unless the main system memory is fast, system and software performance will degrade. Caches help to regain the performance lost through system memory wait states but they are never 100% efficient; a system with no wait states always provides the best performance. Given that a cache is required, there are effectively two methods of practical implementation – discrete and integrated.

Discrete cache designs

Discrete caches are space consuming, place artificial limits on system speed, prevent multiprocessor designs and are generally underestimated in their design complexity. A discrete cache can take up to 70 chips to implement – about 70% of a VMEboard. Figure 5.32 compares a discrete design cache with one using the Motorola MC88200 Cache Memory Management Unit. The CMMU solution takes less board space, has fewer pin connections (which dramatically improves reliability) and, additionally, provides greater functionality. The biggest restriction with discrete implementations is upgrading the system clock speed.

Most of today's M68000 family designs are capable of running different speed processors on the same hardware by simply replacing the processor and retaining the original memory system and peripherals. The insertion of wait states does not degrade the system performance too much. With a RISC architecture, both the processor and its cache memory need upgrading to prevent waitstates on the processor buses from destroying performance. Faster processors need faster caches which need faster memory chips which will become available.

The problem comes with the interface logic and buffering that is needed. Buffering delays of a few nanoseconds start becoming very significant as cycle times become shorter. In addition, the effect of impedance mismatch and capacitive loading, due to design layout and printed circuit board track lengths, start exaggerating the problems. In effect, it will be virtually impossible to speed upgrade such designs without redesigning the board. The only sensible method of solving these problems is to integrate the various functions on to one piece of silicon manufactured in the same technology. With both the processor and its cache memory system using similar fabrication techniques, they can easily track each other as the faster

Discrete 64 Kbyte cache with write buffering:

Device Type	Quantity	No.of Pins	Total No. of Pins	Pack area	Total Pack Area
374A octal latch	18	20	360	0.3392	6.1056
373A octal register	8	20	160	0.3392	2.7136
240 octal buffer	4	20	80	0.3392	1.3568
3020 write buffer	4	68	272	1.25	5.0000
16k x 4 SRAM	30	24	720	0.4032	12.096
	64		**1592**		**27.272**

Integrated 64 Kbyte cache with write buffering, and bus snooping:

Device Type	Quantity	No.of Pins	Total No. of Pins	Pack area	Total Pack Area
MC88200 CMMU	4	180	720	3.16	12.64
	4		**720**		**12.64**

n.b:
1. All package areas in square inches and are based on maximum package dimensions.
2. All packages are either 300 mil DIP or PGA.

Figure 5.32   *Discrete v. integrated caches*

versions become available. A board upgrade simply becomes a processor and integrated cache replacement, without the need for a total redesign.

Conclusions

The most obvious conclusion is that designing a memory system for today's high performance processors is extremely complicated compared with that of a few years ago. This is further compounded by the unfortunate fact that many of the design trade-offs are so system and software dependent, it is difficult to draw parallels from other systems. However, there are some general statements which can be made.

CISC processors are the most tolerant of slow memory compared with DSP and RISC processors, although the effect on performance is different in each case. The design technique of inserting wait states but increasing the processor clock generally increases CISC performance but decreases RISC and DSP performance. In practice, RISC processors with two or three wait states may be a waste of time.

For higher-speed performance, cache memories provide an ideal buffer between the processor and slow memory but their complexity must not be underestimated. Special care must be taken to ensure cache coherency and integrated solutions are preferable to discrete implementations.

The inclusion of DRAM, memory management and caches can involve additional 'pseudo-random' delays during memory accesses, caused by memory refresh, page faults, cache flushing, etc. These cause distortion within DSP applications and usually are not to be recommended. They can cause problems within real-time applications running on other applications and these timing differences should be taken into consideration within the design.

6 Real-time software, interrupts and exceptions

What is real-time software?

Real-time software differentiates itself from many other types of software by its reaction to external stimuli. For software to be described as 'real time' it must respond in a known maximum time interval to outside stimuli such as interrupts. Many process control applications require this ability to control machinery like conveyor belts, which are fitted with limit switches to prevent objects from falling off. The switch is located such that when it is tripped, the control system can respond and stop the belt before the object being carried falls off the end. Within such a system, the software must demonstrate real-time characteristics to guarantee that it will respond and switch off the belt within a certain time interval when the limit switch is tripped. The actual response time can be 3 ms or 300 seconds, as long as it is guaranteed. In the conveyor belt example, a longer guaranteed response would require positioning the limit switch further up the belt.

The easiest way to obtain real-time characteristics is to use a real-time operating system, like VRTX, OS–9 or pDOS. These operating systems, and others like them, are built around a central real-time kernel which controls the basic processor hardware and provides facilities for software applications to use. The kernels are multitasking, allowing multiple applications to execute simultaneously and respond directly to interrupts, etc. With these kernels, there is basically one key time measurement – the context switch. When a context switch occurs, the currently executing application is replaced by another. This may happen as part of the normal multitasking operation or when an interrupt needs servicing. In the latter case, the servicing application is switched in as part of the system response. A context switch involves saving the processor's registers into an application control block and replacing them with data from another application control block. Using today's processors, context switch times of about 100 μs are quite normal.

Responding to an interrupt

There are four general operations involved with generating a real-time response to an external interrupt:
1   interrupting the processor,
2   servicing the interrupt at the kernel level,
3   table searching to locate the service task and, finally,
4   performing a context switch to load it.
The speed of these operations is dependent both on the efficiency of the software and on the performance of the processor.

Interrupting the processor

At this stage, the main factor in determining response time is the execution time of each processor instruction. With many of today's processors, an interrupt can be acknowledged only on completion of the current instruction and this execution time can be anything from two to two hundred clock cycles if complex addressing modes and operations are executed (Figure 6.1). Once the processor has been interrupted, it has to

Figure 6.1   *A typical processor interrupt sequence*

store enough information to allow it to return to its activities prior to the interrupt. External memory is often used for this operation, holding the vector table containing pointers to the individual interrupt service routines. At this stage, performance is almost entirely dependent on hardware design, primarily memory access times and processor speeds.

Servicing the interrupt

The interrupt service routine is the first software to deal with the interrupt. It operates at a very low level as part of the kernel and is closely associated with the processor itself. The speed of this operation depends both on the efficiency of the kernel software and on the performance of the processor executing it.

The basic flow is simple: the interrupt routine services the kernel's needs and proceeds to locate the task attached to the interrupt. If a timer-generated interrupt is received, the service routine may update the kernel's system clock and perform other housekeeping functions before activating the tasks associated with that interrupt vector. This service software is critical to correct operation and its characteristics determine the response times offered by the operating system. For instance, extensive checking may be carried out to ensure system integrity at the expense of speed. More trusting software may make the opposite trade-off and sacrifice system checking for speed. Once the basic kernel needs have been completed, a higher-level routine takes over.

Locating associated tasks

Application tasks running under the kernel's control may be waiting for the interrupt to occur and trigger some task response. This may be the activation of a dormant task to perform some specific routine (e.g. switch the conveyor belt off). The normal method of determining who is interested is extensive table-searching. The actual implementation differs between kernels, but the basic operation is similar to that shown in Figure 6.2. Various table or linked lists are interrogated to establish which tasks have declared an interest in the particular interrupt. Each interested party is then informed through a message passed by the kernel's location routine. If

Figure 6.2   *Real-time kernel operation*

multiple tasks are attached, each task is notified in turn, usually on a priority basis, allowing the more critical functions to be informed first. Invariably, a context switch is performed to allow a higher priority task to action its message. In our example, if the conveyor belt needs to be switched off, the task that performs it cannot wait until the current task completes its operation. A context switch is required to replace it and allow the new task to switch off the belt. Again, the speed of this operation is dependent on the efficiency of the software and similar trade-off decisions as before.

Context switches

If a task needs to be activated and executed to action the interrupt, the context switch time needs to be added to the previous times to provide the total response time. The time taken to perform a context switch depends on the number of processor registers that require saving, memory access times and the software algorithms used for housekeeping within the kernel. Context switch times quoted by many operating system vendors include the system overheads associated with deciding which task is selected for the next execution time slot. Once the new task is switched, it can take whatever action is required.

For an M68000 processor, interrupt sequences and responses are determined by a combination of the currently executing instruction and the time taken to build the appropriate external stack frame. To generate an interrupt, the level is encoded in binary on to the three interrupt pins. These pins are sampled regularly and the interrupt must be present and steady for a minimum of two system clocks before it is recognized. However, Motorola's specifications recommend that an interrupt level is maintained until the processor acknowledges it. In other words, do not assume that a pulse width of two or more clocks will always generate an interrupt – it won't! The processor compares this interrupt level against the interrupt mask stored in the status word. If the incoming level is higher than that of the mask the processor services the interrupt; if the interrupt is of a lower level, it is ignored. A level 7 interrupt is always taken and cannot be masked.

The processor can service an interrupt only on instruction boundaries, i.e. when it has completed executing the current instruction but before the next one commences. As stated previously, this can be a long time if complex addressing modes and instructions are being used. At the boundary, the processor checks the interrupt level status and, if needed, starts to process the interrupt. It switches into SUPERVISOR mode, makes an internal copy of the status register, suppresses any tracing and raises the interrupt mask to that of the external interrupt. This last action is necessary to prevent the same interrupt from repeatedly generating interrupts. The processor then starts an interrupt acknowledgement cycle where it either receives a vector number or assumes it is to use a predefined autovector assigned to that particular level. It then builds the external stack frame comprising four words which store the status register and program counter, along with a vector offset and frame identifier. The processor can now locate the service routine from the vector location within the vector table and, several microseconds after the interrupt was recognized, the service routine is started.

After servicing the interrupt, the RTE (ReTurn from Exception) instruction is executed. The information from the stack frame is read back into the processor and normal processing commences.

Improving performance

The M68000 sequence follows the classical interrupt process. The use of an external stack frame allows the nesting of interrupts and other exceptions until the stack runs out of memory. There are two ways in which this sequence can be shortened. The first removes the need to wait for the current execution to complete. However, the corresponding stack frame is larger, due to the extra processor context information that is stored. All the intermediate and internal data, microcode and pipeline contents have to be saved externally. A second method involves the use of a hardware stack where the time-consuming stacking operations are performed internally with a far shorter time. The M88000 and DSP56000 use variations on these ideas to reduce their interrupt latency.

Interrupting an MC88100

The MC88100 has a single interrupt pin which is used to signal an external interrupt. If this level-sensitive pin is asserted for two successive falling clock edges, an interrupt is signalled internally and the processor context saved to an internal set of shadow registers – not to external memory. The current instruction does not have to complete and the only variable in the latency calculation is the time taken to complete any data and instruction unit memory accesses. Worse cases are four operations for the data unit and two for the instruction unit. A typical value is six clock cycles which, at 25 MHz, is less than 0.25 μs, at least an order of magnitude faster than more conventional architectures. Figure 6.3 shows the sequence for both architectures.

Once interrupted, the shadow registers are frozen and no further updating can take place. If another interrupt occurs while shadowing is frozen, the processor cannot preserve its context and takes another

Figure 6.3   *Interrupting an MC88100*

ERROR exception. Such interrupt routines should therefore execute without exception, or the shadow registers saved to external memory and shadowing enabled.

MC88100 interrupt service routines

RISC architectures trust software far more than conventional processors and allow far greater control over exception handling. The interrupt service routine is selected by a vector passed by the interrupting device. The vector table, shown in Figure 6.4, is different from conventional processors in that each vector contains the first two instructions of the handler and not an address pointer, so allowing instant execution of the routine. One of the instructions must jump or branch to the remainder of the routine. Usually,

Figure 6.4   *The MC88100 vector table*

this is a delayed branch which prevents unnecessary pipeline flushing and maintains single-cycle instruction execution. If shadowing is re-enabled, further interrupts and exceptions can be nested. The decision to allow this is totally under software control. Software can decide if it wishes to trade system checking for speed. If speed is chosen, software must be written so that no further exceptions occur. The code must be readily available and now swapped out to disc, stack and memory resources must be adequate, further interrupts require masking and memory systems, especially those with error detection and correction, must not return an error.

The next stage involves executing the kernel's routines to decide what action is required.

Improving software performance

RISC processors achieve their greater performance by simplifying instructions so that they execute in a single cycle and creating the more conventional complex instructions as a series of RISC instructions. Although multiple instructions are executed, overall execution time should be shorter. However, the more complex and powerful the RISC instructions that are executed while still maintaining single-cycle execution, the more work the processor performs. The M88000 instruction set has been optimized rather than reduced, which means that many conventional CISC instructions can be replaced on a one-to-one basis, so helping to keep code expansion ratios as close to this ratio as possible. This rich instruction set has tremendous importance, when considering how fast the kernel software routines execute. Three important areas are table indexing and addressing, data fetching and condition testing.

Addressing data

Unlike many RISC architectures, which have only one address mode and require addresses to be calculated prior to every external access, the M88000 instruction set supports five. Probably the most useful is the register indirect with an index, which can be scaled. This allows a pointer to be assigned to a head of a table or set of tables and allows other registers to index into it, dramatically reducing the number of address calculations and instructions required. Simply changing the main pointer register to that of another table allows rapid searching of tables and linked lists, which reduces the number of instructions needed per function and increases throughput.

Fetching data

Having located the data, it now requires fetching. The M88000 is based on a load-store architecture, which does not operate directly on external memory – data is loaded into a register, modified and written out again. This effectively removes memory access time from instruction execution time. Such operations take only three instructions and, therefore, three cycles to complete. Direct memory modifying architectures take three instruction times, plus the time for two memory accesses.

Further consideration must be given to how much data can be fetched and how this is performed. Most compiler-generated data, like 'C' variables such as char, short and int, are 8 or 16 bits in length, yet current RISC architectures are 32-bit in data size. While many RISC architectures can deal with the corresponding byte and halfword data sizes internally, they have to fetch such data using a multiple instruction sequence. The first instruction calculates the address and loads it into the address register, a 32-bit wide word of data is fetched into a register and, finally, a third instruction is needed to extract the relevant byte or halfword from that register and store it in yet another register. The MC88100 has four data byte enable signals which allow it to fetch individual bytes and halfwords directly in a single cycle. This again reduces the code expansion, the number of cycles needed to perform the task and, ultimately, improves system performance.

The combination of these two factors can reduce the number of instructions needed to access a byte of data from a table by a factor of three, compared with other RISC architectures; an example is shown in Figure 6.5. The MC88100 can access data directly by fetching a byte from a table pointed to by a register and indexed by a second. With a poor RISC

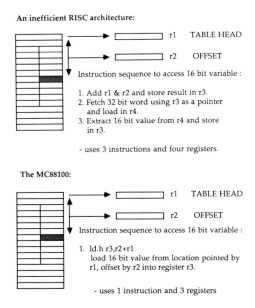

Figure 6.5   *Accessing data within memory tables*

instruction set, the address is calculated and loaded into a register. A 32-bit value is then loaded and, finally, the byte is extracted, making three instructions in total. This operation is repeated many times by a kernel – savings in this area are essential to maximizing performance. With data located and loaded, the kernel must now test it.

Testing data

Conventional processors have a condition code register which is usually updated at the end of every instruction, allowing easy condition testing. Various combinations of bits within the register indicate if the certain conditions exist. Maintaining this register imposes a large overhead on the processor and it is no surprise that the M88000 family, like most RISC architectures, does not have a specific condition code register. Instead, any general-purpose register can be used temporarily as a condition code register. To compare two values held in two registers, the MC88100 compare instruction can be used. This tests for all conditions and sets appropriate bits within a third specified register. The next instruction is a branch on bit set or clear, which redirects program flow as necessary. With further bit masking, etc., extremely complex conditions can be tested for. To test for five particular conditions requires only six instructions – a compare followed by five branch on bit condition instructions. In addition, delayed branch versions of the instruction are available, which improve efficiency by removing pipeline stalls caused by flushing.

However, the MC88100 has another, more efficient, method of branching on condition. The previous example compared two values and needed a two-instruction sequence. There is a branch on condition instruction which compares, tests and branches in a single instruction and, with the delayed slot version, executes effectively in a single cycle. This instruction compares a single value with zero and has an interesting effect on compiler and operating system software. Instead of counting upwards within loops, it is more efficient to count down to zero. A high-level language procedure may require a loop variable starting at 0, incrementing by 1 and causing termination at value 10; this causes ten iterations of the loop. The compiler, for maximum efficiency, should code this as a loop variable initialized with 10, decrementing by 1 and terminating at 0. Such type of optimization can be performed only if the loop variable is of limited scope and not referenced elsewhere. For maximum performance, loops and other counters should count down rather than up.

Saving and restoring register sets

Having tested the data, the decision to perform a context switch has been taken. The context switch simply saves the current processor register contents and replaces them from memory. The time taken is dependent on the number of registers and the number of memory accesses to save/restore each register. RISC architectures require more registers than other architecture, especially to hold data locally, which other architectures would manipulate directly in memory. A cause of concern with many of today's processors is the large number of registers and the number of clock cycles required per memory access. However, with reference to context switching times of real time operating systems, actual register swapping is a small part of the overall time. To save 20 registers, at three clocks per register, takes only 60 clocks. At a 20 MHz clock rate, this is equivalent to 3 µs of processing time. With a typical context switch of 100 µs and four save or restore operations during the kernel processing, this is still only equivalent to about 12% of the total time.

With the register-intensive characteristics of RISC, caused by no direct data manipulation in memory, larger register sets are necessary to maintain performance. However, they require storing during context switching and this potentially increases context switching times. The MC88100 has only 32 general purpose registers, which it can save in 32 clocks. This is still 50% less than conventional processors. Decreasing the number of registers can decrease this time, but any such decision must be carefully considered. If software restricts register usage too much, increased stacking operations may result, which actually make the kernel, application execution and processing less efficient and therefore slower.

Interrupting the DSP56000

Interrupting the DSP56000 from external sources is different from both the M68000 and M88000 processor families. External interrupts normally generate a fast interrupt routine exception. The external interrupt is synchronized with the processor clock for two successive clocks, at which point the processor fetches the two instructions from the appropriate vector location and executes them. Once completed, the program counter simply carries on as if nothing has happened. The advantage is that there is no stack frame building or any other such delays. The disadvantage concerns the size of the routine that can be executed and the resources allocated. When using such a technique, it is usual to allocate a couple of address registers for the fast interrupt routine to use. This allows coefficient tables to be built, almost in parallel with normal execution.

When the interrupt service routine needs more than two instructions, a JSR (Jump SubRoutine) instruction is located in one of the two fast interrupt locations to transfer control to a long interrupt handler. Any change of instruction flow can be used to convert the exception handling to a long exception interrupt routine. With a long interrupt routine, both the program counter and status register are saved on the stack to allow normal processing to resume when the ReTurn from Interrupt (RTI) instruction is executed at the end of the routine.

These two interrupt mechanisms can be used to control communication between a host CPU and a DSP56000, as described in Chapter 8, or can be used to time an external event which is greater than the resolution capabilities of its SCI timer (Figure 6.6). The SCI timer is programmed to

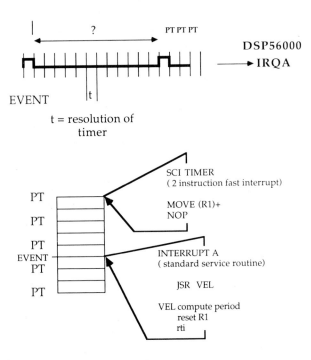

Figure 6.6 *Using interrupts to time an event*

generate a two-instruction fast interrupt which simply autoincrements register R1. This acts as a simple counter which times the period between events. The event itself generates an IRQA interrupt, which forces a standard service routine. The exception handler jumps to routine VEL which processes the data (i.e. takes the value of R and uses it to compute the period), resets R1 and returns from the interrupt.

Dyadic v. triadic instruction sets

One major difference between the M68000, the DSP56000 and the M88000 family instruction sets is the number of source and destination addresses that each instruction can specify. The M68000 family uses a diadic set with two components forming two data sources, the instruction results being returned in one of the sources. The M88000 RISC processor uses a triadic model with two sources and a third, separate destination. The DSP56000 is essentially a diadic model but has some instructions that can perform parallel moves with extra addresses. What are the advantages?

The obvious advantage concerns the preservation of data within the register set or in memory. The dyadic instruction destroys the contents of one of the sources on its completion, which either forces the data to be fetched once more, or inserts an instruction to copy the destroyed sources's contents to the stack or another register, prior to the instruction. Compilers often generate an instruction pair which can be replaced by a single triadic instruction. In this case, the M88000 reduced instruction set, with its triadic operations, is actually more efficient than the complex instruction set of the M68000. However, encoding three operands into a single fixed length instruction can restrict the number and different types of operatives that can be executed. With a 32-bit op code and 32 registers, the M88000 uses 15 bits for register encoding and leaves 17 bits to describe the operation or for immediate values, etc. With a register set of 256 registers, there are only 8 bits left to encode the operation, etc. With their single-cycle execution, RISC processors must have a fixed op code length and cannot do as the M68000 and DSP56000 families, i.e. simply extend the op code as necessary.

CISC processors, with their memory-to-memory architectures which need variable-length instructions to accommodate direct addresses with scaling, etc., have an average instruction length of 24–32 bits rather than the minimum 16 bit op code. Comparing lengths between MC68020 and M88000 code gives a typical expansion of about 30%. This gives a good indication of how powerful the M88000 instruction set actually is. With its greater power, it performs more work per clock cycle, i.e. its MIPS are worth more than other architectures!

Instruction restart v. instruction continuation

Another aspect of real-time performance concerns the mechanism used to restore processor context during exception processing caused through a bus error or a page fault. Instruction restart effectively backs up the machine to the point in the instruction flow where the error occurred. The processor re-executes the instruction and carries on. The instruction continuation stores all the internal data and allows the errant bus cycle to be restarted, even if it is in the middle of an instruction. The continuation mechanism is undoubtedly easier for software to handle, yet pays the penalty of having extremely large stack frames. The restart mechanism is easier from a hardware perspective, yet can pose increased software overheads. The handler has to determine how far back to restart the machine and must ensure that resources are in the correct state before commencing.

While the majority of the M68000 family are of the continuation type, the MC68040 and the M88000 family are of the restart type. As processors increase in speed and complexity, the penalty of large stack frames shifts the balance in favour of the restart model.

The effect of external memory on real time performance

While all RISC systems should be designed with single-cycle memory access for optimum performance, the practicalities are that memory cycles often incur wait states or bus delays. Unfortunately, RISC architectures cannot tolerate such delays – one wait state halves the performance, two reduce performance to a third. This can have a dramatic effect on real-time performance and all the advantages gained with the new architecture may be lost. The MC88200 CMMU can allow slower and more cost-effective memory to be used, without the performance penalties. It provides wait-state free cache memory, which prevents such delays from affecting the MC88100 CPU performance. The MC88100 can save its registers into the MC88200 cache memory on a single-cycle basis, irrespective of how slow the external memory subsystem is. In addition, critical software routines can be cached in another CMMU on the instruction bus, again allowing single-cycle access and execution. If instructions have to be fetched from dynamic memory, with typical times ranging from four to forty clocks, the kernel execution time becomes the dominant factor within the context switch time. Again, any advantage offered by RISC may be lost through a poor memory subsystem.

However, there are some potential penalties for any system that uses caches and memory management which must be considered. Consider the system in Figure 6.7. The processor is using an Harvard architecture with combined caches and memory management units to buffer it from the slower main memory. The caches are operating in copyback mode to provide further speed improvements. The processor receives an interrupt and immediately starts exception processing. Although the internal context is preserved in shadow registers, the vector table, exception routines and data exist in external memory.

In this example, the first data fetch causes a cache miss. All the cache lines are full and contain some dirty data, therefore the cache must update main memory with a cache line before fetching the instruction. This involves an address translation, which causes a page fault. The MMU now has to perform an external table walk before the data can be stored. This has to complete before the cache line can be written out which, in turn, must complete before the first instruction of the exception routine can be executed. The effect is staggering – the quick six-cycle interrupt latency is

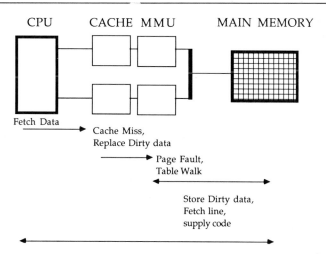

Figure 6.7   *The impact of a cache miss*

totally overshadowed by the 12 or so memory accesses that must be completed simply to get the first instruction. This may be a 'worst-case' scenario, but it has to be considered in any real-time design. The problem can be contained by declaring exception routines and data as non–cachable, or through the use of a BATC or transparent window to remove the page fault and table walk. These techniques couple the CPU directly to external memory which, if slow, can be extremely detrimental to performance. Small areas of very fast memory can be reserved for exception handling to solve this problem; locking routines in cache can also be solutions, at the expense of performance in other system functions.

Register windowing

Another architectural feature often put forward as a good way of improving processor context switch and procedural call times is the idea of register windows. A small area of onchip memory is divided into register banks which can be switched to store the old contents and give a new clear set without having to store the data on an external stack frame. This solution has one drawback – what happens when all the register windows have been used? The answer is that data must be saved out to memory to free up a window. The next question concerns which window is saved. In practice, the whole set of windows is transferred out with the inevitable transfer delays. A typical number may be about eight windows, which may or may not be enough to support an operating system call. For real-time applications, the worst case scenario of a complete window set transfer must be assumed.

Combining architectures

The most obvious method of improving real-time performance within embedded control systems is to increase the processing power. Faced with the task of sending and receiving serial data at 1 Mbit/s, or detecting missing teeth on a gear wheel to generate ignition timings at 7000r/min, this appears to be the most sensible choice. Such systems generate a lot of interrupts and require fairly intensive data processing to perform serial data checking or timing measurements between these events. Where microprocessors have been used to implement such designs, the system has centred around a single processor controlling standard timer and serial comms peripherals. This approach started with 8-bit microprocessors and, as demands have increased, faster generations have simply been slotted in to solve the problem.

With the advent of microprocessors like the Motorola M88000 and the DSP56000/DSP96000 Digital Signal Processors augmenting the M68000 family, a designer has several options to solve the problem. The most obvious is to select the fastest, most performant processor available and use its increased power to reduce interrupt latency and increase data processing. However, each of these families has its strengths and careful consideration must be made of system needs. As the processor increases in power, demands on the memory system increase and, as previously described, cache systems can be used; they, too can introduce further difficulties.

An alternative approach to this problem is to adopt a multiprocessing system where extra processing is distributed throughout the system. This has been used in many VMEbus systems, as in Figure 6.8 for example. Rather than use a single, higher-cost processor, several lower-cost processors are used and the work load is distributed across the system. In this configuration, serial and parallel I/O is controlled by separate processors located on each I/O board. With this intelligence, the overhead of servicing interrupts, etc. is handled onboard and frees up the main processor to perform other tasks. The onboard processors may not be the

Figure 6.8   *A VMEbus-based system*

same as the main CPU, but instead can be matched to have the right characteristics required by the interface software to control the I/O.

Such a solution is often not possible for many implementations, due to the higher component count costs involved with designing the bus interfaces, the processor to processor communication, bus arbitration, etc. However, silicon technology which has increased clock speeds and device density to provide today's high-performance processors can equally be used to integrate a distributed processor system on to one chip, with the resultant reduced chip count and costs.

The M68300 family

Two members of the family are currently available, with many more to come. They combine a M68000 family processor and its asynchronous memory interface, with all the standard interface logic of chip selects, wait state generators, bus and watchdog timers, into a system interface module and use a second RISC type processor to handle specific I/O functions.

The MC68302 uses a 16 MHz MC68000 processor core with power down modes and either an 8- or a 16-bit external bus (Figure 6.9). The System Interface Block contains 1152 bytes of dual-port RAM, 28 pins of

Figure 6.9 *The MC68302 integrated multiprotocol processor*

parallel I/O, an interrupt controller and a DMA device, as well as the standard glue logic. The communications processor is a RISC machine that controls three multiprotocol channels, each with their own pair of DMA channels. The channels support BISYNC, DDCMP, V.110, HDLC synchronous modes and standard UART functions. This processor takes buffer structures from either the internal or external RAM and takes care of the day-to-day activities of the serial channels. It programs the DMA channel to transfer the data, performs the character and address comparisons and cyclic redundancy check (CRC) generation and checking. The processor has sufficient power to cope with a combined data rate of 2 Mbits per second across the three channels. Assuming an eight-bit character and a single interrupt to poll all three channels, the processor is handling the equivalent of an interrupt every 12 µs. In addition, it is performing all the data framing, etc. While this is going on, the onchip M68000 is free to perform other functions, like the higher layers of X.25 or other OSI protocols as shown in Figure 6.10.

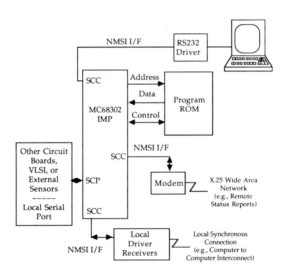

Figure 6.10   *A typical X25–ISDN terminal interface*

The MC68332 is similar to the MC68302, except that it has a CPU32 processor (MC68020 based) running at 16 MHz and a timer–processor unit instead of a communications processor (Figure 6.11). This has 16 channels which are controlled by a RISC-like processor to perform virtually any timing function. The timing resolution is down to 250 ns with an external clock source, or 500 ns with an internal one. The timer–processor can perform the common timer algorithms on any of the 16 channels without

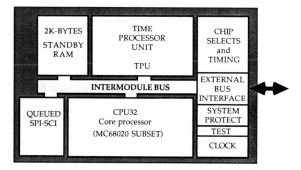

Figure 6.11 *The MC68332 block diagram*

placing any overhead on the CPU32. A queued serial channel and 2 kbits of power down static RAM are also onchip and for many applications; all that is required to complete a working system is an external program EPROM and a clock.

Software considerations

Another benefit of these highly integrated distributed processing chips is the reduction in software that is needed to be written. For a more traditional communications controller, the low-level interrupt handlers, framers, etc. can be extremely difficult to write, especially with the tight timing restraints often encountered. To program the MC68302 comms controller, a memory-based buffer structure is used which consists of a frame status, a data counter and a data pointer to the receive and transmit data resident in memory; this can simply be defined as a structure in C. There is no low-level bit manipulation, interrupt handling, data checking, etc., as they are handled already by the other processor and its embedded code.

Similarly with the MC68332. To perform the missing tooth calculation for generating ignition timing, a set of parameters is calculated by the CPU32 and loaded into a parameter block (Figure 6.12) which commands the timer–processor to perform the algorithm. Again, no interrupt routines and no periodic peripheral bit manipulation are needed by the CPU32. The M68000 instruction set compatibility shown by both processors has other advantages – compilers, applications and real-time operating system are freely available, allowing the easy migration or development of code.

Combining DSP processors

This technique need not be confined to integrated processors. Both the DSP56000 and DSP96000 processors can be configured to act as subordi-

$00	REF TIME	CHANNEL_CONTROL
$01	MAX_MISSING	NUM_OF_TEETH
$02	BANK_SIGNAL/ MISSING_COUNT	ROLLOVER_COUNT
$03	RATIO	TCR2_MAX_VALUE
$04	PERIOD_HIGH_WORD	
$05	PERIOD_LOW_WORD	

ERROR	TCR2_VALUE

☐ updated by CPU32 host

Figure 6.12 *The parameter block for a period mesurement with missing transition detection*

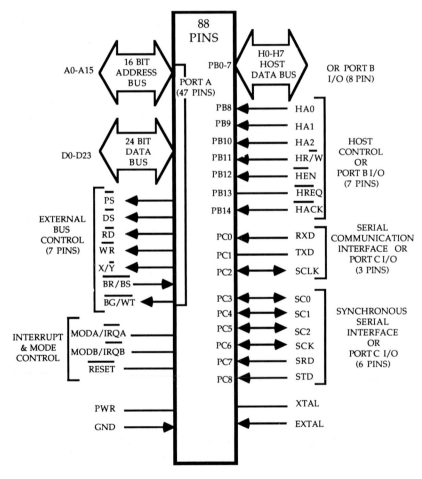

Figure 6.13 *The DSP56000/56001 processor*

nate to an MC68000 or similar type of processor. This is performed easily using their host interface ports (Figure 6.13), which act as memory windows into the processor, allowing processor to processor communication via memory and interrupts. The interface logic is minimal and thus meets the low component requirements of many applications.

Why use a DSP chip? It combines good processing power with internal memory and has extremely quick interrupt latency, typically a couple of clocks for a fast interrupt. This is achieved through the use of a hardware stack and the absence of automatic stack building. The device is highly integrated, with parallel and serial I/O channels, onboard memory, memory interface logic etc. The register model has general-purpose address registers and a dual accumulator data model and, although a little different from an M68000 or M88000, is capable of high-level programming in C. The processor throughput is good – in 75 ns the DSP56000 can perform a multiply accumulate and two data transfers simultaneously. The DSP96000 can also do this but performs the operations in IEEE floating-

Figure 6.14 *An MC68000/DSO56000 multiprocessor configuration*

point precision and calculates differences as well. In MIPS figures, these processors are performing at about 13 MIPS and peaking at over 40 MIPS.

Figure 6.14 shows a typical configuration. The DSP56001 loads its program from external EPROM and then executes from internal memory, not needing external memory. The program/data can be altered or downloaded by the M68000 passing data via the host interface and forcing the DSP56001 to execute a fast interrupt. There are 16 routines that can be selected by the M68000 and they effectively force the DSP56001 to execute a simple two-instruction sequence with no interrupt overhead. Using this technique, 24 bits of data can be loaded into the host interface receive registers and a fast interrupt can be used to force the DSP to load the data into its memory. A sequence of such transfers can be used prior to redirecting the DSP56001 to another set of data or routine.

This simple combination provides very fast interrupt handling and processing from the DSP56001 and good general-purpose processing from the M68000. Multiple DSP processors can be controlled in this way to create arrays. Typical examples are adaptive filtering for digital audio, suspension systems and graphics acclerators. The NEXT computer, designed by Steve Jobs, has used this principle, coupling an MC68030 and a DSP56000 together. The MC68030 runs UNIX while the DSP56000, by virtue of different algorithms and control, provides the system with a modern, fax machine, CD quality sound and speech synthesis and recognition. To implement these facilities with discrete peripherals would place a tremendous overhead on the processor. While a faster processor, like the MC68040, could cope with that burden, the DSP56000 dispenses with the peripherals and removes the burden at a much lower cost.

Conclusions

RISC, CISC and DSP processors all have different methods of handling interrupts and exceptions which, in turn, have their various trade-offs. When considering the whole aspect of interrupt latency and context switching, it is important to examine the complete process involved, from the interrupt generation through to performing the required service. It is all too easy to blinker the process to functions which are thought to be critical when other areas are impacting performance far more. While the lure of the latest and most powerful processors is extremely attractive, multiprocessing or integrated systems may actually achieve the needed goals with less effort and cost.

7 Multiprocessing

The use of multiple processors to improve performance within a system has been common for many years but, with the advent of fast processors, memory subsystems and buses, there has been an almost unparalleled interest in more recent years. Again, there are many differeing types of arrangements and considerations which need careful consideration. The most important aspect of any multiprocessor design centres around the nature of the task(s) to be performed and the method of communication used. While it may be easy to believe the hype associated with some of the larger multiprocessor systems, i.e. that performance increases linearly with the number of processors, the reality is totally different. If the communication overhead is greater than the performance gain, the system will plateau and adding extra processing units will result in minimal performance gain. Gene Amdahl, who designed IBM's mainframes before his own computers, expresses this relationship as:

$$N/\log N$$

where N is the number of processors. Many multiprocessor systems make several assumptions about the type of software program that is going to be executed and this often limits their use to niche applications. In other words, a 100 CPU parallel processor computer is unlikely to run a spreadsheet or wordprocessing application any faster than a single processor system, but will be able to model weather systems. The difference depends on the nature of the application – a spreadsheet has serial data and program execution and cannot subsequently be broken into components which can be executed in parallel. An environmental model can.

Every processor has a separate data and instruction stream associated with it and this gives four main types of processor design, depending on whether multiple or single streams are used.

SISD – Single instruction, single data

The single-instruction, single-data stream machine is the most commonly implemented design and was the basis of many early mainframe and super computer designs. All the processors described so far, ranging from the M6800 through to the M88000 series, are essentially single-instruction, single-data machines. This definition can include pipelined arrangements, multiple functional units and Harvard memory organization. The basic

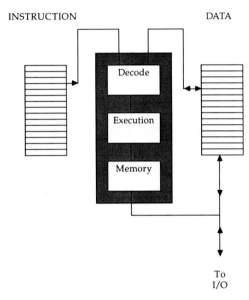

Figure 7.1 *Basic SISD architecture*

architecture is shown in Figure 7.1. Two independent streams supply the instructions and data to the processor unit within the shaded box. The three-stage pipeline processes the data according to the instruction and stores the results or performs an I/O function. This type of machine is essentially a serial execution machine, although multiple resources and overlapping may be used to reduce the time taken to perform each instruction.

SIMD – Single instruction, multiple data

In this configuration, used in array processors, one instruction stream is used to process multiple data streams using many processing elements. A single instruction is received at a time but may be executed conditionally by

Figure 7.2 *Basic SIMD architecture*

the individual processing units on their own individual data, stored in local memory. This conditional execution is necessary for systems or program sequences which require serial execution and cannot make use of parallelism. The communication methods used are based around ring, mesh and broadcast networks. Figure 7.2 shows the basic principles. A Master processor performs the basic I/O functions and issues the instruction ($\times 4$) to each processing element via the communication network. Each element then processes the data stored within its own local memory (patterned box). This process is repeated until all the data has been processed successfully. At this point the results are passed to the Master for consolidation and further data dispersed through the network, ready for the next set of processing. This data collation and dispersion adds system overhead and increases dramatically as the number of elements goes up.

MIMD – Multiple instruction, multiple data

The multiple-instruction, multiple-data machine is the traditional multi-processor system which can execute multiple programs operating on multiple data streams. Each instruction stream has its own data stream which may come from shared or local memory. Processor-to-processor communication can be based around shared memory, serial networks and other links, like crossbar switches and multiport memory. Figure 7.3 shows a typical example.

MISD – Multiple instruction, single data

This design is essentially hypothetical as there are no real implementations, although the execution pipeline fits the description. Each stage of the

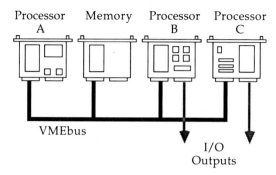

Figure 7.3   *An example MIMD system*

pipeline acts as an independent processing unit that operates on the data passing through it and before passing it on to the next stage in the chain.

Constructing a MIMD architecture

The MIMD architecture is the most often implemented with micropro-cessors and, with the advent of fast processors with multiprocessing support and reduced external memory bandwidth, is becoming increasingly attractive for designers to implement. The basic communication method involves the use of shared memory, which is used for passing data, program and control information between the processors. Access to such areas is controlled using a semaphore technique implemented with the M68000 TAS (Test And Set) instruction, or with the M88000 xmem instruction. This allows each processor to handshake for access, preventing simulta-neous access and the system corruption it produces. Such configurations are easy to design but careful consideration must be made of the bandwidth needs and memory organization.

It is essential that each processor has its own local memory and that the bulk of its processing uses this memory, thus reserving the shared memory solely for message passing. The amount of message passing determines the number of processors the system can support. For practical reasons, such systems usually have a central I/O system for mass storage, serial comms, etc. This creates a single resource which competes, as shown in Figure 7.4, with the message passing traffic and reduces the number of supported processors.

The solution is to take the I/O traffic off the message-passing bus, as shown in Figure 7.5. A variation on this design is to use part of the dual-ported memory on the processor boards as the message area. This again appears to be desirable on first inspection but can greatly reduce performance. Most 'dual-port' memory systems are constructed using a

Figure 7.4 *Using a VMEbus for a shared memory system*

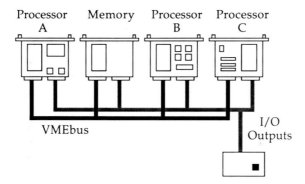

Figure 7.5 *A dual bus system to increase bus bandwidth*

shared memory technique where two or more processors can access the same memory – one at a time. The difficulty arises when the message-passing area is used by another processor. It gets access and effectively prevents the local processor accessing its own local memory. Although message passing is not stopped, the local processing is halted and thus the system loses performance. In such configurations, local memory effectively appears on the same bus as the message passing area and local processing consumes message-passing bandwidth. For a system where message-passing bandwidth is crucial to the design success, this is clearly unacceptable.

The key to such designs lies in optimizing the memory interface so that the memory hierarchy is matched to the needs of the various levels within the system.

Processor bandwidths

The M68000 family has steadily decreased its external bus bandwidth requirements by the adoption of internal caches, reducing the number of clocks per memory access and through the use of burst filling. Figure 7.6 shows the trend. The bus bandwidth figures refer to the processor's needs and indicate that the more advanced parts are more suitable than their predecessors for multiprocessing systems. These figures do not take into

	MC68000	MC68020	MC68030	MC68040
Clocks per Cycle	4	3	2	2
Bus Bandwidth	80%	60%	50%	30%
Nominal Clock Frequency	8	16	20	25

Figure 7.6 *The M68000 memory needs*

account the beneficial effect of local memory and caches. Figure 7.7 shows the benefit of local memory. The vertical axis shows the amount of global or shared memory access for a given amount of total memory access. The data for the bus bandwidth figure of 80% is from Figure 7.6. The graph shows that large amounts of local memory dramatically reduce the bus bandwidth requirement. To achieve an overall external bus bandwidth of about 20%, enough local memory must be present to meet about 75% of the processor's need. A comparative bandwidth figure for a M88100 with two MC88200 CMMUs is about 25%, while the figures for a DSP56000 are harder to calculate. If the program and data can be stored internally, the external bus needs are effectively zero. If external memory is used, the

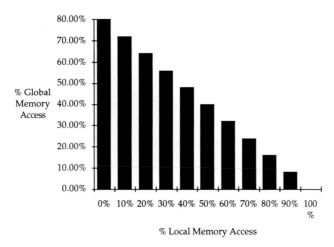

Figure 7.7 *M68000 memory access*

figure becomes 100%. A typical figure is in between and totally software dependent.

These figures indicate the number of processors which can effectively be linked in a multiprocessor system, while sharing a single resource or memory. For both the MC68040 and MC88100/MC88200 configurations, this boundary is reached at about four processors. To go beyond requires additional memory resources, like secondary caches and local memory, or the use of other communication techniques, such as serial networks, cross bar switches, etc. The question immediately arises of how to profile such a system and therefore know how to make the trade-offs. By profiling a system, a good understanding of how the individual processors within a MIMD machine interact and use resources is derived. The basic techniques involve breaking down the overall system into its individual elements and establishing each individual element's needs.

Profiling

First, determine the basic level of performance needed to carry out the given task, i.e. processing throughput, memory needs and speeds, any time-critical operations and the amount of data access v. computation. Frequently, this type of information can be obtained only from running specific benchmarks and code sequences, and from a good system knowledge. In the past, real hardware was often used to provide this data. While providing definitive data on how fast, given a certain configuration, it was impossible to determine the number of data accesses, branches taken, cache hit ratios, etc. With the advent of simulators, this type of data is easily available and is worth its weight in gold. The Oasys M88000 simulator can run code and provide the number of instructions executed, the different types, MMU ATC cache hits and misses, external cache hit-and-miss ratios and the number of data and instruction fetches performed. The DSP56000 simulator can perform a similar function and is also capable of simulating a multiprocessor system. Coupled with this type of information, the system profile can be determined.

Cost of memory access

All processor systems use differing types of memory within their design, depending on the costs, access times and density needed. The hierarchy, shown in Figure 7.8, shows some interesting characteristics. The fastest access is undoubtedly using processor registers or onchip caches. Moving down the hierarchy increases access time, increases density and decreases the cost per bit. However, if the main processor access is to lower levels, there is a far higher performance impact. Cache memories help by restricting the number of memory accesses the processor has to perform to

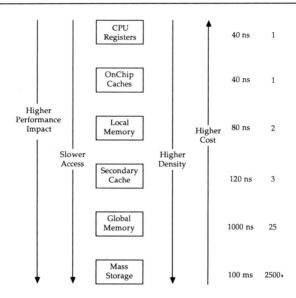

Figure 7.8　*The memory hierarchy*

the levels below the cache. The cache does not help on the first access, but by copying data, provides a benefit on any subsequent accesses. The figures on the righthand side give an indication of the speed differential. CPU register access is some 2500 times faster than mass storage! The system profile can be matched to provide the right trade-offs.

If a system needs very fast data access, allocating storage on a hard disc greatly impacts performance. In reality, the storage is allocated as close to the processor as possible. If the profile shows that the majority of system functions are computation bound, the ideal is to move code storage up to local memory or onchip cache and move variable storage down. If a system spends much of its time page swapping, an increase in local or global memory results in tremendous gains in performance. It can be seen that a good understanding of systems and what they do allows the optimum design to be built. A similar approach can be done for a multiprocessing system where the points of communication replace the storage needs.

Figure 7.9 shows an hierarchy for two processors. Communication links are possible at the register level; however, this type of transfer can be implemented only at a VLSI level and has been left out. Standard communication at the global or shared memory is the fastest available but mass storage using shared files or pages and various speed serial networks can also be used, albeit with greater overhead. Comparing this diagram with its predecessor, the fastest communication network (i.e. global memory) is about halfway up the memory hierarchy. To reduce the communication overhead further, the ideal solution would be to couple

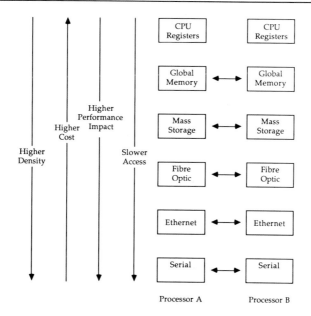

Figure 7.9   *A communication link hierarchy*

caches together, allowing the extra speed of cache memory to be used. This can be done using a bus snooping mechanism. These mechanisms were described in Chapter 5, with reference to cache and data coherency. Using bus snooping to aid processor-to-processor communication is the same principle viewed from a different aspect. In the example in Figure 7.10, the processors themselves are responsible for ensuring that shared data is updated correctly – this effectively couples the processor with slow memory and impacts performance. By using the cache, the processor is buffered and only accesses slow memory when the data has been changed. This creates an effective link between the two caches – high up in the hierarchy, for maximum performance.

Shared memory schemes can be implemented with any M68000, M88000 or DSP56000 processor. All that is needed is some multiport memory and semaphore signalling, using either bit testing or register to memory swaps, to provide control. Links using caches require onchip caches and, for higher performance, bus snooping protocols. The MC68020, MC68030 and MC68040 all have them but only the MC68040 has snooping protocols. The MC88200 CMMU provides both the cache function and bus snooping necessary for the MC88100. The DSP56000 does not have any cache but can use its host interface port to provide a fast memory-to-memory link. It does, however, have a fast synchronous serial interface which can allow data transfers of several megabits per second. Using it, arrays can easily be built.

Figure 7.10 *A bus snooping link*

Fault-tolerant systems

Fault-tolerant systems are a special type of multiprocessor design, where the goal is increased availability rather than higher performance. Such systems can tolerate component and system failure, albeit with degradation of overall system performance. The basic approach is to use redundancy, so if one component fails there is a backup immediately available to take over. While it is relatively easy to provide uninterruptable power supplies, error detecting and correcting memory, mirror discs, etc., to prevent a peripheral failure from bringing down the system, there are several challenges in the processor design. The biggest problem concerns how the faults are detected and the amount of work necessary to restore the status quo. As with memory and communication links, there is an effective hierarchy for fault detection and backup.

Any fault-tolerant system must have multiple processors. Figure 7.11 shows a two-processor system and the points within the system hierarchy where comparison and checks can be performed to detect any failures. As the fault detection point moves down, the cost of detection decreases but system granularity (i.e. the amount of work that may be suspect) increases, as does the amount of restoration work needed.

One detection method is the comparison of data files stored on a hard disc. This is easy to implement but the main processor must effectively be stopped while the comparison is made and the amount of work needed to correct faults is large. The backup process is a byte-for-byte comparison and is relatively slow, due to increased access times. Backup copies of all data files are maintained to provide a known reference in case of a fault, so the system can take the known good backup and simply repeat the processing on another processor. Again, performance impact is large.

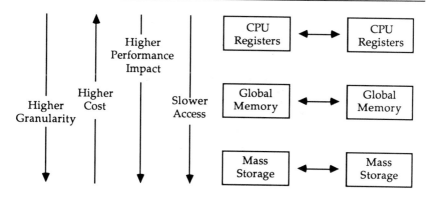

Figure 7.11   *Fault tolerant hierachy*

Comparing memory structures is another technique. Here, memory is split into four separate entities which are accessed by two processors. As with the file comparison method, two of the memory areas are used to hold two copies of a known reference point, while the other two are usable for new data structures and comparison. Figure 7.12 shows the basic principle. Granularity is broken down to a smaller level, such as the memory resident pages of a task, and the operation is terminated by a context switch, system call, cache flush or similar event. The new areas are compared and, if there is no error, the new blocks become the backups and the system has successfully completed a processing operation. If an error occurs, execution can be repeated using backup data and replacement processors, memory or other hardware. Performance is better than that of file comparison but an error still causes a considerable amount of data to be recalculated. With a file comparison configuration, the repair time is measurable in seconds, while that of a memory comparison is in milliseconds.

An alternative is to run pairs of processors in a lock step, where each operation is checked for errors. This provides the earliest possible error warning but at the highest component cost. Devices like the M68000 family can easily be configured for such designs. Typically, a control signal such as the address strobe is used to start the signal comparison. The strobe is synchronized from both processors and is used to enable signal comparators which check the address bus, read/write lines, etc. These should be stable when the address strobe is' issued. If an error occurs, a bus error can be generated which terminates the cycle and starts exception processing which can investigate the problem. To check data activities, the data strobes can be used in a similar way. There are several considerations however.

The M68000 processor stack frames contain a mask revision which could cause a data comparison problem. It is important to make sure that processor pairs have the same mask revision. A second problem concerns

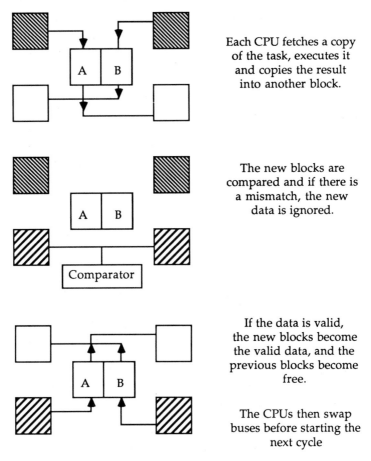

Each CPU fetches a copy of the task, executes it and copies the result into another block.

The new blocks are compared and if there is a mismatch, the new data is ignored.

If the data is valid, the new blocks become the valid data, and the previous blocks become free.

The CPUs then swap buses before starting the next cycle

Figure 7.12 *A memory comparison fault tolerance scheme*

setting up any internal resources, such as caches and memory management units. The comparison can be disabled while the processor resets and starts up but there is no guarantee that the two processors will be synchronized exactly. A simple solution is to build a common stack frame in external memory and to execute an RTE instruction. This loads back the stack frame and allows the processors to start in a pre-determined way. External address translation tables and floating point frames can be loaded to set up other resources. Caches can be preloaded by simple execution of NOPs or simple data moves.

The main difficulty concerns hardware comparators and synchronizers. These insert timing delays which can prevent a processor from running as fast as it can – a 20 MHz processor may be capable of only 16 MHz operation when the propagation delays caused by the synchronization logic are added. This effectively places artificial limitations on the performance that can be obtained from such a design.

The M88000 family allows two processor nodes (i.e. an MC88100 and its associated MC88200s) to be run in lock step without any performance impact. Each device can be configured as either a Master or a Checker. The signals are paralleled up but only the Master actually drives the bus. The Checker receives the signals and if they correspond with its signal, the processor is allowed to continue. If there is a mismatch, an error signal is asserted and processing is effectively stopped. By bringing the comparison logic onchip, performance degradation is removed, allowing such designs to improve performance through speed upgrades.

Single- and multiple-threaded operating systems

Given a good hardware implementation of a MIMD machine, there is yet another system layer to consider. Most operating systems have been written to support a single processor and therefore need modification to cope with multiple processors. The two methods used are described as single- and multi-threaded, which refers to the way the system handles operating system calls. In a single processor, the supervisor state effectively handles all operating system matters and can be viewed as a separate processor dedicated to that function. The supervisor processor has a single entry point (the trap instruction) and a single exit point (the RTE instruction). With a multiprocessor system, there is a choice – either only one processor can act as the supervisor at a time, the single-threaded approach, or multiple processors can – the multi-threaded design.

With the single-threaded approach, the operating system software is common to all processors and access to the routines and resources is controlled by semaphores. A task running on a processor makes a system call which causes the processor to switch into its supervisor state, as shown in Figure 7.13. It checks to see if any other processor is acting as a supervisor and, if so, waits until the access semaphore is clear. It then sets it and

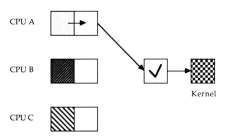

Figure 7.13 *Single threaded operation – stage 1*

effectively performs a context switch so that its supervisor state is exactly that of the last user. It can now access whatever resource it needs to complete the call. At any one time, only one processor is performing operating system tasks. Figure 7.14 shows another processor trying to execute a system call and being blocked by the semaphore. This type of system is easy to implement; the only real modification is the addition of the semaphore software and associated routines. The bulk of the kernel is still executed by a single processor and needs no modification. The disadvantage of the system is the poor system call performance. There is still only a single processor actually executing the kernel and therefore the system performance in this area is no better off than in a single-processor system. Applications will run faster, however, and examination of systems which show this type of characteristic are indicative of a single-threaded system.

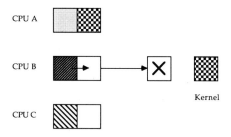

Figure 7.14   *Single threaded operation – stage 2*

However, this configuration is inefficient, considering it is quite common for differing processors and their tasks to need quite separate functions to be performed by the operating system. Obviously, turns must be taken when accessing common resources, such as hard discs, but for other functions it should be possible for the kernel to be split into parts to allow multiprocessing within itself. The multiple-threaded kernel takes exactly this idea. Providing there is no conflict of interest, any processor can perform system functions. The advantage is the speed improvement shown by system intensive applications, but this is offset by the additional software and reworking needed to modify an operating system kernel.

Both the M68000 and M88000 families have versions of UNIX and real-time operating systems that offer single- and multiple-threaded multiprocessing.

8 Application ideas

1 MC68020 and MC68030 design techniques for high-reliability applications

All microprocessors depend on the integrity of the memory subsystem to allow the system to execute reliably. Many early microprocessor families suffered from the execution of illegal op codes, caused by memory corruption, which often put the processor into an indeterminate state — with disastrous results for the external system. To prevent this, parity and/or error detection and correction schemes for memory systems were implemented. Unfortunately, processors were not capable of detecting such memory faults directly; the bus cycle is terminated normally and a non-maskable interrupt generated, allowing software to resolve the situation. This is complex and time consuming. The M68000 family solved these problems by allowing external logic to terminate the bus cycle with an error flag and restart it if required.

Due to the internal microcoding present in M68000 family processors, any attempt to execute an illegal instruction causes an exception to take place. This immediately starts the illegal op code handler software routine which determines what has gone wrong and, more importantly, what to do about it. The processor also identifies incorrect memory addressing, privilege violations, divide by zero and many other errors. Each has its own vector in the vector table and associated software handler, allowing such errors to be controlled, the system repaired and restarted.

This neatly takes care of any obviously wrong memory corruptions but fails to identify corruptions resulting in valid instructions or addresses. To prevent the processor outputting garbage, garbage must be prevented from being input which requires some external memory checking. The most common methods use either parity bit generation or error detection and correction. Both of these methods rely on check bits being fetched and compared with the stored data. Parity is capable of detecting only a single bit failure while EDC (Error Detection and Correction) can reconstitute the original data and recover from the corruption. However, such memory protection often cannot signal the error condition until late in the bus cycle or requires extra time to place the correct data on the bus.

Synchronous systems, which have fixed cycle times, incur either additional software overhead in repairing the damage caused by receiving invalid data, or have to run permanently slower to allow time for recovery. Both of these schemes place unacceptable burdens on design.

If invalid data is presented to the processor (due to some bus fault, etc.), which is a legal instruction or corrupt data, the software may not recognize the error and start to perform unexpected operations, such as addressing non-existent memory. This is often the first indication that something has gone wrong with software execution. If such a non-existent address is accessed via its asynchronous bus, the processor waits indefinitely for a valid response and appears to hang up. This is easily solved by using a watchdog timer, such as a monostable or clock counter, which is enabled and reset by the address strobe at the start and completion of a bus cycle. Failure to reply with DTACK causes the timer to timeout and assert the BERR line and start bus error or exception processing. This technique not only identifies addressing errors, but can also be used to highlight 'bus hogging' errors in multiple master systems with additional processors and DMA devices.

If the frame building operation for the bus error exception encounters another bus error, the processor assumes that all is lost with its external circuitry, and halts. Assertion of the HALT line could fire another timer which attempts to reset the processor and restart the system by asserting RESET and HALT lines. Alternatively, with the processor in a halted state, there is no software resetting of a software timer to reset the processor on expiry. By using investigative software routines within the power up sequence, battery backed up RAM can be examined and damage repaired, or some assessment made of data lost, etc.

The above methods can provide protection from memory corruption caused by hardware failures but do not prevent software overwriting programs or data in error.

Partitioning the system

Many earlier 8-bit microprocessor systems could easily be crashed by bad programming and/or software errors, associated usually with application tasks rather than with the operating systems used. The reason was quite simple. There was little or no separation or protection of the controlling software and application tasks running under it. Applications could easily manipulate system tables and stacks and even overwrite kernel areas.

Obviously, this was not acceptable for high reliability and is one of the many reasons behind the slower uptake of microprocessors in critical designs. To solve this deficiency, the M68000 family uses the concept of two different states, with separate and protected resources. The processor normally executes code in the USER state but when an exception occurs, it switches into the SUPERVISOR state, with its own separate stack pointer and access to the processor control registers. This transition can be caused by a processing error, external interrupts or a software interrupt TRAP instruction. Using these two states allows application and operating system software to be separated, preventing rogue applications from corrupting the whole system.

The processor's dual status needs to be repeated in the external design. If the whole of external memory were available to both the USER and SUPERVISOR states, each others programs would be put at risk from corruption. The memory system must be partitioned so that programs can be protected. This function is performed by the three function code signals which are driven with the address bus on the start of every memory cycle. The three pins offer eight codes indicating the type of transfer taking place, i.e. program or data, SUPERVISOR or USER, interrupt acknowledge-/CPU space cycle. By taking these outputs and including them in the address decode logic, blocks of memory can be reserved for specific use.

Care must be taken with system design if such hardware partitioning is used. Data which is accessed on start up may be stored in the program boot up ROMs. While instruction accesses create the correct address and function code information for the decode logic, any data access is inhibited, resulting in a major system problem. It may be impractical to have additional ROMs onboard. Both the MC68020 and the MC68030 have a solution. The SUPERVISOR has access to two additional registers which allow user-definable function codes to be stored. These can be used with the MOVES instruction to transfer data from one address space to another. When this instruction is executed, the normal function code is replaced by the contents of either the source or destination function code register, depending on which way the data transfer is performed. This allows the correct code to be output, fooling the decode logic and allowing the correct data access.

This ability can also be used to restrict access to I/O devices by mapping them into an undefined address space. Normally, all access to I/O devices is performed in the same way as normal memory access, using the same instructions and addressing modes. If a system breaks down, corrupting its memory, it is possible for the system I/O to be corrupted and left in an indeterminate state. An addressing error can change a parallel port's status instead of a memory location in a data structure. By placing the I/O addressing in a separate address space, access can only be via the SUPERVISOR, executing the MOVES instruction, with the alternate function code registers set correctly. This reduces the possibility of any corruption and results in such a low level of accidental access that it can be ignored. In addition, any access can occur only via the SUPERVISOR and it can, therefore, be carefully checked.

For many critical applications, additional testing is needed – software requires mathematical verification to provide confidence in its functionality and to establish if there are any design or coding errors. This often places additional restrictions on software design and can prohibit the use of interrupts or exceptions, complicated branching and addressing modes. Indeed, some implementations do not use subroutines, relying solely on inline code and explicit addressing modes. Restricting the instruction set is a simple matter for the compiler. The major problem arises with preventing exceptions.

Consider some safety critical software that has been written and mathematically verified. Such verification inevitably prohibits the use of interrupts and exceptions. Should any occur, software and hardware validity is broken and the system becomes suspect. Such cases should result in the system halting, preventing any erroneous action and possibly allowing a redundant unit to take over. While the majority of exceptions can be either not used or masked, there are some, such as level 7 interrupt, that cannot be excluded. Although the hardware design can pull the interrupts pins permanently high, an external hardware failure could generate such an interrupt, even though all three pins would need to be asserted simultaneously. Interrupt handlers can be written to return execution to the point prior to the interrupt. If the system has started to malfunction, there is no guarantee that this software will work.

There is a similar problem with the bus error signal. If asserted during a memory cycle, it can cause the bus error exception to be taken. Again, this destroys the mathematical verification and system integrity.

Inhibiting exceptions

Both the MC68020 and the MC68030 have three stack pointer registers available to the programmer. Two are restricted for supervisor use and the third is for the user. The user stack pointer, A7 or USP, is used normally for information and subroutine stacking operations. The supervisor uses either its Master stack pointer or Interrupt stack pointer, depending on the exception cause and the status of the M bit in the status register. If this bit is clear, all stack operations default to the A7' stack pointer. If it is set, interrupt stack frames are stored, using the Interrupt stack pointer, while other operations use the Master pointer, thus effectively allowing the system to maintain two separate stacks. What is important is that a throwaway stack is built on to the Master stack before the complete frame is built using the interrupt stack pointer (Figure 8.1). If either of these

EXCEPTION

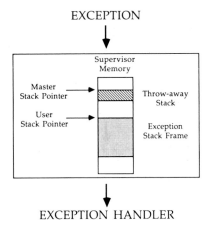

EXCEPTION HANDLER

Figure 8.1   *Normal exception stack frame building*

operations encounters a bus error while building either of these stacks, the
processor takes a double bus error and halts. The combination of these two
characteristics allows the selective disabling of all exceptions or interrupts
only under software control.

A 'No Exception' scheme can be implemented using the various stack
pointers. On entry to a critical software routine, the stack pointer register is
loaded with the address of a non-existent memory location, any stack
frame building results in a bus error and halts the processor without any
software intervention. If the interrupt stack pointer is so manipulated, only
external interrupts effectively result in such a processor halt (Figure 8.2). If

EXCEPTION

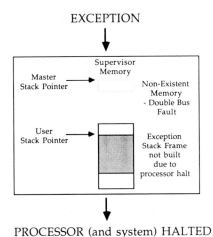

PROCESSOR (and system) HALTED

Figure 8.2   *Forcing exceptions to halt the processor*

the Master stack pointer is used, all exceptions result in a halted processor by virtue of the throwaway stack which is always created on the MSP. All that is needed is a single instruction at the beginning of the critical routine and another at its completion to implement this concept and increase the overall reliability of the system.

There is another option available which is even more selective. It uses the vector base register (VBR) to relocate the processor vector table to a different memory location. With a new table, individual vector locations can be corrupted so that they cause an address error (Figure 8.3), forcing the processor to take the appropriate exception which, if it causes an address error, forces the processor to take the double bus fault, and halt. This corruption can be caused by making the exception handler pointer stored in the vector table an odd value. Alternatively, the vector and the bus error vector could point to non-existent memory and generate the double bus error this way. This technique can be performed on the original vector table but it uses a lot of overhead to save, modify and restore the vector table. Using the VBR allows one instruction to switch into the protected mode, and another to switch back.

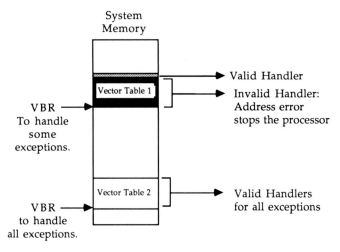

Figure 8.3 *Using the VBR to inhibit exceptions*

The above technique can be performed by using the software handler to simply execute the STOP instruction. The previous method uses the processor hardware and does not rely on external software and its integrity.

Implementing the system

Figure 8.4 depicts a MC68020–based computer system and its hardware interfaces to external systems. The various memory chips and peripherals are decoded from the full address bus, function code and read/write signals, which are driven at the start of each external bus cycle. To save time, they are decoded and then validated by the address strobe signal AS★. The full address bus must be decoded to ensure that each memory block can be accessed only by addresses within a specific range. If partial decoding is used, each memory block is repeated throughout the entire memory map. This may save on circuitry but does allow access via incorrect addresses. Should an address pointer or an external hardware failure occur, it may access such a multiple mapped block — with disastrous results.

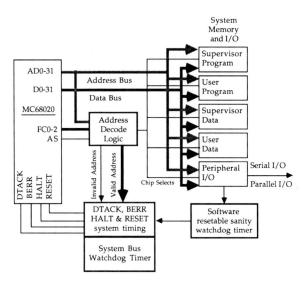

Figure 8.4 *An MC68020 system block diagram*

As previously described, it is desirable to limit any I/O access to a specific code sequence using a single privileged instruction to reduce the probability of an error generating a code sequence that might access the critical I/O to virtually zero. This is done by fully decoding the function codes to split the system memory into various blocks – SUPERVISOR, USER, data and program and I/O space. I/O space is defined by using one of the spare undefined codes for critical peripherals. Normal instruction execution cannot generate the right function code to access the I/O space. The address may be generated in error but, without the correct function code, no physical access is performed. Only the Supervisor can access such peripherals, executing the MOVES command after the source and destination registers have been loaded with the correct function codes. This limits access to a single instruction requiring several correct register contents, rather than virtually any valid instruction.

It is important to ensure that the RESET vector is present at location $00000000 and is mapped into the SUPERVISOR data space, so that it can be accessed correctly on power up. A common technique is to remap EPROMs so that for the first few memory cycles, they appear at address $00000000 instead of their normal location (Figure 8.5). This allows the processor to get its RESET vector, locate the first instructions and jump to the correctly mapped routines in EPROM. The vector table can now be written into RAM at location $00000000 which neatly saves the problem of reconciling a RAM-based vector table with non-volatile storage of the RESET vector. This system can be synthesized in software using the VBR (vector base register). The EPROMs are mapped at $00000000 with RAM located above. Once the EPROM resident software has started, it writes into the VBR, relocates the vector table into RAM and copies its contents

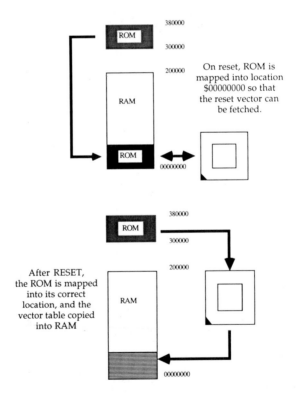

Figure 8.5 *A hardware method of providing both a ROMed RESET vector and a vector table in RAM*

from EPROM to RAM. The former solution relocates the EPROM using additional logic; the latter uses a couple of instructions and no additional logic (Figure 8.6). If any data is stored in EPROM, either the EPROM must be mapped into the data space as well or software must transfer all data into RAM using the MOVES instruction during the system set up. This is often neglected and can be a very costly mistake.

Figure 8.6 *Using the vector base register to provide a RAM-based vector table*

Further protection is supplied by a system sanity timer, which requires periodic resetting by software to prevent it from expiring and asserting a combination of system HALT and RESET lines. To prevent accidental access, this timer is mapped into the I/O space with other critical I/O functions. Depending on the required system characteristics, it could either reset the system or halt it.

Bus error handling

The most likely cause of an unexpected exception is the bus error. The initial problem is to determine where the error occurred and then to decide if it is a transitory or a permanent fault. By investigating the stack frame built by the processor, the access address, function codes and status of the read/write line, together with the instruction and status registers at the time of the error can be examined. By comparing this information with a system resource map compiled during initialization, the fault can be diagnosed as an external hardware fault (i.e. an access to an invalid address), or the result of corrupt program or data. If it is hardware, the instruction can be restarted just in case it was a transient problem. With a software fault, all that can really be done is to reset stack areas, note the failure and restart at a known point, i.e. execute the STOP instruction and wait for the next interrupt. If everything is bad, a software reset may be called for. This is achieved by noting the time and nature of the fault in the system parameters memory area, placing the processor in a halted state by executing the STOP instruction and waiting for the external reset watchdog timer to reset the system.

The MC68020 and MC68030 processors provide some additional protection against bus errors generated due to transient errors. If the error occurs during a data fetch, the exception is always taken. If it happens while an instruction is fetched, the exception is only taken if the instruction is executed. The processor prefetch mechanism often fetches instructions which are not executed due to program flow changes, external interrupts, etc. This improves system reliability with respect to transient errors.

Other exceptions

The MC68020 processor will trap other exception conditions and allow their separate handling. Some of them, like divide by zero, misaligned addressing, check bounds violation, etc., are due primarily to hardware faults. All 256 vectors are handled, albeit with a general handler that simply notes the exception and returns. This is essential because any vector can be selected if there is an external hardware fault during a vectored interrupt acknowledgement cycle. For this reason, an autovectored interrupt hardware scheme is used which limits the choice to the vector for that particular interrupt level and does not use an externally supplied vector to find the exception handler. However, all the vectors are covered in case of a hardware fault.

2   Upgrading 8-bit systems

The main reason for moving away from an 8-bit processor design to 16 or 32 bits is to provide the next level of performance or functionality within the system. Increased performance either for greater functionality or higher throughput is obvious but many upgrades are done for other reasons. The need to go beyond a 64 Kbyte address range or bank switching to allow more data or program space, or to change from assembler to a high-level language to reduce program development and reduce maintenance are often reasons. In some cases, there may only be a need to prepare for a 16/32 bit platform or be able to offer such a solution which pre-empts the move. Given that an upgrade is needed, there are several ways to proceed. The first is simply to create a 16/32-bit processor design from scratch. This may be the only solution if the new specification is radically

Figure 8.7 *An MC68008 basic system*

different from its predecessor but for many, this is costly, time consuming and effectively scraps the previous design investment.

Comparing a 16-bit M68000 design with that of a M6800 or Z80 8-bit system shows that there is remarkable similarity between the systems; often the main difference is simply the wider memory. A simple transition can be made by using an 8-bit external bus MC68008 processor to allow the memory and peripherals to be used with an internal 16/32-bit processor architecture (Figure 8.7). The memory array, MC68901 Multi-Function Peripheral and EPROM are byte wide; 16- and 32-bit accesses are performed automatically as a sequence of byte accesses. The processor can provide up to 4 Mbytes of direct addressing and achieves about 60% of the throughput of the full 16-bit M68000. The figure is greater than half because byte data fetches take the same time with the M68000 and M68008 but instruction and word fetches take twice the time. This approach has other advantages within a bus-based system, in that it allows a simple processor board replacement.

The M68000 asynchronous bus interface has simpler requirements than many 8-bit processors. It needs only a single clock, which can easily be generated from a combination of a crystal and a 7404 inverter chip (Figure 8.8). This provides the system clock from which the control signals are synchronized, i.e. inputs are recognized, providing a small setup time prior to the clock edge is met, and outputs appear within a fixed time from the clock edge. The non-multiplexed data and address buses remove any need

Figure 8.8 *The MC680 × 0 clock circuit*

for de-multiplexers or latches. The asynchronous bus allows any speed peripheral to talk to the processor and this greatly simplifies interfacing other peripherals to it. For existing M6800 peripherals a MC6800 bus, complete with E clock, is supplied for easy upgrading (Figure 8.9). The E clock is generated from the processor clock by dividing it by 10. For 8 and 10 MHz devices, M68Axx parts are suitable and for higher processor speeds, M68Bxx chips are needed.

With an asynchronous interface, it is possible to force the M68008 to wait indefinitely if the cycle is not terminated either by a DTACK★ or a BERR★ reply. Figure 8.10 shows a circuit which can generate DTACK★ with differing timings and a BERR★ signal if the access is to invalid memory. The counter simply clocks the system clock once it has been enabled by the address strobe, AS★. This happens only with a start of a valid bus cycle; the counted outputs can then be gated with valid address signals to provide the appropriate delay. Using a jumper field allows the user to modify such timings if faster memory, peripherals or processor are added.

For systems that need a full 16- or 32-bit pathway, the MC68008 is not suitable and either a 16- or 32-bit member of the family must be used. The MC68000 and MC68010 have 16-bit external buses and still retain the M6800 interface bus. To upgrade with these processors requires a 16-bit memory path but the 8-bit peripherals can be retained. Many of the M68000 peripherals still have an 8-bit data bus because many of their I/O functions are still based around byte data sizes. A variation on this can be provided by the MC68HC001. This is an HCMOS version of the M68000 running at 16 MHz and has the ability to be configured as either a 8- or 16-bit external bus on reset by using an additional 'mode' pin. The device provides a higher speed, lower power consumption upgrade for the MC68008 and allows dual designs to be built. Such a board would be designed for a full 16-bit memory interface and 8-bit peripherals. For lower

E clock generated from system clock
divided by 10.

For 8,10 MHz CPUs use 68Axx parts
For 12, 16 MHz CPUs use 68Bxx parts

Figure 8.9 *Interfacing an MC68000 to M6800 peripherals*

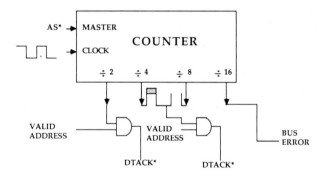

Figure 8.10 *Generating bus error and DTACK*

cost and lower performance systems, the extra components needed for the extra 8 bits would not be inserted into the board and the MC68HC001 jumpered for 8-bit mode. To achieve higher performance, extra memory and associated buffers, etc. are inserted and the processor mode changed to 16 bit. This gives a lot of flexibility for system upgrading without redesigning.

For low-cost 32-bit systems, the MC68020 and MC68030 can offer good

Figure 8.11   *The MC68020 dynamic bus sizing*

performance with the ability to use 1-, 16- or 32-bit wide memory ports without prior knowledge of the port size. This gives the option of mixing and matching 8-, 16- and 32-bit peripherals and buses as necessary. Dynamic bus sizing works by the processor always assuming that the memory port is 32 bits wide. The memory port accepts whatever width of data it can, tells the processor how much data has been taken and how much is left to transfer via a combination of DSACK★ signals (Figure 8.11). The processor simply moves the data up on the bus and performs another bus cycle. The cycle repeats until all the data has been transferred.

3   Transparent update techniques for digital filters using the DSP56000

One of the most frequently used DSP algorithms is the Finite Impulse Response filter (FIR), which is used to perform filtering for tone detection within telecomms applications, tone filters and also for special effects in digital audio and pitch detection within speech recognition systems. The FIR is commonly used because it is non-recursive and therefore inherently stable. It is also easy to adapt through manipulation of its coefficients tables. Coefficients are the analogue equivalent of the resistor–capacitor networks used in analogue filters. These coefficients need to be changed to adapt the filter's response or if the algorithm needs modification. In either case, a controlling microprocessor, like an M68000 or an MC68HC11, can calculate the new values and transfer the data to the signal processor. The challenge is to find the most efficient method of transferring the data.

Method 1

A simple way involves creating a shared memory system between the host processor and the DSP56000. The host processor calculates the new data in its own memory, arbitrates the DSP56000 off the bus, transfers the data, signals the availability of new data and lets the DSP56000 back on to the bus. The DSP56000 checks the semaphore and switches algorithm or coefficients. This solution is viable, but it has certain disadvantages. It is extremely hardware intensive, needing a bus arbiter, dual port or shared memory and controlling logic. The overhead of checking the semaphore is high and occurs irregularly. The DSP56000 either slows down or stops execution during the external fetches or when the host processor is accessing the bus.

Method 2

The DSP56000 has a host interface port which can be used by the host processor to pass data into the chip. The interface, Figure 8.12, simply looks like a memory mapped peripheral to the host processor. The 8-bit port on the left is accessible by the host while the transmit and receive buffers, together with the control and status registers, appear as part of the DSP56000 global data bus. The host processor can force the DSP56000 to execute a fast, two-instruction interrupt routine. With this interface, the block transfer can be made directly into the DSP56000, reducing the necessary hardware and removing any arbitration delays. However, this improvement has some problems. Consider the block transfer time. For a 100 tap filter with 24-bit coefficients, 300 bytes need to be moved. Using a 16 MHz M68000 with a 62.5 ns clock time and three MOVE.B instructions with incremental indirect addressing, takes 275 µs. This may not appear to be a very large overhead but, coupled with the synchronization overhead, it is sufficient to reduce the effective sampling rate to 3.6 kHz.

Method 3

The best method also utilizes the host interface but uses the host command vectors and fast interrupt to effectively cycle steal from the DSP56000.

Figure 8.12 *The DSP56000 host interface port*

Each 24-bit coefficient is written into the host interface and a fast interrupt initiated to force the DSP56000 to execute one of 16 host command vectors. These routines can transfer the data into internal memory and switch coefficient tables as necessary. The block transfer of data from the M68000 to the DSP56000 is done in parallel with the filter execution and is distributed across a larger time period. This effectively places no overhead on signal processing. At 44.1 kHz and one transfer per cycle, throughput is only reduced by 0.9%. In addition, there is no impact on I/O service or sampling rates, minimal hardware is needed (Figure 8.13) and synchronization is controlled by the host.

Figure 8.13 *An MC68000/DSP56000 multiprocessor configuration*

4 Motor and servo control

An increasing need for microprocessor designs is to interface with the real world to drive motors and other mechanical equipment. The hard–disc controller is a good example of such needs and shows how a processor can be used to implement the necessary control and servo algorithms.

Hard–disc mechanics usually consist of two main functions, as shown in Figure 8.14. The disc platter speed must be kept constant and within certain strict tolerances to maintain data integrity. The reason for this is simple – the data is recorded by magnetizing the metal oxide on the surface of the disc platter to form concentric rings of data called tracks. Each track is divided into sectors, with each sector storing a certain number of bytes and error correction codes. The speed of the platter and the resolution of the data head determine the recording density. If the speed changes, the recording density will differ from the time of writing the data and reading

DISC
PLATTER

HEAD CONTROL
Linear or Rotary

SPINDLE MOTOR

Both controls usually three phase brushless DC motors

Figure 8.14 *Hard disc mechanics*

the data. These differences can be so great that the original data cannot be read correctly. In such cases, data is effectively lost, causing much grief to the unfortunate user! This change in speed is the reason IBM format 3.5 in discs are incompatible with Apple Macintosh discs. While the actual floppy discs are identical, the IBM PC format is based on a constant rotational speed; the Apple format changes the rotational speed, depending on which track is being accessed. In both cases, it is essential that the rotational speed during recording and reading is the same.

The head actuator also requires sophisticated control. The tracks are extremely narrow and yet each track must be located repeatedly with great accuracy many hundreds of thousands of times throughout the hard-disc's life. In addition, the seek time taken to locate a track must be the shortest time possible. With a hard–disc system, it is the seek time that plays a large part in determining the data access time and the user-perceived response time.

System needs

Figure 8.15 shows a typical system and how the electronics falls into two main areas. The drive controller takes the data via an interface, like ST506 or SCSI (Small Computer Systems Interface), and the appropriate location data (e.g. track and sector number), passes the data to the read/write electronics and moves the head into the appropriate position. Read/write electronics usually consist of a low–noise analogue amplifier which drives the recording head directly. Digital data is converted by the controller to an analogue serial data stream before being passed to the read/write heads, in a method similar to that used with MODEMs.

The spindle and head control uses standard servo designs where error signals are constantly fed back to the controller so it can detect and compensate for any deviations. This type of function can be performed by any microprocessor with timer, analogue and digital outputs. The servo response time and positional accuracy are determined effectively by the computational powers of the processor. For many lower-performance

Disc Drive Controller Board   Inside Hard Disc Drive

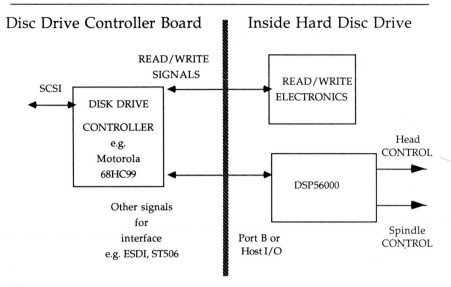

Figure 8.15 *Typical electronics*

designs, higher-performance microcontrollers, like the MC68HC11, are suitable. As performance increases, more and more arithmetic calculations are needed with can be met only by the faster M68020/MC68030, M88000 or DSP families. Considering the space limitation and cost restrictions, the DSP56000 offers a compact, powerful solution. Figure 8.16 shows how the DSP 56000 can be configured. The main control signals require conversion from the analogue to the digital domain and this is performed by the A to D and D to A converters located on the Synchronous Serial Interface (SSI).

Figure 8.16 *DSP56000 functions*

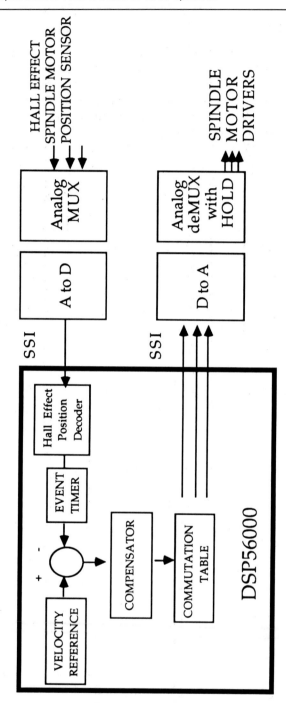

Figure 8.17   *Spindle control*

Spindle control

Figure 8.17 shows the basic algorithm used to control the rotational speed. External Hall-effect position sensors measure the rotational speed of the spindle and generate time-based event data. This is taken into the processor and compared with a standard velocity event generator. The difference in the timing between events can be measured and passed to a compensator which calculates the required compensation and generates the appropriate signals to control the spindle motors and restore or maintain the correct velocity. These functions are performed in software, using simple control techniques.

Control signal generation is the most difficult. The speed and granularity of this data determine the servo response but the generation of sinewave data from digital sources is difficult. There is a further complication involving the constantly changing phase relationships between the three outputs needed to control the three spindle motors. The DSP56000 has an elegant solution; it has a sinewave table digitally encoded within its data ROM and the modulo addressing can be used to cycle through this table without end looping overhead. By using three pointers, differing phase relationships can be created by varying the address space between them, as shown in Figure 8.18.

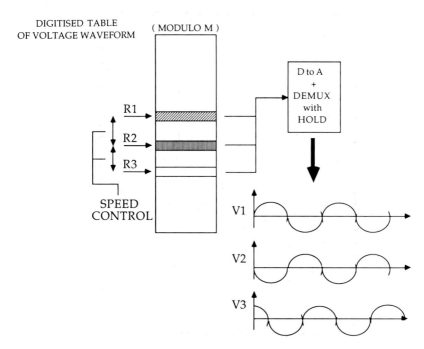

Figure 8.18 *Generating AC voltage waveforms*

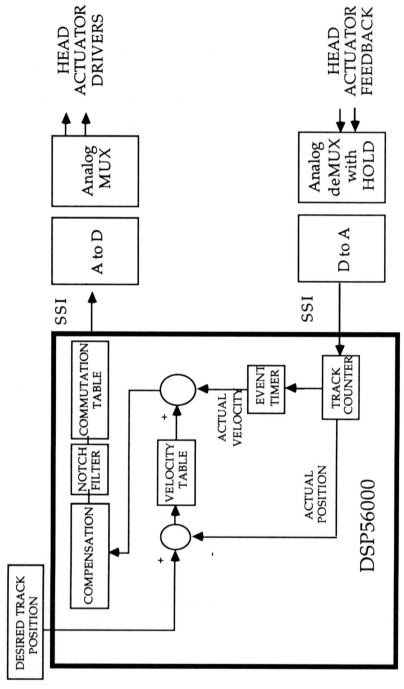

Figure 8.19   *The positioning algorithm*

Head control

The head-positioning algorithm (Figure 8.19) is very similar to that used to control the spindle. The required track position is given to the DSP56001 and this is used for comparison with the current track position and generating the required control signals. If the head is at track 12 and the command to move to track 67 is given, this causes the DSP56000 to start the head actuators moving in the given direction. The movement data is based on current velocity and direction and uses a commutation table and the embedded sinewave table to generate the correct control signals. A notch filter is included to remove effects due to mechanical resonance, etc. There are two main considerations; the first is to detect each track and count it and the second involves adjusting the actuator velocity to compensate for mechanical inertia. In the same way that a vehicle cannot stop dead and needs a stopping distance, the inertia within the actuator requires the stop command to be issued before it actually is positioned over the track. This requires velocity compensation so that the head can be moved quickly over a large number of tracks but can also be moved slowly when fine control is needed.

The technique used with the DSP56000 can provide both the track count and velocity information. The SCI timer is programmed to provide a succession of timer interrupts. This allows the velocity between each track position to be calculated, as shown in Figure 8.20. Each track position generates an IRQA interrupt and the number of timer interrupts give the velocity between tracks. The lower the number of SCI timer events, the faster the velocity. Each timer interrupt generates a fast interrupt which, in turn, causes a pointer to be incremented. When a track position interrupt occurs, the track counter is increased and the velocity processed using the pointer value. Finally, the pointer is reset before restarting the sequence.

Determining track position

The main difficulty with this type of system is providing the track position information. A low-cost solution is to use one of the disc platters to store only track positioning information and keep it as the reference for the other heads within the system. This reduces the drive storage capacity but is relatively simple to implement. This method is sensitive to temperature changes, external shocks and vibrations and component ageing. In addition, the positioning of the servo head may not necessarily correspond with correct data head positioning.

An alternative and more costly method is to embed the servo track positioning information within each track. This frees the servo platter for data storage and increases disc capacity. However, the position control is far greater and requires faster and more accurate responses from the controller.

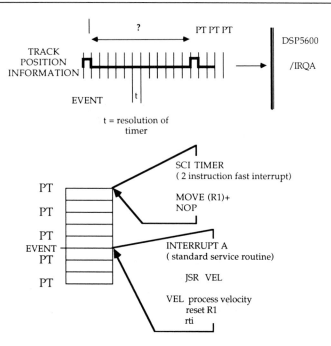

Figure 8.20 *Using the SCI timer*

This increases the processing power needed and, with the control functions using digital processing techniques, a DSP chip is almost mandatory. With such a system, track densities of greater than 1200 per inch are obtainable. The DSP56000 is ideal for such applications because of its 24-bit precision for the control algorithms, its high parallelism and processing throughput.

9 Semiconductor technology

The last decade has seen some unparalleled advances in the semiconductor industry. Memory densities have increased by over a thousand times, the simple 8-bit microprocessors of the late 1970s have matured into 1 million transistor plus processors like the MC68040, and current handling and switching speeds respectively have increased from a few milliamps to tens of amps and from kHz to MHz.

Silicon technology

Integrated circuits are fabricated by taking monocristaline wafers of silicon and diffusing impurities into them under controlled conditions to form semiconducting structures within the material. These are then connected together using aluminium metallization or conductive polysilicon tracks. The tracks and diffusions are performed selectively using a photoresist coating (Figure 9.1), exposing it to a patterned mask, developing the resist to remove the unexposed resist and thus the silicon. Diffusions are achieved using heating within a gaseous atmosphere or by direct ion implantation (Figure 9.2). These processes are carried out on a very small and continually decreasing scale. The metallization tracks used in devices of 10–15 years ago were about 10–20 µm in width. This may be thinner than a human hair but is many times larger than the widths appearing today.

Semiconductor structures are formed around P and N types of diffusions, caused by a lack or excess of electrons within the crystal lattice. With these basic blocks, capacitors, transistors, diodes and resistors can be fabricated and connected in a way similar to that in which discrete components are utilized on a printed circuit board. There are two types of transistor that can be made in this way.

The first type is the bipolar transistor whose structure is shown in Figure 9.3. It consists of three semiconductor diffusions to form a N-P-N or a P-

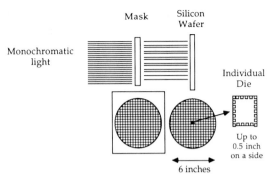

Figure 9.1   *The basic photo-lithography process for integrated circuits*

Figure 9.2   *Diffusing channels into silicon wafers*

Figure 9.3   *Epitaxial bipolar transistor*

N-P sandwich. The central connection is the base and the emitter and collector are the outside connections. In the example shown, the P Diff region is the base, the N + Diff region the collector and the emitter formed from the N EPI material below it. Bipolar transistors have very fast switching speeds of many GHz and good current handling, but their construction is large and their power consumption high.

Figure 9.4 *A conventional MOS transistor*

The second type is the MOS transistor, which is small, with reasonable switching capability but with reduced current capability. It works via a field effect which creates a channel below a very thin layer of silicon oxide dielectric (Figure 9.4), when a voltage is applied above it. This gate voltage can be supplied by a metallization track, in the case of metal gate CMOS, and by polysilicon in most other cases. The MOS transistor forms the basis of most modern digital electronics. For very high speeds, bipolar logic called Emitter Coupled Logic (ECL) is used – but with the penalty of smaller densities and greatly increased power consumption.

CMOS and bipolar technology

The fuel for the processors which have appeared over the recent years is the available semiconductor technology and the transistor density and switching speeds that it can offer. The technology has been based around silicon as the main semiconductor and although more esoteric compounds like gallium arsenide continue to challenge it in raising switching speeds, silicon technology will continue to be the mainstay of the industry. Research teams have developed bipolar silicon transistors with switching speeds of up to 26 GHz. Similar PNP devices have also been reported. Current bipolar technologies will get faster and faster as the transistor size is shrunk. This will increase densities and allow many VLSI devices that currently use CMOS technology to be implemented in bipolar technology, enabling designs like the M88000 RISC family to be implemented in ECL logic and allowing a dramatic increase in processor clock speeds. The version currently being developed by Data General and Motorola will have a clock speed in excess of 140 MHz and should appear in 1991–2.

Over the last ten years, there has been a dramatic swing towards CMOS as the technology of choice for many designs. Its reduced power consumption is essential to maintain acceptably low power dissipation as the number of active transistors and speeds increase (CMOS devices use more power the faster they run). It is likely that this swing will continue. The roadmap for ASIC CMOS technology shows today's 100 000-gate devices being dwarfed by the multimillion-gate chips that will undoubtedly appear. The reason for this increase is the ever-reducing geometries which allow increased densities and reduce propagation delays. Motorola's current high-density CMOS ASICs will almost halve the current propagation delays and line widths by 1994.

The future of CMOS technology on its own to provide the highest-speed processors and memory does appear to be limited. As speeds increase, the required current drive increases to the point where a combination of CMOS logic and bipolar drivers becomes the logical and most effective solution. CMOS is used to provide the logical functions while bipolar outputs are used to provide the high drive. Combination technology, such as BiCMOS, is now starting to appear in memories and will undoubtedly take over as the preferred technology for these types of parts. This combining of technologies is Motorola's aim by the mid to late 1990s. Figure 9.5 shows the overall plan. The three core technologies of Bipolar, CMOS and Power devices will be developed and combined to provide various combinations. Bipolar will continue to be developed through the MOSAIC (MOtorola Self Aligned Integrated Circuit) program and CMOS through the HDCMOS series. These technologies will provide a core of complimentary processes which will allow VLSI designs to combine very fast switching speeds of up to 28 GHz, with current drives of 10 A and high gate density.

This combination allows the integration of digital technology with analogue interfaces, will drive more electronics into the controller world and greatly reduce the need for wholly analogue solutions. As the cost of going digital decreases, the advantages of no component ageing or drift, finer resolution, etc. offered by digital techniques, may prove irresistible. The trends seen in automotive design over the last few years, where mechanical ignition, braking systems and even light switches have been replaced by electronics, are an indicator of what is going to happen.

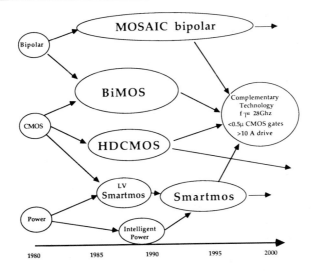

Figure 9.5 *Motorola's technology roadmap for the 1990s*

Fabrication technology

The key to generating the silicon is fabrication technology. The main issue in the 1990s is not whether visible light will be replaced by electron beam or X-rays, but when. Light plays an integral part in building any semiconductor. It is responsible for transferring the patterns from the mask to the silicon surface to allow the selective diffusion and etching necessary to build a transistor, a logic gate or a processor. The resolution of this process determines the size of the transistors that can be built. Today's technology is still predominantly light based and is rapidly reaching its limits. The problem concerns the wavelength of light and, therefore, the resolution of the objects it can expose. As an object's size decreases and approaches that of the wavelength of light, it becomes harder to differentiate it from the background and project it to make the mask or project its pattern on to silicon.

The solution is to use shorter wavelengths which require the use of electron beams or X-rays to replace visible light. Electron beams are used currently to fabricate the masks and in direct etching techniques but, to achieve line widths of 0.25 μm and below, it is likely that X-rays will be needed. This work is already underway. Motorola and IBM are co-funding a $1 billion X-ray lithography research program to develop the appropriate technology.

An interesting implication of this trend will be the exponential increase in capital investment to finance new silicon fabrication plants. It is estimated that a sub-µm fab facility costs about $500 million today. The next generation facility, to cope with 0.25 µm geometries and below, is estimated to cost over $1 billion. For many of today's smaller silicon companies, this level of investment is far greater than their turnover or capitalization and it is likely that between now and the next century many will either merge, be taken over, or simply disappear. This trend has already started. Mostek and Fairchild are a couple of famous names that suffered this fate in the 1980s.

Packaging

The trend in packaging is quite simple. Smaller packages, larger numbers of pins and smaller pin separation – everything that gives board layout engineers nightmares! Analysis of the last ten years has shown a move away from the dual-in-line packages, with about a 64-pin limit, to pin grid array packages of about 200 pins, surface mount packages of 200–300 pins, etc. The differing types of ASIC package options which are currently available give a good indicator of the standards to be seen in the next few years. Currently, Motorola is offering pin counts up to about 500, using a variety of packages ranging from pin grid array, quad flat pack through to TAB bonding. With TAB bonding, the die is inverted and bonded directly to the frame fingers. These fingers are brought outside the package to connect to the outside world. The trend, shown in Figure 9.6, is of decreasing lead pitch.

Packaging sizes will decrease down to chip level (Figure 9.7). This is not new, as hybrids have been around for many years. Here, several dice are

Figure 9.6   *Trends in lead spacing*

Figure 9.7 *Chip v. package areas for the MC68000*

mounted on a substrate and bonded together to form a complete unit in its own right. The flip-chip technique, where the chip is inverted and bonded directly to the substrate, will provide the highest packing density. Motorola has developed a technique which takes this a step further. A silicon substrate is used with the appropriate diffused connections and holes are then etched in the substrate to accept individual dice. In this way, it is possible to achieve a customized 'wafer scale integration', knowing the dice are all functional. The use of silicon dice and substrate prevents many of the thermal mismatching problems.

With surface-mount techniques becoming more and more common, the package options are bound to increase, as shown in Figure 9.8. Currently, Plastic Leaded Chip Carriers (PLCC), Ceramic Leaded Chip Carriers (CLCC) and Plastic and Ceramic Quad Flat Packs (PQFP, CQFP) are the favoured packages, offering high pin densities and low cost. Versions of these packages will appear with even smaller leads and higher densities.

The Pad Array Carrier (PAC) is another package type which may become extremely widespread. It is typically about 10% bigger than the dice and consists of a ceramic body with a matrix of solder bumps arranged on a 0.05 in spacing. The MC88100 and MC88200 are packaged in this form for the Hypermodule to pack up to four MC88100 processors and eight MC88200 cache memory management chips on to a single board measuring 8 × 3 inches. This technology gives extremely high packing density and allows science fiction dreams to become reality. The Motorola micro-ETACS cellular phone, which looks like a Star Trek communicator, and the wrist watch pager are proof that this type of technology is not restricted to niche products but is rapidly entering the consumer market, where size is a premium.

These new generations will need advances in board design, surface-mount techniques and testing before this state of the art becomes routine.

How do you test a PAC device on a board when none of the connections are exposed? The answer is to X-ray it or design the board to provide test points. How do you then rework the board? Solving this sort of problem will require additional help in increasing the testability of a design. JTAG testing, where test signals can be circulated around the pins of a device by putting the device into a special test mode, has just started to appear. The MC68040 has this facility. By the end of the century, probably every VLSI chip will have this or a similar facility and as much attention will be paid to testing systems as designing them.

Figure 9.8   *Surface mount technology progression*

One aspect that will affect all electronic engineers is the need by law to minimize radio-frequency interference (RFI). With chips becoming faster and offering greater current drive, more care will be needed on layout to meet the new EEC and FDI specifications concerning such emissions. This will involve the large-scale adoption of transmission line designs for all active signals and special care will be needed during layout to prevent the physical design from increasing such problems. Fortunately, the techniques used to reduce RFI are good design practices and, apart from a forced renewed interest in electromagnetic design theory, this should pose no problem.

The 1990s may see a greater acceptance of plastic parts in rugged conditions. The first automotive processors used ceramic parts to meet the environmental needs, particularly temperature and humidity. Today, plastic packaging technology has greatly improved so that plastic-encapsulated parts are now used in these applications. With the emphasis of cost reduction within the military market, it is envisaged that plastic packages may be approved in preference to ceramic.

Processor technology

Microprocessors will use higher densities and faster speeds in two ways. The first will be to provide the fastest performance possible and the second will be to provide the highest integration possible. The state-of-the-art performance processor in 1995 will probably have over 15 million transistors and run at over 200 MHz. It is likely that this type of machine will execute multiple instructions per clock, producing 2000 MIPS. This scenario is not too far away – the development of a 1000 MIPS M88000 processor has already been announced by Dolphin Technology and Motorola. Built using bipolar Emitter Coupled Logic running at 125 MHz, this processor has eight execution units and is capable of running eight instructions per machine clock. The first machines should appear in 1992.

At the other end of the scale, a 15 million transistor processor could integrate a complete desk top computer, or provide a system with 75 MC68020 processors on it. It has even been suggested that a mixture of processors could be integrated to run different instruction sets! Integrated processors, like the M68300 family that has recently appeared, are only the beginning.

Memory technology

The industry's memory technology plans (Figure 9.9) indicate an exponential growth in memory size with a density doubling about every three years. DRAM chips tend to have a ten-year design phase from initial process research through to peak demand. The recent peak demand for the

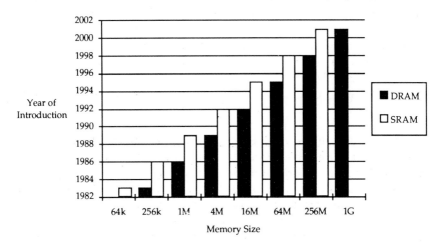

Figure 9.9 *Memory technology predictions*

64 Kbit and 256 Kbit dynamic memory came from work that was started about ten years ago. DRAM memory life cycle falls into three stages. The first involves the development of the technology needed to fabricate the devices and to provide the wafer steppers and associated equipment needed to produce the designs on a large scale. The next stage introduces the parts and starts to ramp up production which normally overlaps with the peak demand and subsequent decline of the preceding generations. This process is repeated throughout the generations. Static RAM follows a similar trend, although the memory densities are a factor of four smaller. Currently, 4 Mbit DRAMs and 1 Mbit SRAMs are being sampled. The reduction in densities is explained by the increased number of transistors needed to build the cell – a DRAM cell uses one transistor while a SRAM cell uses four to six.

The effect of further reductions in the cost per bit is likely to cause more ripples within the computer and processor world. The most obvious is the introduction of solid-state discs. Although this is happening today through the use of wafer scale integration, the cost reductions offered by having 32 Mbytes of RAM on a single chip will make this technology extremely accessible.

Other implications for system designers are equally interesting. Software designers are renowned for underestimating the amount of memory needed for software applications. With the growing trend of more user-friendly interfaces and their insatiable demand for memory, tomorrow's personal computers will use many times the amount of memory compared with today's. Newer technologies, like digital audio, will also benefit. With 1 Gigabit of memory, it would be possible to store sufficient 16-bit words to play over 23 minutes of audio with compact disc quality! The data compression techniques provided by the new generations of processors could easily extend this playtime to hours. The days of revolving media, like records and tape cassettes, may be numbered. Again, the science fiction dream of a solid-state audio cartridge is fast approaching reality.

Science fiction or not?

For many, this glimpse into the future may appear to be too fantastic to believe. However, if the test of hindsight is applied to the last ten years, the developments seen in the eighties also appear as far fetched. Who would have predicted in 1980 that ten years later, most homes would have a computer complete with graphics and large amounts of memory and storage, that most cars would have more computing power in their ignition and control systems than a 1980 mini computer could offer and that credit cards could act as complete data banks? Who would have predicted that the cost of an MC68000 16/32-bit processor would diminish to only 1% of its introductory cost? Some of the predictions are already coming true.

The Motorola-TRW announcement of their CPU-AX superchip, containing over four million transistors and calculating over 200 million floating-point operations a second, reads like a science fiction novel. The die is 1.5 in square and fits into a package 2.1 in square and weighing 42 grams. The CMOS chip uses 0.5 μm technology and dissipates over 17 watts. The system consists of about 146 separate units, but only 64 need to function for it to perform correctly. Through a companion chip, the system can reconfigure itself and repair any faults that may occur during its fabrication or lifetime, providing this system minimum is maintained. The chip is the fruit of a ten-year-old VHSIC (Very High Scale Integrated Circuit) program sponsored by the American Military.

The signs are there to indicate that the future will be even more exciting than what has happened in the past.

10 The changing design cycle

It is usual for a microprocessor system to be designed to meet commercial goals rather than for academic reasons, therefore part of the processor selection procedure has to take into account economic factors as well as engineering ones. The harsh realities of life dictate that the majority of processor designs must meet the required specification and be completed on time to stand any chance of commercial success. It is commercial success that pays everybody's wages and provides the resources for the next development.

The shortening design cycle

Perhaps the biggest change to the actual design process within recent years has been the shortening of both development cycle and product life, as shown in Figure 10.1. In 1984, the average microprocessor development took about two years from concept to preproduction. The product had a life of about three years before any major updating would be required. Today, the same development takes about six months, product life is about 18 months, with two or three mid-life upgrades built in! This contraction is caused essentially by one reason, hitting a market window, although there are several factors that are continuing to fuel these changes.

The importance of getting the product to market at the right time is as great today as it has ever been. Competition within the world marketplace has increased product leap-frogging which, in turn, has caused product life reduction. The rapid introduction of new models to make competitive products obsolete, or appear to be, is an extremely potent commercial weapon. The fuel for these rapid developments is the pushdown effect (Figure 10.2), caused by exponentially expanding silicon technology. The pushdown effect refers to two characteristics of silicon technology. The first is that as new processors appear, the perceived performance of existing products goes down. This does not mean that an 8 MHz MC68000 is

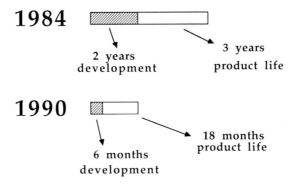

Figure 10.1 *Design cycles*

executing less instructions today than ten years ago, only that the expectations of a high-performance processor in 1979 were met by a MC68000, while today an MC68040 is needed. Coupled with this are the unbelievable cost reductions that come with silicon technology. Comparing the cost of a digital watch in 1979 and today is an excellent example. For an example of this effect on processors, the MC68000 now costs only 1% of its introductory price and, in many cases, is now cheaper than 8-bit processors.

The follow-on effect is that products can be almost obsolete as soon as they appear and that they have to be either continually enhanced to remain in the high-performance perception, or cost reduced to enter higher-volume alternative markets. All this leads to the ever-contracting design cycle.

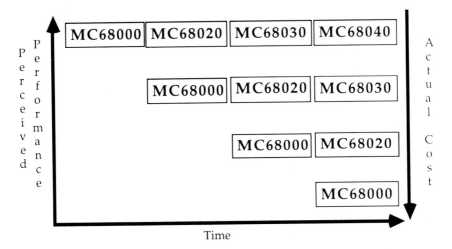

Figure 10.2 *The pushdown effect*

These factors now have to be taken into account and they can pose considerable challenges to a design team. A combination of approaches may be needed. One is to take the new processors as soon as possible and continue to be on that leading edge of technology, thus being able to charge a premium for the product. A second may be to take a leading edge product but continue to cost reduce it so its growth comes from higher volume sales. The PC clone market is a good example of this tactic. A third could combine the two ideas so a particular aspect of the design can be provided on several different platforms, depending on price/performance, etc. Whatever tactics are chosen, it is now almost mandatory to include provisions for these mid-life updates within the original design.

The double-edged sword of technology

For many projects, there will be a time when the double-edged sword of technology[1] will have to be grasped. It is relevant to any design and refers usually to the time when a new technology or production method has to be developed or implemented. The learning curve involved is often underestimated, leading to the problems associated normally with new products. Many companies have policies of waiting for 12–24 months after a product is available before using it. As a result, the learning curve and its associated risk is greatly reduced, but so is any competitive advantage. Leading-edge technology can be a tremendous help but it is equally good at cutting down to size. When successful, as SUN Microsystems found, the rewards are fabulous and quick. When not, the disaster can be equally as swift and final. It is frequently important to gain early access to leading-edge technology but the flipside of such access may be frequent design changes, the joy of being first (but if you have a problem, who do you ask for help?), delays, working without adequate documentation, development tools, etc. This type of environment is very exciting but it is really for the brave and stout-hearted!

For many, the way to solve the dilemma of getting access without the risk is through buying boards or complete systems rather than individual VLSI components. In the past, the argument of Make v. Buy has usually been based on economics, but within the framework of the changing design cycle, it has many other considerations.

Make v. Buy

The economic argument is very simple. With low production runs, the most economic solution involves using a product at its highest integration

---

[1] A phrase I first heard from Tim Coombs at Motorola.

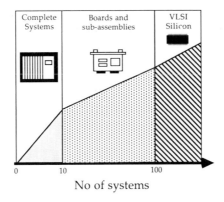

Figure 10.3 *Make v. buy*

level. Figure 10.3 shows a graphical representation of this statement with reference to microprocessor systems. The crossover numbers on the bottom axis are approximations and depend ultimately on the individual situation. For runs of ten systems or less, it is generally better to buy in the complete system and simply add to it. For runs of 11–100 systems, it is more economic to buy in boards and subassemblies and integrate the system. Higher than this, and it is better to design from scratch, buy in the silicon components and build everything.

The first statement that must be made, is that the crossover points are extremely woolly. They involve balancing the costs of increased work against the combined component savings and this can frequently change both from situation to situation and with time. This argument does not take into account other factors which change on moving from one design mode to another.

Design flexibility

Using systems for low production runs has some drawbacks. The design will have compromised the functional need for using an off-the-shelf product. This has several potential follow-ons. The first is that the system may need modifications which could cost more than the savings. The second concerns system architecture. An off-the-shelf system may have all the functionality needed (i.e. processor, memory, peripherals, etc.) but the overall system architecture may not be exactly suitable for the application. A third potential problem concerns future enhancements or cost reductions. Using a proprietary end user system may restrict such upgrades and thus cause difficulties later. It may not be possible to obtain the system with unused functions removed. At this point, the solution may be to move to a board solution.

Building a system using an industry standard bus, like VMEbus or Multibus II, has become an extremely common solution and has led to many hundreds of suppliers providing an extremely wide range of products. This has allowed many companies to buy a core system, develop any specialized boards and integrate the complete system. By using such buses, upgrades are relatively simple and only involve board swaps. The resultant design is more closely matched to needs, although some trade-offs at a lower level may still have to be made. The downside is increased costs and a potentially longer design cycle – but for many, this is a good way of building or developing a product.

If the design has special architectural or build needs, such as a special multiprocessing architecture or military approval, the compromises needed to be able to take advantage of boards or systems may not be acceptable. The only solution is to build the system from scratch. The costs of doing so should not be underestimated and many prototype systems have not seen the light of day because of increased workload. Where the risk is seen as high, it may be better to compromise the design slightly and use bought in subassemblies to enable a prototype to be built. In some cases, this approach has enabled companies to meet early commitments when the full custom system has suffered from delays.

Manufacturing costs

With the move from a system through boards to silicon, manufacturing costs increase dramatically. These costs include the increased development times, inventory costs, capital equipment, etc. and should not be underestimated! Unfortunately, there is often a passionate plea from engineers to design a whole system, rather than concentrating on building the special functions and buying in the more standard parts, such as memory and processor boards. There are cases when manufacturing from silicon is viable for small production runs. The most obvious is when the required function is simply not available off the shelf and has to be built. However, do not be lulled into adopting the approach of 'building a board' and justifying its cost by selling it as an off-the-shelf product; this rarely works. With a VMEbus-based product, there are over 300 vendors supplying product and this competitive market is offered nearly every function needed. To sell a product successfully into this type of environment requires additional software support, service support, etc., which increases the costs or reduces profit margins. In addition, the marketing required is totally different and is more like selling a commodity rather than high technology.

Military approval is another case where the goal of high reliability overrides the normal economic arguments. Even here, this is not as clear cut as it used to be. Many military systems now use commercial product within a sealed environmental chamber so that costs can be reduced but the operational specification is not. With the recent advent of fixed-price contracts, this approach is becoming more common.

The availability of manufacturing facilities and the need to keep them fully loaded is another exception. As system complexity increases, designs are frequently being licensed allowing boards to be used for prototyping but basing the production runs on component costs. The license deal removes the design and development phases.

Quality

Quality has become paramount in recent years and, again, achievable levels can depend on how the product has been engineered. With systems, reliability is dictated by the product quality provided by the system supplier. If the product is bad, it does not matter how good the added value is, the overall system will be deemed as unreliable and unacceptable. The same comment applies to board products; however, system integration and testing are under control and can allow better screening to improve quality, albeit at a cost. At component level, acceptance testing is expensive, requiring sophisticated testers and test program development. Many users are reducing their supplier base to those whose quality is such that the product can be shipped straight to the production line without interim testing.

Upgrading

The opening paragraphs of this chapter described how today's product life was often about 18 months, with two or three mid-life upgrades to ensure the length. It is important to design these upgrades into the system specification from day one. With systems, the upgrade policy is simple to implement – simply go and buy the latest 'go faster' version and transfer the system software and special hardware over. This is a relatively painless process but it does depend on two factors – first, the compatibility between the systems and second, any hardware dependency within the application software. The most common culprits are software loops, which no longer work due to increased processor performance, and the failure to use defined procedures to access physical I/O. It is advisable when designing a system to add an upgrade check to the approval process. It is a good rule to assume nothing or alternatively, document all assumptions and their implications.

The same scenario is true for board designs. Different-speed processor boards can often be interchanged to offer the appropriate performance as needed. However, boards offer greater flexibility and therefore there is an added risk of the production configuration being the one which works on paper but does not work in reality. These problems often occur when functions are added at the same time as performance is upgraded. An onboard Ethernet controller may not be compatible with its separate predecessor or an onboard disc controller may not be able to use existing disc drives that were compatible with the previous discrete controller. These implications can often incur additional costs within the rest of the system which cancel out the advantages of changing in the first place. To ensure these problems do not appear in the field, sufficient resources must be allocated to test any new configurations. Again, the 'How will this affect an upgrade?' test is invaluable.

For silicon designs, the cost of making an unplanned change involving a modification to the printed circuit board or test programs can be very large indeed and should therefore be avoided. Upgrades for discrete designs are fairly limited in scope, compared with board and systems, and invariably have to be catered for at the design inception. Typical techniques include designing the system to support several different processor speeds, memory sizes and speeds and the provision of an expansion port to allow more functionality. Upgrades then become a simple matter of adding different or extra components.

Product differentiation

The question of product differentiation is quite esoteric and concerned primarily with how different a product is and how it stands within a marketplace. Within the electronics industry, there is a large amount of badge engineering where systems are purchased from a supplier by many different companies, who then change the front badge and re-sell the system. In this case, product differentiation is not the product itself – it is the same from each supplier – but the added value, in terms of service backup, application software, networking or just the brand name! When a prospective client can see that the system (well, the hardware anyway) is the XYZ Desktop available from any discount store, it is difficult to prevent incorrect comparisons to be made. The key is to justify the extra cost by the added value, so objections like, 'Why should I pay five times for the system for a bit of software?' can be countered.

With boards, there is a little more that can be done to differentiate it from other versions of it. Making drastic changes to the case, etc. is expensive and more indicative of adopting the board or sub-assembly approach. There is more scope to actually changing the physical appearance and differentiation. Corporate colours and footprints can be adopted to emphasize its presence within an integrated range of products. Although the product may be compatible functionally with the XYZ Desktop, it is harder to make the comparisons and thus raise objections.

With a discrete design, the choices concerning appearance, performance and functionality are not restrained. The product differentiation is at its greatest.

Service and backup

Despite the best efforts of designers, production and quality staff, products do occasionally fail or require regular maintenance. Often a neglected part of the equation, service and backup need to be budgeted for. For systems, the original manufacturer's service organization can be used to provide the backbone of the service, with only hardware specials and software to be catered for. This can save a lot of money and be a major reason for adopting a system solution for even high run rates. The types of services offered are usually based on a 24-hour, on-site repair scheme.

With boards, more responsibility must be taken by the end manufacturer. Board manufacturers often offer a 24-hour replacement by post or courier service, which allows the end manufacturer to maintain a small inventory of spares and provide a higher level of service. This obviously increases costs. With a discrete system, the design and implementation are in the hands of the end manufacturer, therefore the entire service costs are his responsibility.

Production technology

The production tools needed range from screwdrivers for a system implementation, to a full production line with PCB design facilities, etc. The costs can be quite prohibitive and, in reality, much use is made of sub-contractors for PCB manufacture, board stuffing and testing. However, the implicit costs of using certain types of packaging or achieving certain component densities are still there, irrelevant of in house or outside manufacturing.

The problem concerns the ever-increasing trend of more pins within smaller areas running at faster speeds. The first 8-bit micros had a state-of-the-art pin count of about 40 pins in a dual in-line package based on a 0.6 in pitch. The M68000 went up to 64 pins in a dual in-line package which occupied about three square inches. To many, it was known affectionately as a caterpillar! The same device is now available in a surface-mount FN package which is less than 0.75 square inches in area. The MC68020 came out as a large pin grid array package with 114 pins and, for many PCB designers, was a nightmare come true. It is now accepted as a standard package, with the nightmare being an MC68030 surface-mount package that has 132 leads on a 0.025 in pitch! What is important to remember is that the layout tools have improved, so that while the new packages can present a challenge, they are still within the current technology. The decision has then to be made whether this challenge is accepted or deferred until later, when implementation is easier.

The same comments are true for PCB production. A four-layer board with two power and two signal planes was once state of the art. Fourteen layer boards are now commonplace, with six power planes and eight signal planes. Track widths have reduced so that two tracks can be laid between adjacent pins. This type of technology is needed to make the large numbers of connections present in a modern high-density board. Coupled with this need for more connections is the increase in processor clocks, which forces more care to be taken to prevent transmission-line effects from distorting previously clean edges.

The pushdown effect previously described for processors also holds true for production technology.

Simulation v. emulation

The methods used to develop and debug systems within the design cycle have also had to change to meet the new requirements. The in-circuit emulator has been the usual method used for debugging microprocessor systems. It gives basic facilities for software testing, hardware debugging and system integration, by providing a window into the system via the processor. Its ability to simulate a simple target (i.e. a processor with memory) has allowed software to be developed and tested in parallel with the hardware. The target hardware was then debugged using the emulator, to ensure that the basic functions worked before the task of total system integration was attempted.

However, emulators are not the perfect replacements for microprocessor silicon. The logic needed to intercept processor signals, substitute functions and drive other signals causes slight timing differences. These differences are further aggravated by the delays caused in moving signals up and down the cable connecting the probe between the target and the emulator. With processor pin counts fast approaching the 200-pin barrier and beyond (resulting in large probes), the target board must often be laid out to accommodate the emulator rather than the processor! Surface-mount packages and the ever-decreasing pin width are further obstacles to the use of emulators.

As systems have become more complex, the associated problems have required logic analyser functions to provide a wider picture than that of the processor environment. To solve these problems, data must be provided by the processor and other functions, to give an overall view. This data often needs further qualification to isolate the critical events from the background. With the promise of faster and more powerful processors, how are such systems going to be developed? The answer is to provide better tools earlier in the design cycle. The emulator has traditionally been used to debug hardware, identify any prototyping problems and eventually provide a stable hardware target. With the high cost of complex multilayer circuit boards, the cost of any modification is high. This draws a parallel with ASIC development – in this environment, mistakes cannot be solved simply by the addition of blue wires – the designer has to get it right. With ASIC design, the key to achieving this is the right simulation tools.

Motorola realized that the new generation of processors, like the M88000 family, was going to offer single-cycle performances with fast clocks (20–33 MHz) where emulation would be virtually impossible to use. Designers are already using the fastest logic and keeping PCB track lengths to a minimum to reduce transmission-line effects and delays. With their inherent timing differences, emulators are not suitable. The problems with noise and crosstalk effectively prevent wirewrapping, and it has become apparent that many customers were going straight to PCB for prototyping. The multilayer boards involved to achieve the density and noise immunity are expensive and it was therefore essential to get the design right first time. The solution was simple – take the ASIC example and develop simulation tools to allow both the hardware and software to be simulated and tested early in the design.

The first tool was a software simulator which could allow cross compiled code to be tested and debugged on a basic system and so allowed software development in parallel with the target design. The M88000 simulator provides symbolic level debugging, single stepping, register and memory display and modification, breakpoints, etc. It has been integrated with the Greenhills compilers by Oasys and is available from Real Time Products. To help speed this development, Motorola recently placed a debug monitor into the public domain for both the M68000 and M88000 processor families. The debugger, FBUG, is written in 'C' and can easily be configured for any system.

A second set of simulation tools was developed in conjunction with Logic Automation. This provides hardware models for Motorola's processors and peripherals and allows complete target systems to be designed and simulated. System timings can be checked to identify any errors. Smartmodel simulations allow software to be executed on the system and can be used to integrate software on to the target and test it. The beauty of this technique is that the system can be tested as a whole and modified without the expense of new prototypes, reworking, etc. New design ideas can be tested on a 'what if' basis. The emphasis is on solving problems when modifications are inexpensive to carry out, i.e. early in the design cycle.

Once simulated, the basic target board can be built and the full software tested. Compared with previous generations, today's systems are more complex and often feature multiprocessors with cache memory systems, etc. Many of the problems that now occur are subsystem interactions, where either communication or synchronization has failed. Identifying such problems with only an emulator is like looking at a room via a keyhole. It provides a view into the system but one cannot see everything or be sure that something isn't lurking out of sight. In an effort to widen this

Figure 10.4   *A Gould CLAS4000 logic analyser timing display*

view, many emulators now provide basic logic analysis support or, in the case of the MC68302 ADS, special decoded processor signals for logic analysers. Simple analysers have their disadvantages – whilst they can unobtrusively collect vast quantities of data, they often cannot display it in a readily accessible form, such as op codes.

The solution is to provide the new generation of analysers with a disassembly capability and sophisticated event qualification, such as those from Gould, Hewlett Packard and Tektronix (Figures 10.4 and 10.5). These analysers provide very large numbers of channels, essential for a processor with 4×32-bit wide ports, which can disassemble data streams either side of the MC88200 cache memory management unit. In this way,

File Edit Control Transfer Windows Options

State [LA 1−Last]

C1 = 0   C2 = 25   C2−C1 = 0025 samples Previous   Next

C	Line	Address	Data	Status		C	Line	Address	Data	Status
C1	0000	F5F4	F7F6	F9F8			0037	3938	3B3A	3D3C
	0001	E9E8	EBEA	EDEC			0038	2D2C	2F2E	3130
	0002	DDDC	DFDE	E1E0			0039	2120	2322	2524
	0003	D1D0	D3D2	D5D4			0040	1514	1716	1918
	0004	C5C4	C7C6	C9C8			0041	0908	0B0A	0D0C
	0005	B9B8	BBBA	BDBC			0042	FDFC	FFFE	0100
	0006	ADAC	AFAE	B1B0			0043	F1F0	F3F2	F5F4
	0007	A1A0	A3A2	A5A4			0044	E5E4	E7E6	E9E8
	0008	9594	9796	9998			0045	D9D8	DBDA	DDDC
	0009	8988	8B8A	8D8C			0046	CDCC	CFCE	D1D0
	0010	7D7C	7F7E	8180			0047	C1C0	C3C2	C5C4
	0011	7170	7372	7574			0048	B5B4	B7B6	B9B8
	0012	6564	6766	6968			0049	A9A8	ABAA	ADAC
	0013	5958	5B5A	5D5C			0050	9D9C	9F9E	A1A0
	0014	4D4C	4F4E	5150			0051	9190	9392	9594
	0015	4140	4342	4544			0052	8584	8786	8988
	0016	3534	3736	3938			0053	7978	7B7A	7D7C
	0017	2928	2B2A	2D2C			0054	6D6C	6F6E	7170
	0018	1D1C	1F1E	2120			0055	6160	6362	6564
	0019	1110	1312	1514			0056	5554	5756	5958
	0020	0504	0706	0908			0057	4948	4B4A	4D4C
	0021	F9F8	FBFA	FDFC			0058	3D3C	3F3E	4140
	0022	EDEC	EFEE	F1F0			0059	3130	3332	3534
	0023	E1E0	E3E2	E5E4			0060	2524	2726	2928
	0024	D5D4	D7D6	D9D8			0061	1918	1B1A	1D1C
C2	0025	C9C8	CBCA	CDCC			0062	0D0C	0F0E	1110
	0026	BDBC	BFBE	C1C0			0063	0100	0302	0504
	0027	B1B0	B3B2	B5B4			0064	F5F4	F7F6	F9F8
	0028	A5A4	A7A6	A9A8			0065	E9E8	EBEA	EDEC
	0029	9998	9B9A	9D9C			0066	DDDC	DFDE	E1E0
	0030	8D8C	8F8E	9190			0067	D1D0	D3D2	D5D4
	0031	8180	8382	8584			0068	C5C4	C7C6	C9C8
	0032	7574	7776	7978			0069	B9B8	BBBA	BDBC
	0033	6968	6B6A	6D6C			0070	ADAC	AFAE	B1B0
	0034	5D5C	5F5E	6160			0071	A1A0	A3A2	A5A4
	0035	5150	5352	5554			0072	9594	9796	9998
	0036	4544	4746	4948			0073	8988	8B8A	8D8C

Figure 10.5 *A Gould CLAS4000 logic analyser hexadecimal decoded display*

both logical and physical bus signals can be combined with other data signals to provide the data base for further event qualification. This can be so powerful that it is easy to isolate even erratic random failures and trace the before and after status. The general-purpose nature of this instrumentation is another benefit – it can support a wide range of processors and will analyse data from any system. To switch from M68000 to M88000 disassembly is often a single software module change.

These techniques are not the abrupt end of the emulator; for slower speeds and less complex designs, it can still provide an efficient debugging environment. Both the recently announced Motorola MC68332 and MC68302 have in-circuit emulation tools and, as emulation technology improves, undoubtedly systems will appear for faster processors. However, technology is increasing exponentially and observers are predicting that 200 MHz processors with 512 + connections and with the chip bonded directly to a substrate will be here before the turn of the century. Only time will tell whether emulation or simulation techniques will have kept pace.

11   The next generations

Enter the MC68040

The MC68040 is the latest member of the MC68000 CISC processor family. Fabricated in 0.8 μm HCMOS technology and using 1.2 million transistor sites, it incorporates separate integer and floating-point units, giving sustained performances of 20 integer MIPS and 3.5 double precision Linpack MFLOPS, dual 4 Kbyte instruction and data caches, dual memory management units and an extremely sophisticated bus interface unit. The block diagram in Figure 11.1 shows how the processor is partitioned into several separate functional units which can all execute concurrently. It features a full Harvard architecture internally and is remarkably similar, at the block level, to the M88000 RISC processor.

Revolutionary rather than evolutionary, the design takes the ideas of overlapping instruction execution and pipelining to a new level for CISC processors. The floating-point and integer execution units work in parallel with the onchip caches and memory management to increase overlapping so that many instructions are executed in a single cycle, so giving the processor its performance. Examination of the pinout (Figure 11.2) reveals a large number of new signals. One major difference with the MC68040 is its high drive capability – it can be configured on reset to provide drive currents of either 5 or 55 mA per bus or control pin. This removes the need for external buffers, reducing chip count and the associated propagation delays, which often inflict a high speed design.

The 32-bit address and 32-bit data buses are similar to their predecessors, although the signals can be optionally tied together to form a single, 32-bit multiplexed data/address bus. The User Programmable Attributes, UPA0 and UPA1, are driven according to the setting of two bits within each page descriptor. They are used by the onboard memory management units to enable the MC68040 Bus Snooping protocols and also to give additional

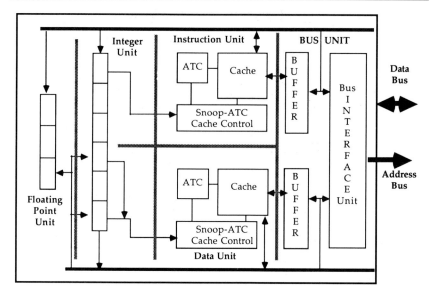

Figure 11.1 *The MC68040 block diagram*

address bits and provide software control for external caches and other such functions.

The two size pins, SIZ0 and SIZ1, no longer indicate the number of remaining bytes left to be transferred as they did on the MC68020 and MC68030, but are used to generate byte enables for memory ports. They now indicate the size of the current transfer. Dynamic bus sizing is supported via external hardware, if required. Misaligned accesses are supported by splitting a transfer into a series of aligned accesses of differing sizes. The transfer type signals, TT1 and TT2, indicate the type of transfer taking place and the three Transfer Modifier pins, TM0–TM2, provide further information. These five pins together effectively replace the three function code pins. The TLN0 and TLN1 pins indicate the current longword number within a burst fill access.

The synchronous bus is controlled by the Master and Slave transfer control signals. Transfer Start (TS★) indicates a valid address on the bus, while the Transfer in Progress (TIP★) signal is asserted during all external bus cycles and can be used to power up/down external memory to conserve power in portable applications. These two Master signals are complemented by the slave signals – Transfer Acknowledge (TA★) successfully terminates the bus cycle, while Transfer Error Acknowledge (TEA★) terminates the cycle and the burst fill as a result of an error. If both these signals are asserted on the first access of the burst, the cycle is terminated and immediately re-run. On the 2nd, 3rd and 4th accesses, a retry attempt is not

Figure 11.2   *The MC68040 pinout*

allowed and the processor simply assumes that an error has occurred and terminates the burst as normal.

The processor can be configured to use a different signal, Data Latch Enable (DLE) to latch read data instead of the rising edge of the BCLK clock. The internal caches and memory management units can be disabled via the CDIS★ and MDIS★ pins respectively. The four processor status signals, PST0–PST3, provide information on exactly what the processor is doing internally (Figure 11.3). This data can identify supervisor and user activities and usually bears little relationship to the current bus cycle. This is provided for instrumentation support.

JTAG testing is supported via the TEST signals. This allows bit patterns to be output from the device under controlled conditions to test peripherals, etc., without having to isolate the processor. There are two clock signals, PCLK and BCLK; the processor clock, PCLK, runs at twice the speed of the bus clock, BCLK, allowing the internal nodes and execution units to run at twice the speed. The 25 MHz MC68040 actually executes internally at 50 MHz.

<u>PST0-3 TABLE</u>

PST3-0	INTERNAL STATUS
0000	User start/continue current instruction.
0001	User end current instruction.
0010	User branch taken and end current
0011	User branch not taken and end current.
0100	User table search.
0101	Halted state (double-bus fault)
0110	Reserved
0111	Reserved
1000	Supervisor start/continue current instruction.
1001	Supervisor end current instruction
1010	Supervisor branch taken and end current.
1011	Supervisor branch not taken and end current.
1100	Supervisor table search
1101	Stopped state (supervisor instruction).
1110	RTS executed.
1111	Exception stacking

Figure 11.3   *The PST signal meanings*

The instruction execution unit

The instruction execution unit consists of a six-stage pipeline which sequentially fetches an instruction, decodes it, calculates the effective address, fetches an address operands, executes the instruction and finally writes back the results. To prevent pipeline stalling, an internal Harvard architecture is used to allow simultaneous instruction and operand fetches. It has been optimized for many instructions and addressing modes, so that single-cycle execution can be achieved. The early pipeline stages are effectively duplicated to allow both paths of a branch instruction to be processed until the path decision is taken, which removes pipeline stalls and the subsequent performance degradation. While integer instructions are being executed, the floating-point unit is free to execute floating-point instructions.

The programming model, Figure 11.4, is essentially the same as that of the MC68030, although only two bits are used in the CACR register to enable or disable either of the two onchip caches.

The floating-point execution unit

The MC68040 has its own floating-point unit on chip offering >3.5 MFlops performance. It provides hardware support for the four arithmetic functions and executes the other transcendental functions via a software emulation package. This combination provides support for the

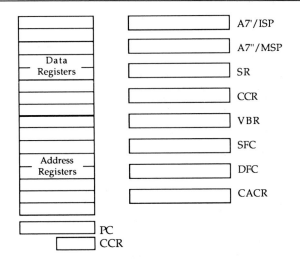

Figure 11.4   *The MC68040 integer unit programming model*

existing MC68881/882 floating point coprocessor instruction sets and the
performance improvements are shown in Figure 11.5.

Memory management

The MC68040 has two memory management units, one allocated for data
and the other for instructions. The MMUs are a subset of the MC68030
MMU and are extremely simple to program and control. Two root pointers
are supported, one each for user and supervisor use. Page sizes of either 4 or
8 Kbytes are selected by bits within the translation control register and are
supported via a fixed three-level set of table descriptors. To prevent
external table walking, each MMU has a 64-entry, 4-way set associative
Address Translation Cache which contains the most recently accessed page
descriptors. The MC68030 concept of transparent windows has been
utilized, with four transparent windows being shared between the two
MMUs to allow memory areas to be mapped without using the ATCs.

Instruction and data caches

To keep instructions and data flowing into the execution units, the
MC68040 has two, four-way set associative physical caches, each 4 Kbytes
in size. One cache is dedicated to instructions, the other to data. The caches
provide the single-cycle access necessary to maintain the single-cycle
execution within the integer and floating-point unit pipelines.

   The caches are organized as four sets, each with 64 lines per set and a line
size of 16 bytes. Each line has a valid bit and is divided into four longwords,

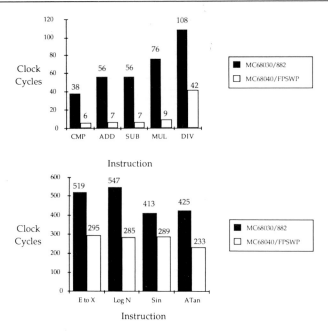

Figure 11.5 *MC68040 FPU instruction timings*

each with a 'dirty' bit to indicate whether the data has been modified. The cache is on the physical side of the onchip memory management units and thus does not need flushing on a context switch. This is important to maintain performance. Each cache is coupled with its associated MMU so that ATC lookups are performed in parallel with cache lookups and there is no performance delay. If there is a data miss and a line must be replaced, any dirty data is written out to main memory and the replacement line brought in as a burst fill of a whole cache line. This is a development of the synchronous burst memory interface, which appeared on the MC68030 and uses page mode memory to access memory on cycles 2, 3 and 4 on successive cycles, although the first access may incur wait states. The caches support four main coherency schemes:

- cacheable with data writethrough
- cacheable with copy back
- non-cacheable
- special access

Selecting 'Cacheable with writethrough' via a page descriptor forces all data writes through to main memory, thus enforcing data coherency, i.e. cache and memory data are identical. This couples the processor un-necessarily to slow memory and so the copyback scheme is also supported.

Here, cache data is updated but the main memory is not immediately written to, which reduces the number of external memory accesses and associated delays. Cache data is marked as dirty, using a tag bit, and is written out only as the result of a cache flush or if it is to be replaced. To ensure data coherency, bus snooping is supported which monitors the external bus to detect any access to an address where the main memory data is stale.

Non-cacheable is straightforward and is used to prevent data being cached as would be needed when accessing I/O, for example. Special accesses, such as table walks, exception stack frame building and the new MOVE16 instruction which moves 16 bytes anywhere within the memory space, are not cached.

The bus interface unit

The key to maintaining the internal execution units is to provide extremely fast accesses to memory so that the internal caches can be updated quickly and any delays through to main memory are kept as short as possible. The basic interface uses a 32-bit data and address bus which can be either multiplexed or non-multiplexed as required. The interface is synchronous but allows the inclusion of wait states, enabling it to communicate to different-speed peripherals or memory. It uses a burst fill interface, similar to that of the MC68030, Figure 11.6, where the first access takes a minimum of two cycles and the remaining three are single cycle. The processor always assumes that the external ports are 32-bit, aligned and capable of supporting burst filling. Where this is not possible, as with a peripheral, burst filling can be inhibited by asserting the TBI★ signal during the first access. Similarly, asserting the TCI★ signal inhibits internal data caching.

The BIU is intelligent enough not to discard valid cache lines until the replacement line has been fetched completely from memory. This is achieved by flushing the line into a buffer, performing the external access and then moving the cache line into the cache RAM. If an error occurs during the external fetch, the old line is reinstated into the cache. If the error occurs while fetching data needed by the execution units, a full bus error exception is taken. If the error happens during the remainder of the burst fill and the data is not needed, the good data from the earlier cycles is taken and the bus error exception deferred. In practice, data is not cached, ensuring that it is always fetched again from external memory. If the error then occurs, the exception is taken. This effectively provides an additional automatic retry mechanism to the available hardware retry. In addition, the BIU does not use burst fills for accesses that do not allocate data cache on a read miss such as table searches, vector fetches, exception unstacking and writing a single dirty long word from a cache line. In these cases, it performs a single byte, word, or longword transfer.

Figure 11.6   *A typical MC68040 burst fill access*

The bus cycle commences by the MC68040 issuing a bus request, BR★, waiting for bus grant, BG★ to be asserted and bus busy, BB★ to be negated, before claiming ownership of the bus. Unlike its predecessors, the MC68040 does not automatically have the highest priority within any system. The priority and arbitration scheme is user defined and can have any implementation.

Associated with the arbitration mechanism is the locked cycle support for indivisible cycles. The LOCK★ signal indicates an indivisible bus cycle to the arbiter so it can enforce the locked sequence. The LOCKE★ signal is issued on the last transfer of any locked sequence, allowing bus arbitration to overlap the last transfer and indicating when to remove the BG★ signal without breaking a locked transfer. The processor supports implicit bus ownership where the arbiter asserts BG★ to the processor but neither it nor another processor needs it. In this case, the processor implicitly owns the bus and drives the address bus and transfer attributes with undefined values.

Exception handling

The MC68040 uses the standard M68000 seven-level external interrupt mechanism with both autovectored and vector number exceptions. Hardware support is via the IPL0–2★ with the AVEC★ and IPEND★ signals. The Supervisor/User model is maintained to handle these and other exceptions, although the processor exception model is different. Five-stack frame formats are used for the different exceptions. The MC68040 uses an instruction restart exception model to handle bus transfer errors – sufficient information is stored in the 30-word stack frame to allow safe system continuation. This has several advantages, in that it reduces the exception stackframe size needed to store the internal contents and allows software and, therefore, the system designer, to decide how the system will handle such interruptions to normal processing. It is up to the exception handler to decide whether outstanding memory accesses are to be completed, for example.

Bus snooping

The Bus Snooping protocol used on the MC68040 is different from that of the M88000 by virtue of how the stale data is updated. With the M88000, the attempted access is snooped, aborted, the main memory updated and the original access automatically restarted. With the MC68040, the access is snooped but the processor decides whether to act as the memory block or allow the memory to be enabled. There are two snoop control pins, SC0★ and SC1★, which control exactly how the processor responds, as shown in Figure 11.7. Typically, these are connected to the user attribute pins,

SC1	SC0	READ ACCESS	WRITE ACCESS
0	0	inhibit snooping	inhibit snooping
0	1	supply dirty data and leave dirty	sink byte/word long-word data
1	0	supply dirty data and mark line invalid	invalidate line
1	1	reserved snoop inhibited	reserved snoop inhibited

Figure 11.7 *The MC68040 bus snooping*

allowing software to control which mechanism to use via the page descriptors. The MI★ output allows the processor to inhibit the external memory so it can act as memory and supply or accept the correct data as determined by the SC0–1★ coding. Snooping can be used with copyback or writethrough modes, depending on the number of external masters and their caching capabilities.

The MC68040, with its high performance and integration, now offers CISC users the power previously only available from RISC – coupled with the World's largest base of 32-bit software. For many workstation and other power-hungry applications, this will be an irresistible combination.

An alternative direction: system integration

For many applications, the promise of higher performance does not, in itself, satisfy the design needs. A design may need low chip counts and small packaging instead. Fortunately, the silicon technology which has increased clock speeds and device density to provide today's high-performance processors can equally be used to integrate a distributed processor system on to one chip with its reduced chip count and costs.

The MC68300 family

This family of integrated MC68000 processors bridges the gap between 8-bit microcontrollers and the 16/32-bit M68000 families. The idea was simple – take an MC68000 family processor core, add all the interface logic needed for chip select, some on chip memory and some intelligent peripherals controlled by another dedicated processor. This type of configuration is almost identical to that of an MC68HC11 MCU, except that processing power is greatly increased. Two members of the family are currently available, with many more to come.

The first part, the MC68332, was developed for General Motors to satisfy its automotive requirements. The invasion of the microprocessor into this industry has been enormous in recent years. Microprocessors now control ignition and fuel injection systems, anti-lock braking, gearbox control, dashboard instrumentation and even folding roofs in some up-market convertibles. These functions are now being performed by essential 8-bit and derivative architectures and an immediate question comes to mind – 'Why move to a 16/32-bit architecture?'

The answer is simple. Microprocessors allow finer control of the systems and can compensate for mechanical wear and tear within a mechanical component's life. Both these attributes are essential for an engine to maintain peak performance and, more importantly, emission control. They reduce the amount of servicing needed which, in turn, improves

Ignition

Engine
Management

Measure Engine RPM

Measures Acceleration

Measures Driver commands

Computes fuel mixture

Computes spark timing and

duration

upto 7000 times a
second

Fuel
Injectors

Figure 11.8 *A typical engine management system*

reliability and decreases costs. However, if they fail, there is little a motorist can do to rectify a fault. A modern car has no distributor, optical timing sensors, integrated high-tension supply for the spark plugs, and so on. Even the electronics are encapsulated! The continuous need to improve environmental aspects without increasing costs demands more and more processing power.

Figure 11.8 shows a simplified engine management system and identifies many of the tasks performed by the processor within the system. The work load is even greater for 6, 8 or 12 cylinder engines, or those used within a racing environment. A typical V12 Formula 1 engine may have two spark plugs and fuel injectors per cylinder and rev up to 20 000 r/min. The computing power needed to perform the calculations in real time is phenomenal!

The MC68332 has a CPU32 processor (MC68020 based) running at 16 MHz and a timer/processor unit (Figure 11.9) which has 16 channels controlled by a RISC-like processor to perform virtually any timing function. The resolution is down to 250 ns with an external clock source or 500 ns with an internal one. The timer/processor can perform the following timer algorithms on any of the 16 channels without placing any overhead on the CPU32:

- Discrete input/output
- Pulse-width modulation
- Input capture and transition
- Period measurement with additional transition detection
- Period measurement with missing transition detection
- Position-synchronized pulse generation

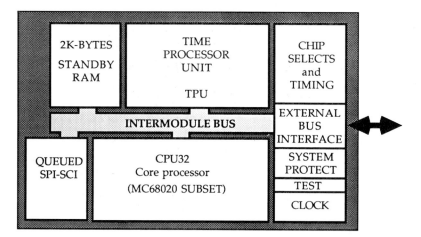

Figure 11.9 *The MC68332 block diagram*

- Stepper-motor control
- Output match
- Period/pulse-width accumulator

A queued serial channel and 2 Kbytes of power down static RAM are also onchip and again, for many applications, all that is required to complete a working system is an external program EPROM and a clock.

The advantages of an integrated processor are not restricted to the automotive industry. The MC68302 uses a 16 MHz MC68000 processor core with power down modes and either an 8- or 16-bit external bus (Figure 11.10). The System Interface Block contains 1152 bytes of dual-port RAM, 28 pins of parallel I/O, an interrupt controller and a DMA device, as well as the standard glue logic. The communications processor is a RISC machine that controls three multiprotocol channels, each with their own pair of DMA channels. The processor takes buffer structures from either the internal or external RAM and takes care of the day-to-day activities of the serial channels. It programs the DMA channel to transfer the data, performs the character and address comparisons and cyclic redundancy check (CRC) generation and checking.

The processor has sufficient processing power to cope with a combined data rate of 2 Mbits per second across the three channels. Assuming an eight-bit character and a single interrupt to poll all three channels, the processor is handling the equivalent of an interrupt every 12 μs. In addition, it is performing all the data framing, etc. While this is going on, the onchip M68000 is free to perform other functions, like the higher layers of X.25 or other OSI protocols. The three communications channels support BISYNC, DDCMP, V.110 and HDLC synchronous modes and standard

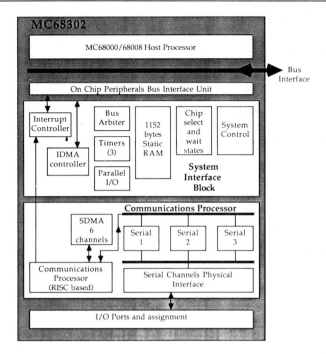

Figure 11.10 *The MC68302 integrated multiprotocol processor*

UART functions. This part essentially combines a whole single-board computer bar memory and is applicable to any such application. One interesting offshoot is its use as an intelligent peripheral for both M88000 and MC68040 systems, where the MC68302 performs all the low–level I/O functions and communicates via shared memory to the main processor.

Increasing the clock rates

Ever since the appearance of commercially available reduced instruction set computers (RISC), there has been a debate concerning which architecture provides the best performance. The argument centres around the ability of RISC architectures to execute their instructions within a single cycle, either through the use of pipelines or by reducing the instructions to a simple operation and synthesizing complex operations with compiler-generated code sequences. These sequences take less time than a Complex Instruction Set Computer takes to execute its single cycle, thus producing the performance advantage. Recent developments have centred around the adoption of RISC architectures by more esoteric silicon and gallium arsenide to increase the processor clock and performance. This is possible, it is argued, only with the relatively simple processor execution units used by RISC machines.

Due to their relative simplicity, RISC processors are easier to fabricate in ECL technology but their memory subsystems require very fast memory, which is expensive, or need complex memory caches and cache coherency systems. Comparing transistor counts for similar performance CISC and RISC processors reveals a similar system count. The MC68040 CISC processor has 1.2 million transistors, while its M88100 RISC counterpart with two MC88200 Cache Memory Management Units has 1.86 million, albeit distributed over three chips. Both systems have integer and floating point execution units, dual memory management and caches with cache coherency. RISC systems may have simpler processors but their memory systems are more complex.

Technology trends indicate that increased speeds are accompanied by higher densities. Silicon technology is therefore applicable to both architectures. It is sobering to reflect that the fastest CMOS merchant processor currently is still a CISC MC68030 running at 50 MHz.

Improving the instruction set

Recently the RISC camp has been challenged further by the latest generation of CISC processors, like the MC68040, which executes complex instructions in a single clock cycle. As CISC processors approach the one-per-clock figure, their more powerful instruction set can actually deliver more work than a RISC counterpart. When RISC machines first appeared, CISC machines were taking about 6–10 clocks per instruction. This allowed RISC machines the time to execute a sequence of simpler instructions with a single clock per instruction and still offer better performance. However, as CISC processors have steadily decreased their average clock-per-instruction figures, this has placed pressure on RISC instruction sets.

The philosophy behind the MC88100 instruction set was simple. If a complex instruction could be executed in a single cycle and was shown to be beneficial to system performance, it would be included. This has resulted in an extremely rich set with many addressing modes, bit field data support, floating-point operations, etc. It is more accurate to describe the instruction set as optimized, rather than reduced. The advantages of a powerful instruction set are many. It reduces the code expansion experienced when moving from a complex to a reduced instruction set and, by reducing the number of instructions, increases the amount of work that can be performed. This may appear to be embracing the CISC philosophy of making instructions more complex to do more work, but should not be interpreted as such. Careful upgrading of RISC instruction sets, where single-cycle execution and the architectural integrity can be maintained, will undoubtedly improve performance.

Upgrading instruction sets

Upgrades may not be as simple to implement as with CISC processors like the M68000 family. The difficulty concerns the fixed op code length needed by RISC machines to allow single-cycle instruction fetches and simplify the instruction decode. The MC68020 could supplement the M68000 instruction set by using operands to extend the effective op code size from two bytes to a maximum of ten. With this size, there is little difficulty in allocating bits to encode new operations. This variable length is a potential obstacle to performance improvements in that it is difficult to predict how many memory fetches are needed to fetch complete or multiple op codes in a single cycle without assuming the maximum length. The hardware difficulties of fetching 8×10 bytes instructions are considerable.

With a 32-bit fixed op code, the size favoured by nearly all today's RISC processors, the majority of coding bits are taken by the triadic register operands. Each instruction usually has two sources and a destination to be specified and, with a register file size of 32, this takes 15 bits – leaving 17 bits for the operation and addressing modes to be encoded. As the register file increases, each addition requires three times as many bits to encode it. With a file of over 128 registers, there are only 8 bits left to encode the instruction and any addressing mode. In these cases, the power of the instruction set is very poor and inefficient. Without destroying binary compatibility or lengthening op code size, it is difficult to see how these instruction sets can be improved.

The MC88100 already has seven groups of 256 instructions reserved for future special function units. If these instructions are executed without the relevant hardware support, the processor takes an exception to allow their simulation in software. This is similar to the F line and A line exceptions of the MC68000, where software simulation was replaced by integrated hardware support in later processor generations.

Executing multiple instructions per clock

Increasing the power of an instruction set is difficult to do once it has been defined and, therefore, is of limited scope. A more interesting approach is that taken by Motorola and Dolphin Technology with the development of a 1000 MIPS single processor based on M88000 RISC architecture. The processor, fabricated in Emitter Coupled Logic and running at a 125 MHz clock rate, has eight execution units and in burst can execute $8 \times$ M88000 instructions per clock cycle. It is this breaking of the single-cycle barrier that will be the main emphasis of RISC designs in the future – and yet many current implementations have aspects within their design which will handicap such developments. While no further data has been released on this project to date, it is worthwhile examining some of the problems associated with implementing multiple execution machines, identifying some of the architectural requisites for such designs and showing how M88000 architecture fulfils them.

General principles

Multiple-execution machines (MEM) should not be confused with multiprocessor or parallel processing designs, although they are very similar in that they have the capability of executing multiple instructions every clock. The main difference is the level at which the allocation of resources is performed. With most parallel or multiple processor computers, the execution units virtually act independently and can be likened to several computer systems that simply reside in a single chassis with a single controlling program. This system software controls resource allocation, which may or may not be transparent to the user; applications may have to be adapted accordingly. The MEM design performs this role at the VLSI hardware level so that the resource allocation is transparent to the user, thus enabling binary compatibility across a range of machines, irrespective of the number of instructions that can be executed per clock.

The general principles behind a multiple-execution unit processor are relatively simple (Figure 11.11). The execution unit is replicated, so there are multiple units, each of which is capable of executing an instruction per clock cycle. These units are fed via an extremely wide bus (an eight-unit design with a 32-bit op code needs a 256-bit bus), so that a very large word, a multiple instruction, can be presented. Each individual op code within it is allocated to a particular execution unit on every clock cycle. For efficiency, this requires a fixed op code length with no additional operands, so single-cycle memory accesses can be maintained and hardware needed to detect an op code overspill into the next allocated slot is removed. Fortunately, most RISC designs, including the M88000, use a fixed-side op code.

The next problem to overcome concerns the validity of the results. Although eight instructions may have been executed, not all the results are necessarily valid. If a branch instruction is encountered and taken, the instructions executed with it but located after it would not normally have been executed and their results should be discarded. Similarly, instructions which use results from previous instructions may not be valid because the data was not ready when they were executed. It is this type of problem that must be overcome before multiple-execution machines can realize their potential performance.

Data dependency refers not only to data or registers encoded within the

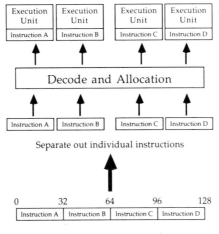

Figure 11.11   *A four execution unit design*

op code but also to any unique resource within the programming model, such as condition codes or status bits. If a programming model has a single condition code register, this immediately places restrictions on which instructions can be executed in parallel. Only one such instruction can be executed per clock, even though there may be tens of execution units available. In addition, there can be no automatic updating of the condition code bits as in the M68000 family – which instruction should be used for the updating? Architectures with dedicated condition code registers are not ideal for multiple-execution units. Conventional processors have a condition code register which is usually updated at the end of every instruction and allows easy condition testing. Various combinations of bits within the register indicate if certain conditions exist. Maintaining this register imposes a large overhead on the processor and it is no surprise that the M88000 family does not have a specific condition code register. Instead, any general purpose register can be used temporarily as a condition code register.

Controlling multiple instructions per clock

The real difficulty in controlling a multiple-instruction execution machine is removing or inhibiting the invalid data produced at the end of every clock cycle. There are two basic approaches – prevent the execution of the offending instruction so the erroneous data is not produced, or remove it after execution. To do so after the event is extremely complicated and would require many buffers to act as temporary stores while the execution

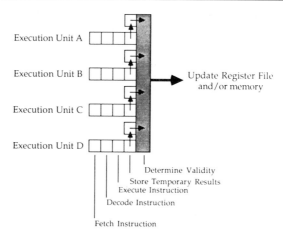

Execution Unit A

Execution Unit B

Update Register File
and/or memory

Execution Unit C

Execution Unit D

Determine Validity
Store Temporary Results
Execute Instruction
Decode Instruction

Fetch Instruction

Figure 11.12 *A post-event hardware mechanism for equal length pipelines*

units progress the instructions. Each unit would need buffers to hold, register contents, a copy of the instruction, and temporary variables. Their contents would then be inspected, decoded and the register files, etc. be updated.

This job is even more complicated if the pipelines are then considered and are of differing lengths, as may be the case with a design with floating-point units, integer units, etc. With pipelines of equal length, the execution units can present their buffered data at the same time and thus provide an accurate snapshot of the processor on every clock cycle. The processing is simply an extra common stage within the pipeline (Figure 11.12). For unequal length pipelines, the temporary data cannot be made available within the same clock cycle and is skewed, as shown in Figure 11.13. The

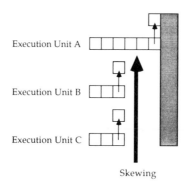

Execution Unit A

Execution Unit B

Execution Unit C

Skewing

Figure 11.13 *A post-event hardware mechanism for different length pipelines*

snapshot has to be delayed until unit A has stored its data. To preserve the temporary data from units B and C, their pipelines must either be stalled or the temporary data stored in a three-stage FIFO buffer, allowing execution to continue. In this case, the pipelines have effectively been lengthened to that of unit A, which can cause further inefficiencies with branching, etc.

While such schemes can be implemented, the hardware is complicated and a better alternative is to prevent the production of invalid data in the first place.

Software control

The software techniques used to synchronize pipelines can be adapted to cope with multiple-execution machines, as depicted in Figure 11.14. The machine shown has four execution units which each receive one instruction per clock. The first and second multiple instructions each contain a pair of data-dependent instructions. This dependency can be removed by re-organizing, as described previously. The last instruction of the first pair and the first instruction of the second pair are interchanged, effectively delaying the former and advancing the latter. However, this does not take into account the potential problem concerned with the execution unit pipelines. Assuming that they are three stages deep, the pairs of dependent instructions need to be separated by at least another instruction and so NOPs or other instructions are inserted accordingly.

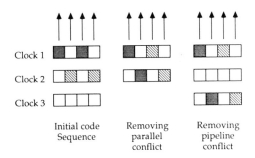

Figure 11.14 *Software reorganization to remove data dependency*
Note: Shaded boxes indicate data dependent instructions

The most promising technique appears to be a variation on the M88000 scoreboard technique, with extra bits to control the pipelines as necessary. Each instruction decode sets these bits accordingly and delays the progress of any instructions so correct operation is maintained. This requires no software intervention to work, although as before, software optimization can increase the performance by infilling the delay slots. It gives a user-transparent interface and allows binary compatibility to be maintained.

The Dolphin M88000-based system, running at 125 MHz with eight execution units, is estimated to run standard M88000 code at about 300–400 MIPS. Optimizing for the architecture should increase this speed to over 500 MIPS, with bursts of 1000 MIPS. For future expansion, the processor has multiprocessor support. The M88000 family has been designed to allow the easy migration of its architecture and software from a single to multiple instructions per clock. It is within this arena that the real differentiation between the various RISC and CISC architectures will appear in the coming years.

DSP96000 – combining integration and performance

The DSP96000 family takes the basic architecture of the DSP56000 and adds extra integration and improved performance to provide an IEEE-compatible, floating-point Digital Signal Processor. While the DSP56000 can cope with the majority of applications with its 24-bit fixed point capabilities, there is a growing need for extra precision and speed which the DSP96000 family offers. The DSP96002 (Figure 11.15) is built using HCMOS technology and has 1024 words of onchip data RAM split between the X and Y data spaces, 1024 words of onchip full speed Program RAM (PRAM) and two preprogrammed onchip ROMs containing data tables, etc. The PRAM areas can be loaded via a bootstrap program from external EPROM. The device has its own onchip support for circuit emulation.

The central processing unit uses three 32-bit execution units, which operate in parallel to perform arithmetic operations, address generation and control and synchronize programs. The device uses a 27 MHz clock, giving a 75 ns cycle time, and can be interfaced with many different memory configurations, depending on the speed needed and the system cost. Static RAMs with access times of 35 ns or better, DRAM using their special page access methods or Video RAM with its serial mode can all be used. The processing throughput that the device can achieve is 13.5 million instructions per second, where an instruction can involve an instruction prefetch, up to three floating point operations like a 32-bit × 32-bit multiply, two data moves and two address pointer updates. This gives a peak performance of some 108 million operations per second. The IEEE floating point is supported via 10×96-bit wide extended precision registers.

Integration has been increased by the addition of two DMA channels, the provision of six onchip memories, two independent expansion bus ports and eight 32-bit buses, three for addresses and five for data. The host interface is supported, as well as the fast interrupt and long interrupt

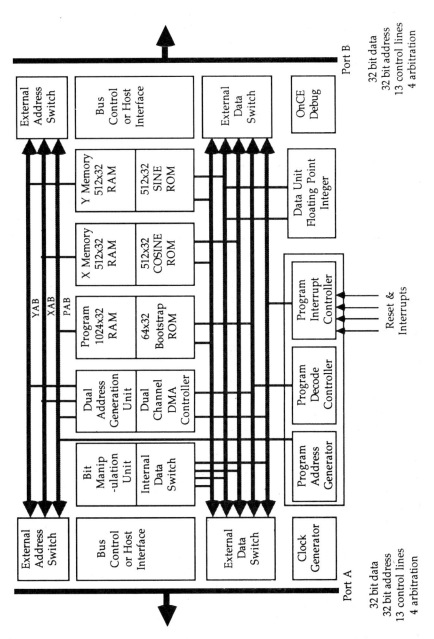

Figure 11.15 *The DSP96002 block diagram*

mechanism, as found on the DSP56000. These use 176 of the device's 214 pins, with 14 reserved for power and 24 for ground.

The instruction set is compatible with that of the DSP56000 but has been expanded to provide floating point and graphics support.

OnCE – a new approach to emulation

The OnCE hardware consists of a serial port and a history buffer, which stores the last five instructions executed. Additional hardware allows single stepping, execution freezing and the setting of breakpoints on any X, Y or P address. The control is located onchip and data is passed to and from a host via the serial line. In effect, the DSP96002 can act as its own emulator in this case, without the problems caused by long cables, etc. The system will match any further speed increases because of its integration into the processor itself. The device can provide a performance upgrade path beyond the simple clock speed increases available to the DSP56000 family and is equally applicable to any system that needs floating-point accleration or extremely fast processing. Applications that can benefit include graphics systems, image processing and numeric analysis.

Integration and higher performance

All three processor families will develop higher performance and higher integration parts. The M68000 family will follow both lines to produce a large number of offerings with high functionality and performance, providing the broadest range of platforms. This is partially because of the ten or so years that the architecture has had to establish itself and the several generations that have already appeared. Currently, there has been only a single RISC generation and only two generations of DSP processors; it is therefore unfair to conclude that these families will not develop a similarly broad range of platforms in the future. The M68000 family has the advantage of time, some 30 million parts in use and over $4 million worth of software.

The M88000 should be viewed as the start of a family, as was the M68000 in 1979. The misconceptions that it is a one-off or that its performance is so good that it will be very difficult to improve upon, must be forgotten – the M88000 RISC family will provide the highest available performance from a general-purpose processor. The DSP56000 and DSP96000 should not be considered just as signal processors; their integration and performance make them equally suitable to many embedded control functions. While missing many functions such as memory management, which a more general-purpose architecture needs, they are indeed a microprocessor and their use in other applications should not be ignored. In terms of 'bangs per buck', they are extremely competitive.

12 Selecting a microprocessor architecture

It will have become apparent that there is not a single processor architecture which is the panacea to every application and, however much manufacturers attempt to declare that a processor is meant for a particular application or market, it is the ultimate use of the product that determines its suitability. This choice is made by the end user and not the supplier. Every processor has its strengths and weaknesses, its obvious and hidden applications and it can be very difficult to determine exactly the ranking the various attributes should have and their appropriate weighting. This chapter does not predetermine or dictate how processors should be used but suggests the criteria which should be considered in making such a choice.

Meeting performance needs

Until recently, the most dominant factor in choosing a processor architecture was whether it met the performance needs or not. This greatly simplified the selection process and led to a performance drive in product offerings. The manufacturer with the fastest processor generally had a big edge over any competitor. However, with the diversification of architectures available, which overlap each other in terms of performance, a far greater understanding of other factors, such as system cost and upgrading, starts to come into play. With a choice of processors offering the needed throughput, these other factors become very critical.

Choice of platforms

With the shortening design cycle and the higher competitive nature of many electronics industries, the planning of mid-life upgrades and new products becomes extremely critical. One market strategy may be to remain at the top end of the performance spectrum, in which case the overriding need for maximum throughput is the main consideration. In the case of a general-purpose design, the fastest generation of RISC processors, like the M88000, will always have the performance edge. An alternative plan may be to offer a wide portfolio of systems running common software, while providing differing performances at differing costs. In this case, the M68000 family is an ideal option. While the cost of a minimum M88000 system will come down, it still is far higher than a lower performing M68000 or M68300-based system. While the fastest M68000 may be about 18 months behind its M88000 counterparts, the performance increases, coupled with the wide choice of platforms, may tip the balance. In the DSP arena, code compatibility between the DSP56000 and the DSP96000 can provide another choice of platforms with different speed variations.

Whatever the choice, the system should be designed for easy upgrade-ability, to meet any competitive threat, improve profit margins or simply increase market share.

Anticipating future needs

The preoccupation with increasing processor throughput overshadows the other revolution that is starting within the microprocessor industry – the advent of highly integrated processors. Many applications do not need more processing throughput but require instead a higher integration level to reduce system costs and improve overall system performance. With this aspect in mind, the obvious choice is the M68000 family, with its M68300 integrated processors, or the DSP56000 with its combination of peripherals and powerful processor. The M88000 family will undoubtedly increase the integration that it offers but the trend will be towards solving processing bottlenecks rather than increasing functionality. In some cases, it may be worth increasing some system costs to make an architectural switch earlier than expected, thus allowing plenty of time to become familiar with new ideas and to make the changeover in more controlled conditions, rather than under a 'make-or-break' regime.

Software support

Many analysts predict that software will become the dominant cost of any development involving processors and the issue of software support has quite rightly become extremely relevant. Software needs range from assemblers, compilers, debuggers and operating systems to applications and frequently the cost is under estimated. For established architectures like the M68000, M88000 and DSP56000 families, there is a wealth of assemblers and language support available on a multitude of hosts, ranging from simple home computers to sophisticated multiuser systems. In these situations, a selection process to determine the best software environment is necessary. The situation is similar to that of buying a hi-fi system where all the various configurations will play records and tapes, yet they offer different quality and features. In many cases, the choice may be reduced to the simple question of how much money is available.

One area that should not be forgotten is the cost of porting software to a particular hardware platform. Any system will generally be different to everybody else's and will require even basic software, such as monitors and run time libraries, to be converted. While these ports are frequently simple to perform, they can be time consuming and costly, especially if things go wrong. Fortunately, most software companies providing these tools offer a large amount of customization to cater for such developments. But this is not often the case for applications – each application is usually ported to a particular set of hardware and operating system, which creates large porting revenues and is frequently a barrier for many.

This situation had developed over time and it has only recently been recognized that open standards are the key to the future. For all the criticism levelled at the IBM PC hardware, the one thing it has achieved is to awaken everyone to the advantages of shrink-wrapped software. For new architectures, such as the M88000, it has been possible from day one to develop a Binary Compatibility Standard (BCS) which allows shrink-wrap software without having to enforce a 'hardware clone' on any hardware manufacturer. Cloning restricts the architectural variation that can differentiate systems. The BCS is explained in Appendix B. This work is now being applied to the M68000, where the integration of the MC68040 and the UNIX 5.4 operating system provides a consistent platform to build on. The M88000 BCS provides a large market for software houses to attack with a single port and some 200 applications now available. The M68000 family has over \$4 billion of 32-bit software written for it and it is likely that virtually every need is catered for. There are even MSDOS emulators for those who want to move MSDOS software across!

The provision of software is essential for the success of a new processor family and, rather than seen as an afterthought, it is now considered as part of the initial design program.

Development support

In the early days, the answer to this problem was simple – the manufacturer was the only source of such equipment. With the advent of cheap workstations and personal computers, this monopoly has rapidly disappeared and been replaced by a more open approach. Development support includes providing the compiler tools and debugging support, emulation to give a window into the target environment and occasionally, some analyser tools. The trend of moving towards system simulation using behavioural models, as described in Chapter 10, is rapidly increasing. Again, the three Motorola processors are well provided for. With the M68000 family, there are many third-party products with which, instead of asking what support is available, the question of 'how much do you want to spend?' is raised! One aspect that does remain is the undeniable fact that the more costly and complex the system, the more sophisticated and expensive the tools will be. The standard and traditional method of system debugging was to use an emulator but this approach has been augmented by other cheaper methods.

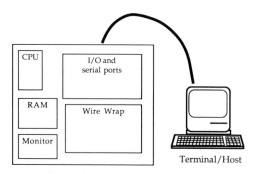

Figure 12.1   *An EVM system*

The cheapest support is provided usually by an EVM (EValuation Module), a simple board with a processor, memory, resident debugger and I/O interfaces (Figure 12.1). In many cases the board has EPROM programming facilities. Developed initially for 8-bit microcontrollers, the approach has now been brought into the 16 and 32-bit arenas. EVMs frequently come with assembler and compiler software to run on a PC or Apple Macintosh. The aim is to provide a very low-cost environment, where software can be written, developed and tested and simple hardware interfaces built. Software is developed on the PC and downloaded, via a serial line to the board, where it can be run and debugged. However, they do not provide true emulation capability, i.e. the ability to replace a processor within a target system. A variation on the EVM idea is the ADS (Advanced Development System), where the 'EVM' is expanded by the addition of an interface card to the host and a processor probe, as shown in Figure 12.2. These systems are very simple, low-cost emulators and can be used to debug a separate target system. Their facilities are not sophisticated, although they can be augmented by external logic analysers if necessary. For many simple projects, they are more than adequate.

Figure 12.2 *The ADS board for the MC68302*

The full-blown emulator has evolved into a full-blown and sophisticated piece of instrumentation (Figure 12.3). The software tools that are available allow simulation and primary testing to be performed without any target system and frequently the actual use of an emulator is transparent to the engineer. Such systems have trace buffers, event qualification facilities and the ability to replace or overlay target memory with emulation memory within the emulator itself. Breakpoints can be set when instructions are executed or if particular signal states or addresses appear. Many such systems can actually provide multiprocessor support.

It is possible to buy an M68000 assembler, C compiler and a simple evaluation board for about £500. An emulator costs around £2,500. Similarly, a DSP56000 simulator, assembler and C compiler with a development board capable of emulation is about £3,000. System support for an M88000 is currently far more than this! The reason is simple – the faster clock speeds and hardware require even faster hardware to gain the timing advantages necessary to provide the emulation.

Such instrumentation is therefore at least as expensive as the systems it is helping to develop. An emulator has a processor, memory, software, etc. The software tools are state-of-the-art and the many man-years of development have to be paid for. In other words, development system costs frequently reflect overall system costs and sophistication.

Standards

Standards are becoming more important to control the costs of software development and as higher system connectivity is demanded. Standards may define communication links, quality, software conformance, etc. Apart from the standards involved with shrinkwrap software, the need for

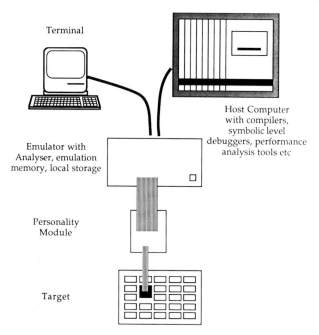

Terminal

Host Computer
with compilers,
symbolic level
debuggers, performance
analysis tools etc

Emulator with
Analyser, emulation
memory, local storage

Personality
Module

Target

Figure 12.3   *An integrated emulator/analyser with software development tools*

military specification components may be another factor, either for defence projects or because of hostile environments.

Again for the M68000, M88000 and DSP56000, there are well-defined military programs in place. Typically, military spec parts conform to one or more of the established standards, such as 883-C or CECC. These standards define the conformance testing and associated documentation that each part has to go through before it can be supplied with its certificate of conformance and used in the end application. There are different levels of screening, depending on whether the parts have been simply processed using the standards or the appropriate Institutes have actually qualified the process(es) involved. In many cases, it is the traceability in cases of failure that provide the guarantee. While screening can ensure the outgoing quality is good, it does not prevent field failures and, where a failure occurs, the product must be traced so that others of the batch can be replaced or checked.

When a new commercial part becomes available, it takes about 12 months for the first hi-rel versions to appear. Generally, they are slower than the current commercial parts, due usually to their higher operating temperature specification: −55 to +125 degrees Celsius, compared with

0–70 degrees for commercial parts. Electrical timings are frequently the same, although this is not always the case. Packages are almost certainly ceramic.

Built-in obsolescence

Is a design limited by the production technology or by the silicon technology? For many designs where production technology is the limitation, there is a great danger of the product becoming obsolete as soon as it comes to market. Semiconductors will continue to go faster and this frequently forces the pace within the market-place. However, this increase has to be followed by a matched increase in production technologies. If a design is using older methods but stretched to the limit, the cost of changing in mid-life is far higher. The cost and difficulty of changing a circuit board may be far greater than the additional costs of faster processors and memory and therefore the upgrade path is effectively stopped, potentially making the board obsolete. The market advantage of having the highest performance system can be lost or devalued through the additional upgrade costs.

It makes sense, for a lot of systems, to design either for the highest available speed or different processor options so the design can be changed to give other advantages, such as higher speeds or a change to cheaper alternative parts.

Market changes

In the end, very few processor designs are performed simply for academic or non-commercial reason. For the majority, commercial success is as important as the engineering goals. It is now important that products are designed to provide mid-life upgrades, so a response can be made to any other competitive threat. There are various ways in which such upgrades can be designed in. The obvious way is to provide differing processor speed and memory options within a design. This is frequently the reasoning behind the provision of a standard bus interface, like VMEbus or Multibus, which allows standard off-the-shelf products to be added with the minimum of fuss and design effort. Software packages which offer different performance levels are another method of achieving the same goal. By using improved compilers or by the removal of software delay loops, the system can be upgraded without massive costs.

Another alternative is to use the processor developments within a family to run the same system software on a range of platforms. The M68000 family can provide highly integrated low-cost platforms through to super computers, allowing hardware products to be developed for various market segments, yet using a common software base.

Considering all the options

Any architectural decision must be made by considering all the relevant facts. The only way to understand the various aspects of a system and how they relate to a processor architecture is by understanding the relationships and trade-offs that are embodied within a design or application and the processor itself. The weighting given to any individual aspect must reflect the importance or necessity of that function and this, again, can only come from understanding the total system. In the final reckoning, it is the user who will make that decision.

Appendix A   Benchmarking
'Lies, damn lies and benchmarks' (with apologies to Benjamin Disraeli)

When evaluating or investigating processors, it is almost impossible to ignore the many benchmarks and counterclaims that are put forward to defend or establish which product offers the most 'bangs per buck.' In reality, the only accurate benchmark is the application running on the final end system performing real tasks. However, this is often impractical and benchmarks have to be used to give an indication of the achievable performance that can be obtained from a system or architecture. This appendix examines many of the 'tricks' used by some to enhance performance figures.

MIPS, MOPS and MFLOPS

The MIPS measurement, which gauges performance by the number of millions of instructions that are executed in a second, has become a firm favourite with the media for comparing processors. The larger the number, the higher the performance. MIPS actually stands for 'Meaningless Indication of the Performance of Software', 'Meaningless Indication of the Performance of Silicon' or 'Meaningless Indication of the Performance given by Salesmen'. Take your pick, depending on your background. The problem with the MIPS measurement is that it gives no reference to what instructions are being performed and their relevant power. A 21 MIPS machine may appear to be more powerful than a 14 MIPS system but if the former takes three instructions to perform a given task while the latter can do it in one, the 14 MIPS machine will give 14 million iterations of the task to the 21 MIPS processor's 7 million. Such a system may have great MIPS figures but is actually very inefficient in doing anything.

A variation of MIPS is the VAX MIP. Here, performance is normalized to a DEC VAX 11/780 system, where performance is rated at 1 VAX MIP.

This attempts to provide some measure of the task being performed. However, the 'VAX' descriptor is often missed out and VAX MIPS compared with native instruction MIPS to greatly enhance the figures. Another trick is to normalize the performance to a VAX using a particular function in which the VAX performs very badly. This then devalues the VAX MIP rating, allowing the figures to be distorted.

The MOPS (Million Operations Per Second) is even more vague in describing what the actual operation is. Its actual meaning is 'Meaningless and Optimistic Possibility Study'. It is frequently used to enhance MIPS figures by giving even larger MOPS numbers. The argument is simple. If the system is rated at 30 MIPS but is working on ten instructions simultaneously, it is achieving 300 MOPS! What is forgotten, is that the machine has only one pipeline and therefore can only fetch one instruction per clock. The pipeline may be ten stages long, and therefore ten instructions are being processed. However, common sense dictates that this is not the same as executing ten instructions simultaneously. Actual work measurements would be typical of a 30 MIPS not a 300 MIPS machine.

Another way of looking at it is to examine an operation. An ECL NAND gate can perform a logical NAND operation with a propagation delay of 1 ns, allowing 1 000 000 000 logical NAND operations per second. If there were four gates in the package, the combined throughput would be 4000 MOPS! If this is taken to an even further extreme, every transistor in a microprocessor is capable of performing an operation. Imagine the MOPS figures that could be achieved by taking the typical switching times and multiplying by the total number. Again, this system of measurement becomes very nonsensical.

The MFLOP, or Million of Floating-Point Operations per Second, is a combination of MIPS and MOPS applied to floating-point arithmetic. It usually refers to the number of instructions using floating–point data that can be executed per second, although it is sometimes interpreted as operations (whatever they may be!). It suffers from the same disadvantages as MIPS and MOPS.

Unfortunately, these measurements never seem to die.

Dhrystones and Whetstones

The Dhrystone is a benchmark that has been developed for measuring integer processing power but it has been the subject of many 'dirty tricks' which have devalued it as a measurement criterion. The first version, v1.0, was written in C and intended to run on commercially available systems using an operating system such as UNIX. The intention was to provide a test of system and compiler, allowing a user to have a reasonable yardstick with which to measure system performance. The results were distributed on UNIX networks and results from 'hot boxes' or systems coded in assembler or running with no operating system, were not accepted. Unfortunately, Dhrystone figures from such systems started to appear. Some of the figures also appeared to be unbelievable. Examination of the code demonstrated one of the disadvantages – the actual benchmark does nothing except move data and compare it. Nothing is output and so some of the compiler optimizers took advantage of this, reducing the whole benchmark to a loop with a NOP in the middle. Of course the figures from such versions offered phenomenal performance. Version 1.1 fixed a bug with the previous code but was still subject to optimizer abuse. While reduction to a NOP is easy to track, there were still other tricks to be played.

One of the functions the Dhrystone benchmark performs is a string copy and comparison. Many benchmarks used a special handcoded version of these library calls to improve performance, which is not in itself despicable, providing these routines are made available to the system user. Other tricks include taking the loops and unrolling them into straightline code, removing the loop control and branching overheads. The drawback with this is increased code size. If such techniques were applied to normal applications, the resultant code expansion would be prohibitive.

Version 2.1 is now generally accepted as a better version of the benchmark and the rules prohibit loop unrolling and other disreputable practices. Even so, there are rumours of special 'benchmarking' compilers which scan the source for strings like 'Dhrystone' and automatically generate hand-coded routines. In some ways, this is similar to the qualification versions of Formula 1 racing cars, which often have different engines, tyres and chassis from their actual racing counterparts. Yes, more performance may be gained – but it bears little relationship to sustained and actual delivered power.

The Whetstone is a floating-point performance benchmark originally written in Fortran. It suffers from many of the disadvantages of the Dhrystone but is frequently paired with it to give a better measurement of integer and floating-point performance.

Hardware effects

Hardware design is open to manipulation to increase benchmarking performance. One trick frequently used is the creation of 'hot boxes'. Such systems often have small amounts of fast static RAM and run the processor as fast as possible. Some systems even contravened the published timings but, providing they functioned sufficiently to execute the benchmark, this was fine. The problem was that the resultant performance bore little resemblance to that commercially available. A variation of this approach is to distort the comparisons by using different clock speeds. Performance figures for a 50 MHz processor or system when only 16 MHz parts are available are unacceptable. It creates an 'apples and oranges' comparison, where data is distorted and loses its validity.

The appearance of cache memory systems can further confuse the matter. Many benchmarks are small enough to fit within a cache and therefore execute with the best performance. In the real world, other applications or larger routines would be running, the cache would fill up and cause misses. Each miss can impact performance by coupling the processor direct to slow memory and, again, the benchmarked performance is not achieved by the actual system. The use of copyback or write-through schemes can also cause problems.

Optimizing the system

It is very easy to obtain a five times performance increase in a general UNIX benchmark which uses standard I/O calls to disc, etc. In a normal system, such communication to peripherals limits the obtainable performance. There are system variables which can be changed to allow larger buffers, disc caches and page swap areas, forcing many accesses to memory rather than peripherals. One other trick is to initialize the winchester and freshly install the operating system. This prevents file and sector fragmentation, which can degrade system performance by about 20%. Again, the benchmark system will offer the edge over a normal machine. These manipulations may be valid – providing they can be implemented on the end-user system.

Another trick is to remove the operating system completely and call directly to a monitor or debugger to provide the system I/O functions. Again, the benchmarked performance is far greater than practice.

A further practice is that of extrapolation. Benchmarks requiring iterative loops are simply executed by measuring the time for a single loop and extrapolating for all the iterations. This can neatly hide any problems with caches, page swapping, virtual memory, etc.

Some guidelines

Anyone entering the field of benchmarks and system performance is entering a potentially gladiatorial combat with only his wits and agility to compete with. There are three guidelines that should be considered:

1 Establish exactly under what conditions the benchmark was run

Determine which compiler, processor clock speed, memory configuration and speed, operating system and system configuration, etc. were used to perform the benchmark. This information should be relatively easy to obtain; however, it is important to determine other information concerning system tuning parameters. In a UNIX environment, it is relatively easy to improve performance dramatically by re-allocating memory and disc space to paging areas, disc caches, etc. With a 2 Mbyte disc cache, disc I/O performance is dramatically improved – by a factor of four or five.

2 Examine the code and check if it has been over optimized

Loop unrolling, total dead code optimization (replacing everything with a NOP) and inlining can easily be checked. If the binary code is not available, be very suspicious! Again, it is important to determine how the optimization has been achieved. A handcoded routine may be applicable to a real-world environment, providing it is a small part of the overall system code and is frequently used. With large applications, it is nonsensical to expect the improvements offered by handcoding right across the whole application.

3 Apply common sense

Obviously, an MC68000 is not going to achieve the same performance as an MC68040 or an MC88100. Any claims where there appears to be a lack of the appropriate level of horsepower to achieve the performance figures quoted should be investigated thoroughly. It may be that a particular part of a computer system performance is being analysed and taking this in isolation distorts the overall system performance figures.

This is also true of multiprocessor and parallel processor systems. Some benchmark figures for multiprocessor systems are obtained by taking the figure for a single processor and multiplying it by the number of processors within the system. This approach is rarely valid. Such systems frequently compete for memory, mass storage and other unique system resources. The simple scaling of performance also fails to take into account any interprocessor communication overhead.

SPEC benchmarks

The SPEC organization is a group of computer manufacturers (DEC, HP-Apollo, MIPS, Motorola, etc.) which has developed a set of benchmarks and specified the conditions used to run them, in an attempt to provide a consistent environment for performance evaluation. These benchmarks include both processor-intensive tasks and user applications to mimic a real-world user environment. The initial benchmarks allowed some system tuning but this has now been removed.

These benchmarks are reasonable but, like all benchmarks, they are flawed. While providing a consistent approach, their results are based on available computer systems and, therefore, do not reflect the potential performance offered by a particular microprocessor architecture or the performance obtainable within a realtime or embedded control application. System A may be slower than System B simply because the design trade-offs were selected for good price performance rather than out-and-out performance. The benchmarks have been derived from a UNIX environment and their relevance to real-time applications is questionable.

In the end, the best benchmark is your software, running on your hardware and performing your application!

Appendix B Binary compatibility standards

Portable software, and the 88open BCS

One of the enviable features of the IBM Personal Computer was the explosion of software that was developed to the 'IBM PC compatible' standard. With software becoming the dominant cost of any system, it is essential that any new processor or computer system has a good range of software ready. This is recognized by the hardware manufacturer, yet the technique of cloning an established design limits hardware development and innovation.

With the advent of the M88000 RISC processor family, there was a golden opportunity for M88000 users to define a software standard to allow software houses to perform a single port, knowing it would run on any system that complied with that standard. This Utopia has long been sought after but has frequently been thwarted by a failure to establish the right standards before systems appeared on the market and effectively defined their own *de facto* standards. 88open, an organization of M88000 users including Data General, Motorola and Tektronix, looked at the four methods of achieving software interchangeability.

1 System cloning

This sets the standard by defining the hardware and software platforms that will be used. The IBM PC is the most famous example. Its main disadvantage, from a systems vendor viewpoint, is the lack of product differentiation, which makes it extremely difficult to provide a range of systems to users. Such cloning does provide a standard but effectively stifles innovation and choice (Figure B-1).

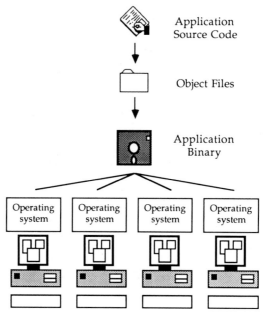

Cloned systems from different vendors

Figure B.1　*System cloning*

2　*Source compatibility*

Source compatibility achieves compatibility by defining languages so they conform to common standards. To port an application to a hardware system, re-compilation and re-linking are required (Figure B-2). This appears to be straightforward but each re-compilation requires separate testing, debugging and support. It is not uncommon for software houses to find their resources tied up in supporting over 100 differing ports, often with differing media and other requirements. In addition, program source is the intellectual property of a software house which, most justifiably, wishes to restrict access to such a product.

3　*Object compatibility*

This method overcomes the concern of access to software but still requires re-linking before the software can be run on a particular system (Figure B-3). It removes the compilation stage but does not solve the testing, debugging and support disadvantages of the previous method. The user is still faced with a potentially complex installation and no real guarantee of success.

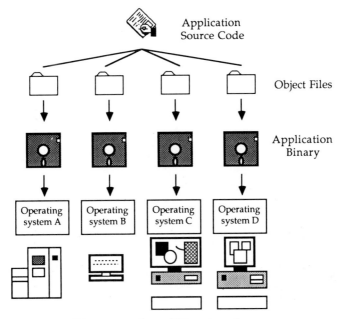

Incompatible systems from different vendors

Figure B.2 *Source compatibility*

4 Binary compatibility

With binary compatibility, only one version is supplied which is simply loaded and executed on any compliant system (Figure B-4). It offers users shrinkwrapped, off-the-shelf software and provides only one product to support, allowing software suppliers to concentrate on enhancing their product, rather than supporting many different versions. In addition, it provides protection for software source and object. This third method has often been talked about but differing hardware standards, such as proprietary memory management hardware, mass storage formats, etc., have prevented it from becoming a reality.

With the advent of the M88000 architecture, which defined a processor, floating-point unit and memory management, there was an opportunity for users to initiate standardization. The work to implement an M88000 Binary Compatibility Standard (BCS) was started by the 88open Consortium in late 1988. By commencing this work prior to general system availability, all systems, from day one, could meet the standard. In addition, the large potential market available to software houses (the 88open Consortium membership supplied over $20 billion of computer systems in 1988) via a single software port, has established a large software portfolio just as the first systems have started being shipped.

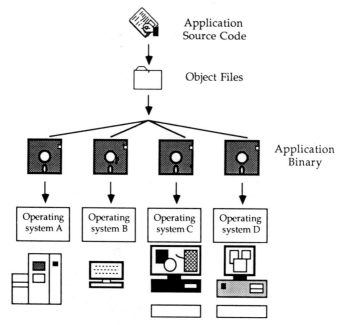

Incompatible systems from different vendors

Figure B.3 *Object compatibility*

BCS – how does it work?

The 88open Consortium decided to implement current standards and the BCS is compliant with POSIX, X/OPEN and AT & T's System V Interface Definition. These standards define the operating system calls, functionality and data structures for a UNIX operating system. In addition, variable sizes, installation procedures, file and resource locations, mass storage media and file formats are all defined. In effect, all access to system are defined so that irrespective of how that system is implemented, it provides the same standard interface, allowing the BCS software to function.

System calls are made using the trap zero 'tb0' instruction with the system call arguments passed using the M88000 register file. Argument 1 is passed via register 1, argument 2 in register 2 and so on. The variable sizes have been extended from many current implementations, such as Xenix, to be fully System V release 4 compatible. It is recommended that all software, both application and operating system, does not use reserved values, execute illegal instructions or calls, cause deliberate system errors and are tolerant of returned arguments. Bits should be tested explicitly and not by

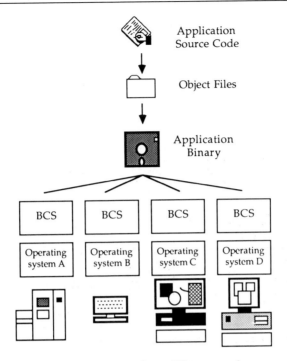

Compatible systems from different vendors

Figure B.4 *Binary compatibility*

value comparison, which may assume reserved bits are returned set or cleared.

Additional hardware support

Any application needs to have some form of direct hardware interface for debugging or auto configuration purposes. The BCS meets this requirement via special calls (Figure B-5). The system configuration call provides over fifty different system parameters, such as memory size, etc., which are essential to any system auto-configuration. The sys_local call provides support for any vendor supplied hardware, such as graphics and vector co-processors. The call requires a vendor and hardware i.d. for each hardware type. Where the hardware is not available or cannot be synthesized in software, the resulting error can be handled simply and a polite message passed back to the user, rather than hanging or crashing the system, which has so often been the case in the past. It is envisaged that some add-ons may become *de facto* system standards, in a fashion similar to recent IBM PC

Figure B.5 *The BCS interface*

developments. The sys_local call provides an elegant method of recognition and driver support.

For debugging purposes, it is essential to have direct access to the hardware to allow debuggers and monitors to function. In the past, this has often been achieved by the use of unreserved exception vectors or by patching with illegal op codes to force an error. Rather than rely on such haphazard methods, the BCS defines a set of vectors for this explicit purpose which will allow the development of standard, portable debuggers and other system utilities.

Benefits

BCS compliant systems and software are interchangeable between each other, irrespective of implementation or source. A single software port will execute without modification on any M88000-based compliant system, be it a deskdtop or a multiprocessor 100 MIPS server. This has great appeal for software houses, which can attack a very large market with a single port. The 88open has set up a subsidiary, Software Initiative Inc., to provide testing and certification of BCS compliant software and systems. Compliant systems are given an 88open BCS certification seal as their guarantee of compliancy. Software Initiative Inc. acts as an independent investigation agent on behalf of a user to determine who is responsible for any non compliancy that may occur. This effectively protects the user from the 'it's the other party's fault' excuse and deadlock. In addition, it provides free system access and technical help to software developers.

Currently, over fifty software suppliers are part of the 88open Software Initiative and about 200 packages are available.

The BCS future

The BCS has met with great approval throughout the UNIX world. It has been adopted by AT & T as the basis of UNIX System V release 4 Application Binary Interface. This will mean that BCS compliant software will run without modification, ensuring a head start for any M88000 BCS compliant products within the marketplace. With the binary level standard achieved, 88open has recognized that for compilers and data base products which require linking, compatibility at object file level is needed. Currently, the Object Compatibility Standard is being developed. It offers tremendous advantages to compiler writers as it will be possible to link together different language modules, without the procedure call problems of today.

Many real-time operating systems now offer SVID compliant run time libraries, allowing UNIX-derived software to execute in a real-time environment. To make use of these features often requires a minimum of re-linking, if not re-compiling. With BCS, the application does not know which UNIX derivative the system is running. It may be single or multiprocessing, the UNISOFT or Data General ports, and therefore it is possible to take BCS applications and run them on another operating system which supports the BCS from the system side but with non-UNIX characteristics. Where additional system calls or hardware access are needed, the existing reserved vectors and sys_local calls could be used to provide these services without compromising the standard. With the ever-increasing software costs, this feature will undoubtedly be exploited.

Index